RED, WHITE & GREENS

RED, WHITE & GREENS

The Italian Way with Vegetables

FAITH WILLINGER

HarperPerennial
A Division of HarperCollins*Publishers*

A hardcover edition of this book was published in 1996 by HarperCollins Publishers.

RED, WHITE AND GREENS. Copyright © 1996 by Faith Willinger. All rights reserved. Printed in the United States of America. No part of this book may be used or reproduced in any manner whatsoever without written permission except in the case of brief quotations embodied in critical articles and reviews. For information address HarperCollins Publishers, Inc., 10 East 53rd Street, New York, NY 10022.

HarperCollins books may be purchased for educational, business, or sales promotional use. For information please write: Special Markets Department, HarperCollins Publishers, Inc., 10 East 53rd Street, New York, NY 10022.

First HarperPerennial edition published 1999.

Designed by Joel Avirom and Jason Snyder

The Library of Congress has catalogued the hardcover edition as follows:

Willinger, Faith Heller.
    Red, white & greens : the Italian way with vegetables / Faith Willinger. — 1st ed.
      p.   cm.
    Includes index.
    ISBN 0-06-018366-7
    1. Cookery (Vegetables). 2. Cookery—Italian. I. Title.
  TX801.W528   1996
   641.6'5—dc20   96-1664

ISBN 0-06-093050-0 (pbk.)

99 00 01 02 03 ❖/RRD 10 9 8 7 6 5 4 3 2 1

tutto fa brodo

———

For Max and Massimo

CONTENTS

Acknowledgments

*M*ost of the recipes in this book are from home cooks, food that I ate with friends or prepared following the cooking advice of farmers or anyone else who wanted to tell me about vegetables. Some of my favorite restaurants in Italy serve home-style food and they've shared their recipes with me.

My husband Massimo introduced me to Tuscan cooking and ingredients and brainwashed me with extra virgin olive oil. His culinary wisdom and unerring palate never cease to astound me. Massimo's father Enzo was a forager of wild greens. He bought olive oil from the mill in the fall, brought home chunks of amazing cheese and treats like mountain chestnuts and smoked herring. Massimo's aunt Enza is a wonderful cook and has a few specialties that simply had to be included in this book.

Torquato Innocenti, my favorite farmer at the Santo Spirito market in Florence, relates recipes for his vegetables, with a Tuscan accent, a sales pitch that has captivated me for years. He sells "unmedicated" produce from his garden on the outskirts of town as well as eggs from his chickens, sacks of cannellini white beans, and a few bottles of homemade tomato puree. He buys stale bread from his customers, two cents a pound, to feed to his chickens and rabbits. Torquato's recipes are always simple, vague, and begin with "a puddle" of oil. Information about cultivars, growth cycles, and the health benefits of his produce is an added bonus. Torquato's advice is scattered throughout this book.

Fabio Picchi and his wife, Benedetta Vitale, own the restaurant, trattoria, and bar Cibreo in Florence and serve the kind of home-style cooking that I love, zapped with garlic and spicy hot pepper. Fabio's antifascist grandfather stayed at home and cooked, the family summered on the Tuscan island of Elba, forming the core of Fabio's culinary memories of land and sea. Fabio and Benedetta's kitchen is footsteps from the Sant'Ambrogio market, one of Florence's best sources of fresh produce from both farmers and retailers and Cibreo takes full advantage of its seasonal wealth. I've spent time in their kitchen and more time in the dining room and come away with wonderful recipes.

I've collected recipes throughout Italy for over twenty years, bringing them all back home to my kitchen in Florence, cooking for my son Max and my husband Massimo, both discriminating diners who endured endless experiments.

GRAZIE AND THANK YOU

To the original Med Like Me crowd from Teverina—Nancy, Arlette, Molly, Paula, and Suzanne and *la banda*—Nancy, Carol, Corby, Fred, and Ed.

To Laura, who kept me organized, and Sarah, who tested everything.

To great friends, traveling companions, farmers, chefs, purveyors, bakers, home cooks, winemakers, producers of extra virgin olive oil, readers, writers, councilors, critics, and vegetable lovers—Aimo, Alan, Alberto, Alfonso, Ann, Anna, Annie, Antonio, Babs, Barbara, Beatrice, Benedetta, Bertha, Bruce, Bruno, Camillo, Catherine, Cesare, Claudia, Claudio, Dania, Dario, Diane, my fantastic agent Doe, Dora, Elio, Enzo, Enza, Ernesto, Fabio, Fausto, Fran, Franca, Franco, Francesca, Francesco, Gail, Gary, George, Giacomo, Giovanna, Giovanni, Giuliana, Graziella, Harry, Henry, Herb, Jeffrey, Johanne, Jon, Judy, Kylie, Leda, Lisa, Livia, Liz, Lorenza, Lotti, Lucio, Marcella, Marco, Margherita, Maria, Marie, Mario, Marlene, Marvino, Mary, Matteo, Maurizio, Nadia, Nancy, Nano, Natale, Nilo, Paola, Paolo, Piermario, Poldo, Riccardo, Roberta, Roberto, Rolando, Romano, Russ, Schultzy, Sergio, Silvana, Silvano, Suzanne, Tonino, Tony, Torquato, Ugo, Victor, Vincenzo, Vinny, the Wags, and Walter.

And to my editor, Susan, for her invaluable advice and enthusiasm for this book.

Introduction

*I*talians do exciting things with vegetables. The same creativity that resulted in twenty-five centuries of world-class art, architecture, technology, fashion, and design applied to the vegetal kingdom has resulted in a thrilling *cucina*. Italians don't have to beg anyone to eat his vegetables. According to ancient texts that discuss the medicinal properties of food, many vegetables commonly eaten in Italy have stimulant or aphrodisiac powers. Intellectual and artistic creativity and a Latin-lover reputation may be the consequences of a diet based on Italian vegetables.

Mussolini called Italy the aircraft carrier of the Mediterranean. Trade routes and exploration constantly expanded the Italian marketplace. The maritime nations of Venice, Amalfi, Pisa, and Genoa brought back global wares. Exotic imports were planted in the gardens of the aristocracy and the church, objects of agricultural and medical study as well as cultural curiosities. This, in part, explains why so many vegetables are available in Italy.

Doctors and monks wrote about the medicinal and digestive effects of herbs, plants, and fruit in thick volumes with hard-to-decipher script and attractive black-and-white botanical prints. Travel and culinary texts document the interest in foreign produce and its impact on local gastronomic traditions. Arab travelers to Sicily, Roman epicures, anonymous fourteenth-century cooks from Tuscany and Veneto, botanical pen pals Ulisse Aldrovandi and Costanzo Felici, expatriot Venetian Castelvetro—all wrote about local and imported ingredients with culinary applications.

Italy's climate favors agriculture. Alpine peaks across all the northern Italian regions form a barrier that blocks the colder weather of northern Europe. Vegetables grow in protected valleys all year round. Throughout most of vegetable-loving Italy the ground barely freezes in the winter. No wonder it's called sunny Italy. The earth yelds a wide variety of vegetables in thousands of microclimates, from lagoons, arid islands, fertile valleys, plains, terraced hills. Inexpensive produce is almost always available and its use is emphasized by an agricultural mentality.

Poverty is also responsible for a mostly vegetal diet. Fields of greens and forests of funghi augment the daily fare free of charge for the forager with a keen eye. Wild asparagus, greens, berries, mushrooms, and truffles are gathered in the countryside.

The Catholic tradition of meatless fast days fostered a dependence on vegetables for everyone, not just poor people who rarely document gastronomy. Court chefs and noble gastronomers wrote cookbooks but embellished lean dishes with exotic, expensive sugar and spice, surely absent in the average household. Home cooking was simpler, rarely written down, but convent and monastery cooks kept records and wrote recipes with cooking time often calculated in Hail Marys.

Regional isolation and cultural incursions molded attitudes toward vegetable cookery. Different squash cultivars, for example, have totally different applications, turning up as a pasta filling in one region, paired with rice in another, pickled, candied, deep-fried, mashed, poached, and braised in other regional recipes. But mention frying to the pickling faction and you'll get a gesture of derision at best. Each region, village, and possibly household feels that its own variety and treatment are the only way to go.

Probably the most important reason why Italians eat so many vegetables is because they taste good. Vegetables, ripe and seasonal, are the stars of Italian *cucina*, treated with respect, rarely combined with more than a few basic ingredients to avoid overwhelming singular flavors. Because components are minimal, super-fresh, just-picked produce is essential. It's useless to attempt a summery raw tomato sauce with tasteless winter hothouse specimens. Or an artichoke recipe with an oversized, flabby, or bruised artichoke. Out-of-season supermarket produce will produce second-rate results and should be avoided.

ITALIAN ATTITUDE

Almost as important as ingredients in the pantry is the Italian attitude about cooking. Italian home-style cooking is based on fresh ingredients straight from the garden or farmers' market (someone else's garden). Cooks set out for the garden or market without a preconceived idea of menu to pick the best, ripest produce, transfer it to the kitchen, and transform it into a meal. Vegetables may turn up as appetizers, soup, risotto, pasta, polenta, side dishes, salad, main course, or even as a raw palate freshener at the end of the meal, along with fruit. With seasonal abundance, cooks have to utilize vegetables creatively, in more than one dish, in more than one course. Thus, asparagus season becomes a series of asparagus-focused dishes that exalt availability with pan-fried frittate, risotto, pasta, boiled, roasted, fried, even raw. Multiply this concept by the number of seasonal vegetables available. Factor in combined vegetable dishes and soups, regional fresh herbs, choice of lipid or carbohydrate, and the reutilization of leftovers. Home-style vegetable preparations are almost endless.

Some dishes seem nearly effortless, like simply boiled asparagus, zucchini, or green beans, dressed with extra virgin olive oil, salt, and pepper. Italians often boil vegetables in a large pot of water, reutilizing the water for pasta.

Most Italian vegetable recipes call for few ingredients—no lengthy lists of exotics that demand hours of special shopping. Many can be made in advance and served at room temperature. Summer dishes tend to be less work since no one wants to exert too much effort in torrid Mediterranean weather.

Seasonal produce is usually inexpensive. With meat and fish reduced to flavor elements, vegetable recipes are generally low-cost, popular peasant food elevated to upper-class tables, too delicious to ignore. The only extravagance is extra virgin olive oil, used with abandon in many Italian regional kitchens. First-rate Italian extra virgin olive oil is expensive but well worth the expense because it's a shortcut to fine flavor. It's not easy to distinguish quality extra virgin olive oil from the selection available to American home cooks. Anything that costs less than ten dollars a bottle isn't Italian extra virgin olive oil, but a rebottled oil from elsewhere. But price alone is no way to determine a fine extra virgin olive oil. Elegant packaging may hide a crummy product. Finding a decent extra virgin olive oil is not easy but is essential for the success of these recipes. See page 4 for invaluable extra virgin olive oil info and sources. To the dismay of my Florentine husband I've reduced olive oil to minimal amounts in all recipes. He adds more at the table.

Italians are extremely casual about quantities. Italian cookbooks use *q.b.,* which stands for *quanto basta,* a sufficient amount, as a term of measurement. Cook until done is normal recipe advice. Relax about quantities. Measuring the ingredients for the following recipes astounded all the Italians who saw me in action. Follow my precise recipes once or twice, until you become comfortable with the recipe—then do it your way.

THE ITALIAN PANTRY

Every Italian pantry contains a few essential ingredients that, combined with fresh produce, can be turned into a meal. It's impossible to prepare decent Italian food without them. Americans have a wide range of imported and domestic products available in markets and mail-order catalogs. Choosing the very best will ensure optimum results but it's not always easy to know what to select.

THE UTTER IMPORTANCE OF EXTRA VIRGIN OLIVE OIL

What's the big deal about extra virgin olive oil? What does cold-pressed or extra virgin mean? Does the temperature or sexual activity of the olive really count? Isn't olive oil greasy and heavy? And how can a consumer who didn't grow up with a Tuscan in the family select a decent oil from a shelf full of bottles with a wide range of prices?

Extra virgin olive oil is the most important ingredient in the Italian kitchen, the foundation of all cooking, the backdrop that sets the stage for flavor, utilized in almost every recipe in this book. First-rate extra virgin olive oil is a shortcut to success and even one tablespoon can dress raw or cooked vegetables with impressive results. Crummy oil offers no thrill and will ruin any culinary efforts.

I live in Tuscany, land of the olive, with a husband who views butter as a product for unevolved palates. He taught me about olive oil, bombarding my taste buds with incredible extra virgins until I got the message. It didn't take long. In other more northerly regions, butter, alone or combined with olive oil, is widely used. But not in Tuscany or Rome, where I learned to cook. There, extra virgin olive oil rules in the kitchen and on the table.

Tuscans use full-flavored extra virgin olive oil because it tastes good but there are other reasons why olive oil is held in esteem. It has no cholesterol, is highly monounsaturated, and is high in vitamin E. It's made by squeezing olives, and unlike almost all other vegetable oils, without chemical solvents. Extra virgin olive oil is pure indeed although unscrupulous industrial olive oil producers take advantage of its immaculate reputation.

Throughout central Italy in late November, green and purple-black ripe olives are handpicked and rushed to a *frantoio*, an olive oil mill, with speed and delicacy, since a massed pile of bumped-around olives may heat up, ferment, acidify, and ruin the oil before it's pressed. In a traditional mill, olives are washed and leaves are removed. The fruit is ground under granite wheels and then kneaded to turn it into an amalgamated paste. The paste is piped onto circular mats, usually synthetic since they're easier to clean, stacked up on a spindle like a bunch of vinyl records, with flat metal disks added every ten layers for stability. The stacks are mechanically pressed, yielding a brownish liquid, a blend of oil and vegetable water, which is separated by a centrifuge. Extra virgin (below 1 percent acidity, although all great oils are far lower) and virgin (below 4 percent acidity) are made with the first pressing. Higher-acidity oils and second pressings obtained with chemical solvents are deodorized, deacidified to 0.5 percent, stripped of color, and then extra virgin is added for flavor. Just say no.

Consumers may have a difficult time choosing a quality extra virgin olive oil. Microclimates, cultivars, geography, and processing all influence flavor and color. Areas in danger of frost during harvest use a mixture of ripe and green olives, producing a peppery, possibly aggressive oil when fresh. More temperate climates where olives can fully ripen will yield a golden, lightly fruity, delicate oil. In the past, oil from southern Italy was often made with overripe or bruised olives harvested from the ground, producing a heavier-flavored oil that easily turned rancid. Irrigation and new harvesting techniques have improved quality, especially in Apulia, which produces 10 percent of the world's olive oil.

Just-pressed extra virgin olive oil, called *olio nuovo*, is a special condiment, available in late November through February, bright green with chlorophyll, peppery and aggressive. Flavors will calm down (polyphenols precipitate) in a few months to the relief of delicate palates. *Olio nuovo* is starting to trickle into the United States and is well worth seeking out.

How can a consumer choose a first-rate oil without tasting? Extra virgin olive oil made with olives from a producer's land is labeled with the words "produced and bottled," *prodotto e imbottigliato*, on the label. This is the only guarantee of quality that can be discerned from the label. Extra virgin olive oil with the word "produced" or "bottled" on the label can be made or simply bottled from olives and/or oil from a neighboring estate, region, country, or even continent. Some cooperatives, mills, and medium-sized producers buy olives and make fine oil but there's no way to tell where the olives are from. Much of the extra virgin olive oil bottled in Tuscany is from elsewhere and the only guarantee of source are the words "produced and bottled." Italian laws are establishing DOC zones for olive oil but I've asked around and no one seems to know when the law will go into effect. The interests of large industrial oil producers with political clout will most likely prevail over smaller quality producers.

Many cookbooks recommend using pure olive oil to cook with, saving extra virgin oil for a condiment, a poor idea. It's like cooking with margarine and putting butter on the table. There is simply no point in using inferior olive oil.

Olive oil exposed to heat and light deteriorates and eventually oxidizes, turning a yellow-orange color. Never purchase or keep olive oil in the sun, stored in a cupboard above a stove, or next to a radiator. Extra virgin olive oil will last up to 2–3 years without spoiling if stored correctly but is at its most flavorful within a year of its production. Quality extra virgin olive oil is often sold in dark bottles or wrapped in foil to protect against light.

Everyone always asks me what my favorite extra virgin olive oil is. I wind up tasting dozens of different oils each season and am enthusiastic about many Tuscan and non-Tuscan extra virgins, most made by wineries that also make great wine. My absolute favorites, which I wind up buying in quantity every year, are Castello di Ama, from central Chianti Classico south of Florence, and Tenuta di Capezzana from the Carmignano area west of Florence, both full-flavored and fruity. I usually use delicately flavored Grattamacco from the Tuscan coast with fish. A new favorite is full-flavored Podere Le Boncie from the southern Chianti Classico area. Maurizio Castelli is the consulting expert at Castello di Volpaia in central Chianti Classico and my *maestro* when it comes to oil. He's a good friend and we've done lots of tastings together—no one executes the olive oil taster's slurp better than Maurizio. At Volpaia, he uses new-wave technology called *sinolea,* which yields elegant extra virgins with milder flavors, and makes oil for many of the nearby wineries, including Castellare and Vistarenne.

If you can't find quality extra virgin olive oil locally, it can be ordered from Balducci's, Telephone: 800-225-3833, Dean & Deluca, Telephone: 800-221-7714, extension 270, and Todaro Brothers, Telephone: 212-679-7766, all in New York; Sutton Place Gourmet, Telephone: 310-564-0006, in Washington,

DC; Zingerman's Delicatessen, Telephone: 313-663-3400, in Ann Arbor, Michigan; Vivande, Telephone: 415-346-4430 in San Francisco; or Manicaretti, Telephone: 800-799-9830, Fax: 510–655–2034, in Oakland, California.

PASTA

Amazing! Two inexpensive ingredients, hard wheat and water, are combined with ingenuity by the Italians, forming endless shapes and forms that beg to be dressed. Countless recipes have been written for pasta, concentrating on sauce preparation, but few mention the crucial step that binds pasta and sauce together, essential for perfect pasta. And there's a secret ingredient that most great cooks use, available in every pasta cooker's kitchen, that's almost never mentioned in recipes. More about that later.

There are two distinct types of pasta in Italy. The older tradition, with variations in almost every region of Italy, is for fresh pasta, *pasta fresca*. Roman recipes document the antecedents of fresh pasta but the first reference I found for homemade pasta is from early in the twelfth century, in papers applying for the beatification of Father William of Malavalle. Dining at the home of a suspected witch, Father William blessed bran-stuffed ravioli and the filling transmogrified into ricotta, miraculous, but probably not sufficient to fulfill the requirements for sainthood.

Fresh pasta is made at home with flour milled from soft wheat, *triticum vulgare aestivum*, opaque, starchier, lower in gluten, and therefore less elastic than hard wheat. Soft wheat is usually milled between metal rollers, flattening vitamin and mineral-rich bran and germ and pulverizing the starchy endosperm, then sifted to separate bran from flour, eliminating the best part in favor of pure white powdery flour. Dough made with this flour is easy to roll because of its low gluten content, and eggs are usually added for flavor and strength. Homemade pasta is at its best hand-rolled, a labor of love that fans find well worth the effort. Fresh pasta is tender, cooks quickly, and should be dressed delicately, with haste.

I'm in love with dry pasta, made commercially, never at home, from higher-in-gluten translucent durum wheat, *triticum durum*. Grains are dampened, allowing water to "wake up" the germ, softening up the outer layer of bran, which is then more easily removed. Branless kernels are milled between deeply ridged cylinders and sifted in a series of up to fourteen "passages" that yield golden-colored, sandlike semolina complete with high-gluten, high-protein germ. Higher gluten means more glutamic acid, the only amino acid that's directly metabolized by the brain. Mental activity is enhanced when glutamic acid is increased. Eating pasta makes you smart! Pasta also contains thiamin or vitamin B_1, which regulates carbohydrate metabolism and has a positive effect on mental attitude. Eating pasta makes you happy!

Even smarter and happier will be those who choose first-rate pasta, which is extruded from bronze dies and slowly dried. It's pale yellow in color with a porous surface that appears to have been sanded. The porous surface holds on to and absorbs sauce better than smooth-surfaced commercial pasta and doesn't become gummy during cooking. First-rate pasta smells sweet and wheaty when cooking. Most large-scale pasta producers extrude dough from Teflon dies and dry pasta quickly, resulting in a smooth surface that doesn't absorb cooking water or sauce. Bronze-extruded pasta is always more expensive but worth the price. It's at its very best when cooked the following way. This also works with industrial pasta made with durum wheat semolina but I have yet to taste a non-Italian brand of pasta that satisfies me. Poor quality pasta is almost impossible to cook correctly.

All recipes begin with a large pot of boiling water. A large quantity of water is necessary so that it quickly returns to a boil when pasta is added. I prefer to use a pasta cooker, a large pot with a colander insert that's lifted to drain pasta, eliminating the need to hoist a heavy pot of boiling water. I've got a beautiful designer pasta cooker by Alessi but any model will do and will also come in handy for cooking vegetables.

Boiling water is salted and pasta is added to the water. The sauce is usually prepared in a wide skillet while the pasta is cooking. When the pasta is cooked extremely *al dente*, offering considerable resistance to the tooth, around three quarters of the normal cooking time, it's drained and added to the skillet of the prepared sauce along with some of the starchy pasta cooking water, the secret ingredient that gives a velvety texture to the sauce. Pasta and sauce are cooked together over highest heat to complete cooking—additional pasta cooking water is added if the sauce dries out. Porous pasta absorbs the sauce and its flavors far better than industrial pasta with its slicker surface. I usually cook short pasta like penne or rigatoni, which are greater in volume than spaghetti, with the sauce (and pasta water, of course) in a pot instead of a skillet because it's easier to manage. When pasta completes its cooking with the sauce it tastes better because it absorbs some of the sauce, which holds on to the pasta instead of sliding around it. Professional chefs usually toss pasta and sauce in the air with a jerking motion that may take a little practice to learn, although stirring with a wooden fork or spoon is perfectly acceptable.

I've never understood why pasta producers would choose to add dehydrated flavorings like tomato, spinach, mushroom, or truffle to pasta. These ingredients are most effectively used fresh, as part of the sauce for pasta. I think flavored pasta is a waste of money.

My favorite brand of pasta is Latini, made in the Marches region of central Italy, packaged in a hand-numbered box that looks like rose-colored granite. Carlo Latini is the only pasta producer who grows his own wheat, all Italian cultivars including high-gluten, low-yield Senatore Cappelli, which he uses to make a single-grain pasta. All Latini pasta is extruded from bronze dies and slowly dried. Latini pasta even tastes great plain, without anything. The bucatini have a smaller hole and are easier to eat, more consistent than regular bucatini. Flat trenette are perfect for pesto or fish sauces. Spaghetti or squared-off spaghetti *alla chitarra*, penne, *maccheroni*, and *strozzapreti* (priest-stranglers) are among my favorite shapes. I order Latini pasta by the case, secure that I can always improvise a meal for unexpected guests.

Fine artisanal pasta extruded from bronze dies and slowly dried is also produced by Rustichella d'Abruzzo (with mostly Italian wheat), Gerardo Di Nola (Italian wheat), and Martelli, Setaro, and Cav. Giuseppe Cocco (Canadian wheat).

Commercially produced pasta, extruded from Teflon dies, produced in Italy or domestically in the United States, will never yield the spectacular results of artisanal pasta. De Cecco is acceptable if none of the other brands I've recommended are available, although first-rate pasta is well worth seeking out or ordering by mail. Look for imported pasta or order it by the box or case from the sources on page 4 [Olive Oil].

RICE

I fell in love with risotto in Veneto. I watched professional chefs cook it and took copious notes on all phases of risotto preparation but never had fantastic results at home until a chef gave me a bag of Carnaroli rice as a gift. And I learned that great risotto requires first-rate rice. Arborio from the supermarket will never yield the spectacular results of superior Carnaroli or Vialone Nano rice.

Around fifty different kinds of rice are grown in Italy, classified by size, from the shortest, *originario*, followed by *semifino*, *fino*, and the largest, *superfino*, more than one-quarter inch long.

Rice shoots are planted in paddies which are drained when the rice is ripe, harvested nowadays mostly by machine, eliminating the grueling stoop-labor depicted in the film *Bitter Rice*. Rice is separated from the stalks and dried to lower moisture so that it can be stored in silos. Milling is a most important step and some of Italy's finest rice is still milled the traditional way: with wooden pestles pounding into bowls that contain a few handfuls of rice; pestles break the husks for easy removal. Most mills run the rice through rubber rollers to remove the husks, which are separated on rocking racks. The outer husk is grated off, leaving a dusting of rice flour on the grains that will eventually thicken some-one's risotto.

Almost all Italians agree that longer-grained *superfino* is the length of choice for risotto. But rice fans from Veneto, Piedmont, and Lombardy don't agree on the variety. Vialone Nano is widely used in Veneto as is Carnaroli, which is also grown in Piedmont and Lombardy. Baldo is a newly developed variety. All have a central core that remains firm under the tooth and contain enough starch to lightly thicken the liquid they're cooked in. Arborio produces a stickier risotto and no one I spoke to recommended it.

Rice should be used within a year of production. Artisanally produced rice is worth searching for because it makes a far better risotto. It's never treated with chemicals and should be stored in the refrigerator. Look for Carnaroli, Vialone Nano, or Baldo in Italian specialty shops or see the mail-order sources on page 4.

TOMATO PULP

Tomatoes are an important part of Italian cooking, used to great advantage, fresh and ripe, during their summer season. They are sometimes peeled, always seeded and juiced, then chopped. For the rest of the year Italians use canned sauce or peeled whole plum tomatoes, a far better choice than insipid hothouse imitations. Tomato sauce is usually too watery and textureless for my taste. Canned whole tomatoes—which are peeled tomatoes packed in juice or concentrate—are drained and then roughly chopped, which is why I almost always use canned tomato pulp—peeled, seeded, and diced tomato without the excess liquid. Best quality tomato pulp is packed alone or in tomato juice, less wonderful brands are packed in tomato concentrate. For the recipes in this book that call for tomato pulp, use fresh tomatoes in season, peeled if necessary, juiced, seeded, and diced. The rest of the year use canned tomato pulp or drained, chopped canned plum tomatoes. Muir Hill organic tomato pulp is a fine choice.

SALT

In Italy salt is an essential ingredient. Historically important, sustaining empires, salt was a state monopoly until 1974. Sea salt is produced in Italy from Mediterranean sea water, in large shallow salt flats close to the coast. Water evaporates from the heat and wind, the salt crystallizes on a base of waterproof clay and is dried in conical piles, a system that works well in hot climates only. Sea salt is saltier than kosher salt but better tasting than American table salt, which pours so well thanks to the addition of aluminum silicate, a metallic-tasting chemical I'd rather do without. Sea salt in Italy pours thanks to the addition of rice in the salt shaker except in the dampest cities. In the dampest climates, salt clogs in shakers and many people use salt cellars. In the kitchen coarse salt is used by the handful. Foods are often flavored with salt-cured products, like pork (*pancetta*, *guanciale*, etc.), fish (salt cod, anchovies, *bottarga* [pressed roe]), or capers (buds of the caper flower, at their best from the Sicilian islands of Pantelleria or Salina), and additional salt is added when necessary. Pasta and risotto simply can't be cooked without salt and sea salt tastes best.

BROTH

Few people in Italy have broth on hand for soups or risotto. When Italians make boiled meats they use the broth as a first course, served in soup bowls with thin strands of pasta, complex filled pastas, or even *minestrina*, tiny shapes of pasta for soup only, topped with a sprinkling of Parmigiano. I don't know anyone with a supply of stock in the freezer. Italian home cooks have mostly opted for the bouillon cube known as a *dado*. But not me. I use water instead of stock or broth for risotto and in soup flavored with vegetables and no one misses the meat. If I've cooked vegetables in my pasta cooker I use their cooking liquid instead of broth. If I'm especially energetic I'll make a simple vegetable broth, boiling some parsley stems, a carrot, onion, garlic clove, and a few fresh herbs for fifteen minutes. Those who insist on using broth for risotto should make lightly flavored, lightly salted broth since it concentrates during cooking.

PARMIGIANO-REGGIANO

It's not really fair to call Parmigiano-Reggiano cheese. It's unique, in a class by itself, complex, nutty, versatile. Bogus grated cheese called Parmesan in a green can in no way resembles the real thing. Parmigiano-Reggiano has been made in the same area of Italy for over 700 years. Each golden-colored, 80-pound wheel is stenciled on the sides with PARMIGIANO-REGGIANO and is made from 170 gallons of milk, heated with rennet in copper cauldrons, stirred, drained in cheesecloth, pressed in a circular wooden mold, soaked in brine, and placed on wooden shelves to age for at least 18 months.

A good cheese dealer will break the cheese along its natural grain, creating a rough textured surface instead of a clean cut. A freshly cut wedge of Parmigiano-Reggiano should be pale gold flecked with white dots, crystallized amino acids, and show no signs of drying out. It's easy enough to keep a hunk of Parmigiano-Reggiano in the refrigerator, wrapped in wax paper, then tightly wrapped in plastic wrap. If the cheese dries out, wrap it with a damp cloth napkin and refrigerate for a day or two, then remove the damp napkin and wrap in aluminum foil or a clean dry napkin. My cheese expert says that fine Parmigiano-Reggiano is ruined by freezing. A few chunks of Parmigiano-

Reggiano topped with a sprinkle of aged balsamic vinegar (for an imitation of this super ingredient see page 215) are wonderful with a glass of sparkling wine. And aged, good quality Parmigiano-Reggiano, paired with green grapes, makes a wonderful dessert.

SALT-CURED PORK

Salt-cured pork products like *pancetta, guanciale,* and *rigatino* are often used to flavor many Italian dishes but they're never exported from Italy. I've never found a satisfactory version of *pancetta* in the United States, but have had good results with salt pork, far less expensive than pseudo-Italian products. Salt pork should be coated with crushed black pepper and stored in a sealed plastic bag in the refrigerator. I don't think the smoky flavor of bacon belongs in Italian cooking and would sooner eliminate the pork rather than use it.

A NOTE FOR VEGETARIANS

I'm not a vegetarian. There are simply too many foods that I'm not willing to exclude from my diet. But I do love vegetables more than meat. In Italy small amounts of cured pork and fish are often combined with vegetables, providing the complexity that a little protein can give a dish. With the popularity of vegetarianism and worry about cholesterol surely the question "Can I skip the meat" is likely to be asked. In most cases meat and fish can be eliminated although the results may not satisfy those used to the depth of the original dish.

ARTICHOKE

Carciofo

I remember my first artichoke, a new-wave vegetable when I was a kid, far more daring than predictable peas, potatoes, and carrots. I loved the distinctly adult flavor and the sloppy ritual of butter-dipping, leaving front-teeth skid marks on the leaves, the danger of the choke, the excitement of arriving at the exposed heart, savored with the remaining butter. And it was expensive.

Years later, when I came to live in Italy I was excited to find a whole new world of artichokes, *carciofi*, light-years beyond boiled, buttered, thick leaves, and a heart. Minimal fuzzy silk that didn't need to be removed. No steaming or boiling. Italians do wild things with artichokes and even eat them raw, peeled at table in the *pinzimonio* treatment (see page 153).

The artichoke, *Cynara cardunculus scolymus,* is a member of the Compositae family, a perennial thistle cultivated for its inflorescence or unripe head, a potential flower on a thick round stem. Scalelike bracts (or leaves) protect the unformed flower or choke. The tender receptacle, located at the stem-vegetable juncture, is usually referred to as the bottom or heart, buttery-bittersweet when cooked, crisp and nutlike when raw. The first uppermost artichoke of the plant is the biggest and best, followed by smaller lateral heads, concluding with even smaller shoots that form under lower leaves on the stalk, best suited for preserving. Ideally, artichokes are harvested with at least 6 inches of stem, jagged fleshy leaves attached.

Who was the ancient botanist who bred the wild cardoon, emphasizing the development of unripe flowers instead of leaf ribs, domesticating a native thistle into the artichoke, then eating the newly improved vegetable's tender bracts and receptacles? Although it goes against current historic wisdom, which considers the artichoke an Arabian import, I'm sure it's Italian, probably from Sicily or southern Italy where both cardoons and artichokes still grow wild.

In some Italian cities vegetable vendors in large markets perform springtime artichoke-cleaning demonstrations: they sculpt away the trim with a sharp, slim paring knife, rub the exposed surfaces with lemon, and drop trimmed specimens in a bucket of acidulated water with a few lemon halves floating around. For those without an Italian vegetable market around the corner and American artichokes to deal with, Marcella Hazan, stellar cooking teacher, illustrates the cleaning process in her most excellent *Essentials of Classic Italian Cooking* (Alfred A. Knopf, 1993)—required reading for anyone interested in Italian food and wine.

American artichokes are tough and woody with a well-developed choke that must be removed. The choke develops as the artichoke matures, on or off the plant, which is why most American artichokes have them. Italian artichokes are harvested earlier and are brought to market quickly. The cut surface of the stem is rusty-looking, but not brownish black like most artichokes in American markets. Italian chokes are usually negligible. American baby green globe artichokes, which are not really babies but lateral shoots, often have less choke. All artichokes, Italian or American, must be trimmed without thought of waste. Stems (or what's left of them) should be peeled to remove the tough outer layer and then cooked and eaten since they have the same structure and flavor as the artichoke bottom. The heart and the bottom are the same, the tender trimmed core of the artichoke. Artichokes will stay fresher if their stems are cut and immersed in water, like flowers. And artichokes can be revived somewhat by immersion in ice cold water for a few hours.

Begin American globe artichoke cleaning by ruthlessly removing one fourth of the tough outer leaves, properly called bracts. Don't feel guilty about throwing away so much stuff because there's more bitter tannins in outer leaves and tips and they're too tough to eat. But they can be used in herbalist infusions which are supposed to be bitter. I quote Marcella's advice on artichoke cleaning: "Begin by bending back the outer leaves, pulling down toward the base of the artichoke, and snapping them off just before you reach the base. Do not take the paler bottom end of the leaf off because at that point it is tender and quite edible. As you take more leaves off and get deeper into the artichoke, the tender part at which the leaves will snap will be farther and farther from the base. Keep pulling off single leaves that are green only at the tip, and whose paler, whitish base is at least 1 1/2 inches high. Slice at least an inch off the top of that central cone to eliminate all of the tough green part. Take the half lemon and rub the cut portions of the artichoke, squeezing juice over them to keep them from discoloring. Look into the exposed center of the artichoke, where you will see at the bottom very small leaves with prickly tips curving inward. Cut off all those little leaves and scrape away the fuzzy 'choke' beneath them, being careful not to cut away any of the tender bottom. If you have a small knife with a rounded point, it will be easier for you to do this part of the trimming. Return to the outside of the artichoke and, where you have snapped off the outer leaves, pare away any of the tough green part that remains . . . Turn the artichoke upside down and you will notice, inspecting the bottom of the stem, that the stem consists of a whitish core surrounded by a layer of green. The green part is tough, the white, when cooked, soft and delicious, so you must pare away the green, leaving the white intact. Pare the stem thus all the way to the base of the artichoke, being careful not to detach it. Rub all the exposed cut surfaces with lemon juice." Marcella's technique of pulling bracts against the thumb, snapping them at their edible bases, is pure Italian home-style, the easiest way. Thank you, Marcella! Artichoke professionals usually clean with a small sharp knife, paring unmercifully, a faster, more efficient method that results in neat, pale chartreuse, flowerlike heads—"like a rose" explains Francesco Mariani, whose family restaurants serve hundreds of artichokes daily. Paula Wolfert recommends removing the choke with a melon-baller, a nifty trick. After cleaning, put the artichokes in 2–3 quarts of water acidulated with 2 lemons (squeeze the juice into the water and then throw in the empty rinds.) Does a 20-minute soak get rid of some of the artichoke's bitterness or is this just folklore? I do it just in case.

The artichoke is a spring tonic of a vegetable, designed by nature to provide a big dose of vitamins and minerals required by the change of season. For maximum health benefits artichokes should be eaten raw. They contain cynarin, which stimulates the production of bile, which in turn emulsifies animal and vegetable fats. Artichokes are low in calories, rich in potassium, phosphorus, folic acid, zinc, vitamin C, flavonoids, tannins, enzymes, salts, and 2 bitter glucosides that indirectly stimulate the appetite. They're laxative, diuretic, and great for the liver, a major concern for Italians. Artichokes are supposedly good for arthritis, gout, diabetes, high blood pressure. Bract and root infusions can be used for eczema. And most of the herbal texts I consulted consider it an aphrodisiac.

If you like artichokes with butter wait until you taste them with a first-rate extra virgin olive oil. Olives and artichokes grow in the same regions and fine Tuscan olive oil often has a hint of artichoke taste in its intense, complicated array of flavors. Since artichokes curdle milk it doesn't seem digestively prudent to dress them with dairy products. If you're willing to invest the time and labor to clean and cook artichokes, please buy the very best olive oil you can get your hands on, even at its priciest costing no more than 15 cents a tablespoon. Splurge!

Italy is the world's largest grower and consumer of artichokes. Italians grow hundreds of different varieties, native sons including the "little purple" and *mazzaferrata* of Tuscany, globular Roman *cimaroli*, the "sweetie" of Genoa, the "little violet" of Liguria, Venetian "castrates" and "canaries," artichokes from Empoli, Naples, Mola, Palermo, Catania, Syracuse, or Sardinia, with or without thorns tipping bracts. Spring markets throughout Italy are stacked with local, inter- and other-regional artichokes. Only four varieties are available in the United States and 98 percent of the commercial crop is the green globe artichoke.

Romans eat globe artichokes braised in olive oil with garlic and mint, served with 4 inches of stem sticking up in the air, or flattened like a flower and twice-fried to a brown crisp. Venetians love sweet and bitter *castraure* grown in the lagoon, eaten as a bar snack (*cicchetto*) in the city's wine bars (*bacari*). Tuscans prefer the purple artichoke raw, paired with peppery extra virgin olive oil. Throughout Italy artichokes flavor rice and pasta, are roasted over embers, baked in the oven, braised, deep-fried with or without a batter, served raw as a salad, stuffed into meat rolls, star in a classic pan-fried flan (*frittata*), or co-star with fava beans and peas in the eggless Sicilian spring vegetable medley (*frittella*).

Pairing wine with artichokes is no easy task since the vegetable's tannins and cynarin clash with wine. Artichokes alter flavors, creating an illusion of sweetness. Red wine's tannins wage war with those of the artichoke. Big, red wines with high tannins are a poor choice. Choose fresh young soft whites, not too acid, like Verdicchio, Soave, Orvieto, Tocai, or Sauvignon or a rosé.

Artichokes can be grown in much of the United States but gardeners in cold climates will have to baby their plants with mulch and black plastic to avoid frost damage. Those who live in Mediterranean-like climates with cool summers and mild winters will have an easier time. Hot weather results in tough artichokes. The best bearing plants are grown from root sections or rooted shoots, never from seed, which attempts to return to its thistle ancestry. I haven't been able to locate anyone selling artichoke plants but Pinetree Garden Seeds, Box 300, New Gloucester, Maine 04260, Telephone: 207–926–3400, and The Cook's Garden, P.O. Box 535, Londonderry, Vermont 05148, Telephone: 802–824–3400, have Violetto seed, and Fratelli Ingegnoli, Corso Buenos Aires 54, Milan 20124, has seed for Violetto and Romanesco artichokes. Start your own selective breeding program.

The recipes that follow have been carefully adapted to the American green globe. Use medium-size artichokes or twice the number of baby artichokes.

History

Roman Columella (first century B.C.) claims the Latin word for artichoke, *cinara,* comes from ash, with which the plant is fertilized. Pliny refers both to artichokes and cardoons. Apicius includes three recipes for cardoons, seven for cardoon bottoms, which are probably artichokes. In "The Greengrocer" (Book III, of Apicius's *De Re Coquinaria),* Chapter I, "Vegetables," suggests adding bicarbonate when cooking all vegetables to keep colors bright. Most of his recipes are unappealing, heavy on the *garum,* fermented anchovy sauce, a Roman favorite, the ketchup of its day. I wouldn't mind trying the only recipe without it—boiled cardoon bottoms are dressed with wine, oil, fresh coriander, salt, and pepper.

Tuscan doctor M. Pietro Andrea Mattioli translates the Latin text of Dioscoride's *Discussions on Material Medicine* and comments at length on "the composition and virtues of medicaments." The original of the first-century text mentions the cardoon ("to be cooked like asparagus") but not the artichoke. Mattioli's commentary is full of information about the artichoke, a domesticated cardoon in his opinion, and notes that they're called *archichiochi* in Lombardy. He goes on to describe dozens of artichoke varieties found in modern sixteenth-century Tuscany—round, long, open, closed, with and without thorns. "The meat of artichokes cooked in broth is eaten with pepper at the end of the meal and with galanga [N.B., an Asian rhizome] to increase amorous appetites."

Domenico Romoli's 1560 *The Singular Doctrine* takes a strong position in the cardoons-artichoke debate, claiming they're the same thing. He includes a formula for chokeless artichokes—soak seeds in laurel oil and pink water (?) for 3–4 days, dry and plant. Romoli warns against eating artichokes with milk because it will curdle. (In fact, dried artichoke flowers are used to make curds for cheese in parts of Italy.) Artichokes should be eaten cooked, according to Romoli, with vinegar, which tames them, and pepper, which eliminates their windiness. It "incites coitus and cleans the mouth too."

Bolognese doctor Baldassare Pisanelli's *Treatise on the Nature of Food and Drink* (1584) is cautionary about vegetables. Cardoons and artichokes are in the same listing although Pisanelli differentiates between their properties. Artichokes open obstructions, provoke urination, produce wind, warm the viscera, increase coitus, and make the member stiff. Raw artichokes are very windy, bad for the head, lay heavy in the stomach, and delay digestion. In his "Natural History" section Pisanelli claims that artichokes are the "pine cardoon" of classic Rome, requiring removal of the "woolly seed," better cooked than raw.

Venetian-in-exile Giacomo Castelvetro wrote *A Brief Account of the Fruit, Herbs & Vegetables of Italy* in 1614 in an effort to convince the English to eat more vegetables. Castelvetro politely points out that spring is the season for artichokes in Italy: ". . . unlike England where you are fortunate enough to have them all the year round . . . We cook them in your English manner, which is not to be despised, and in other ways as well." His best advice is for dressing charcoal-roasted artichokes with oil or butter, salt, pepper, and a squeeze of bitter orange juice.

Notes in front of the vegetable chapters in Vincenzo Corrado's *Of Pythagorean Food* (1781) often have a light dusting of history, careful cultivar descriptions, and general cooking advice. Artichokes are "of various kinds: white, dark and curly, all shaped like a pine cone." According to Corrado, they must be boiled in water with a few drops of vinegar or lemon juice to avoid discoloration and remove impurity unless they are to be roasted. Of all Corrado's elaborate artichoke recipes my favorite is "common-style," with minced anchovies, garlic, thyme, salt, and pepper stuffed between bracts, dressed with olive oil, and baked in charcoal embers or in the oven.

Artichoke Recipes

AUNT ENZA'S RAW ARTICHOKE CONDIMENT
Minced raw artichoke, egg, and caper

———

SHAVED ARTICHOKE SALAD
Thinly sliced raw artichokes and cheese curls

———

ARTICHOKE RISOTTO

———

GIULIANO'S GARLICKY ARTICHOKE SPAGHETTI

———

MARIA'S SPAGHETTI WITH TOMATO AND ARTICHOKE SAUCE

———

PASTA WITH CHECCHINO'S ARTICHOKE-STEM SAUCE
Leftover artichoke stems made into a sauce

———

FLORENTINE ARTICHOKE *TORTINO*
Baked eggs and artichokes

———

BRICK-FLATTENED ARTICHOKES
Carciofi al Mattone

TORQUATO'S BAKED ARTICHOKE "ERECTS"
Carciofi Ritti

———

FRANCESCO GAUDENZIO'S HERB AND GARLIC–STUFFED ARTICHOKES
Artichokes stuffed with herbs and garlic

———

MARIA'S BREAD CRUMB, PECORINO, GARLIC, AND HERB-STUFFED ARTICHOKES

———

ROBERTO'S BATTERLESS DEEP-FRIED ARTICHOKES

———

MARIA'S BRAISED ARTICHOKES
Braised with garlic and parsley

———

BASIC BOILED CARDOONS (OR HUNCHBACKS)

———

CARDOONS BAKED WITH CHEESE
Cardoons boiled, fried, and baked with cheese

———

AUNT ENZA'S STEWED CARDOONS
Cardoons boiled, fried, and stewed with tomato sauce

Aunt Enza's Raw Artichoke Condiment

For 4–6 Servings   Condiment, Appetizer

y husband Massimo's Aunt Enza is a Tuscan classic. She doesn't trust anything electric invented after the iron, does all her laundry by hand, and
brings a sewing kit when she comes for lunch, just in case anything needs to be
mended. She's a mine of information about her childhood, unheard-of holidays, life
in rural Gonfienti, unmentioned on even the most detailed Italian map. She's a wonderful cook, fanatic about extra virgin olive oil, which she uses for everything, even
deep-frying. Aunt Enza's recipe combines the flavor and texture of raw artichoke
with hard-boiled eggs, capers, and anchovy, held together with extra virgin, more
like a paste than an actual sauce. She chops her artichokes with a *mezzaluna*, a two-
handled half-moon-shaped rocking knife commonly used in Italy, which has the
advantage of reducing accidents since both hands are behind the blade. But a rough-
chop in the food processor will do, with a healthy squeeze of lemon to prevent oxi-
dization. Aunt Enza makes her artichoke sauce as a condiment for boiled beef, an
alternative to *salsa verde*—green sauce (see page 220). I think it's too good to save
for boiled meat and serve it as an appetizer, on toasted garlic bread, or as a side dish.

> 2 tablespoons capers, packed in salt if possible
>
> 2 cups water
>
> 2 cleaned artichokes and stems (see page 14)
>
> ½ lemon to rub on artichokes while cleaning
>   plus 2 tablespoons lemon juice
>
> 1 hard-boiled egg
>
> 2 anchovy fillets
>
> ½ cup extra virgin olive oil
>
> Freshly ground pepper and fine sea salt

1 Soak the salt-packed capers in 2 cups water for 15 minutes to remove excess salt. See
page 112 for a source of salt-packed capers—those in brine add little to this dish.

2 Clean the artichokes without mercy of *all* tough inedible parts as directed on page 14 but
don't bother doing open-heart surgery since the artichoke will be quartered and the
choke can easily be removed. Rub the cleaned, quartered artichokes with lemon half.

3 Pulse the artichokes in a food processor (or coarsely chop with a stainless steel *mezzaluna* or knife) with remaining lemon juice, egg, anchovy fillets, capers, and extra
virgin olive oil. For a fine puree, process instead of pulse. Add pepper and salt.

Shaved Artichoke Salad

*I*t started to appear on menus a few years ago, around the same time as raw fish carpaccio, inspired by the raw beef salad created at Harry's Bar in Venice for a countess client. Although it's not traditional, almost anything raw and sliced thin can be called carpaccio on a contemporary Italian menu. No cooking makes this a quick and easy recipe, which may be why it caught on in such a big way. Fresh crisp raw artichokes are thinly sliced, easiest with a mandoline, slicer, or food processor with a slicing blade. I use my Cuisinart blade like a mandoline but those who choose to follow my example should be *very careful*. To eat raw, artichokes must be *fresh* and *tender*—huge flabby artichokes won't even cut well. And they must be trimmed without mercy to leave only tender edible leaves and heart. Parmigiano-Reggiano or Pecorino Romano cheese is scraped with a vegetable peeler, producing wafer-thin curls of cheese for an elegant garnish. Artichokes prepared in this manner must be eaten immediately.

> 2–3 artichokes
> ½ lemon, juiced
> 2–3 tablespoons extra virgin olive oil
> 2 tablespoons chopped parsley
> Sea salt
> Freshly ground pepper
> One 6-ounce chunk of Parmigiano-Reggiano
>   or Pecorino Romano

1 Clean the artichokes without mercy of *all* tough inedible parts as directed on page 14.

2 Cut the cleaned artichokes in half. Slice each half lengthwise, stem end first, with a slicer or mandoline, as thin as possible. Toss the slices with lemon juice.

3 Place the sliced artichokes on a platter, drizzle with extra virgin olive oil, add parsley, season with salt and pepper, and mix well to combine.

4 Run a vegetable peeler over a chunk of Parmigiano-Reggiano or Pecorino Romano to form curls directly over the platter of dressed artichokes, covering the salad with cheese curls. Serve immediately.

Artichoke Risotto

*A*rtichokes are paired with rice in a classic Italian preparation. They're cleaned of tough, outer bracts and truncated as Marcella directs in her master class on peeling (see page 14), but instead of excavating the heart the lower third of artichoke is sliced off, revealing the choke-topped bottom. Peeled stems and clean bottoms are cooked in a simple vegetable stock. Remaining bracts are sliced in skinny strips, sautéed with aromatics, subjected to a lengthy cooking that melts them into a sauce. The rice is toasted, coated lightly with oil, which binds with rice starch, ready to thicken the white wine and vegetable-artichoke stock. For a wonderful herbal kick add a little minced mint (purists will want to hunt down *mentuccia* or *nepitella,* both wild members of the mint family) after the final stirring. Traditionalists may be shocked but I like to finish the final whipping (*mantecatura*) with extra virgin oil. Butter lovers should substitute their favorite lipid for half or even all the oil in this recipe.

> 2 artichokes
>
> 4 cups water acidulated with 1 lemon, juice
>   and whole rind
>
> 8–10 cups lightly salted vegetable broth (1 onion,
>   1 garlic clove, 1 carrot, 1 celery rib, and a few
>   parsley stems cooked for 15 minutes)
>
> 1 shallot or scallion, chopped
>
> 1 garlic clove, chopped
>
> ¼ cup extra virgin olive oil
>
> 1 cup rice for risotto, Carnaroli or Vialone Nano
>   (see page 8 for information on rice)
>
> ¼ cup dry white wine (optional)
>
> ½ cup grated Parmigiano (and additional cheese
>   to top risotto, if desired)
>
> 1 tablespoon chopped parsley
>
> ½ teaspoon chopped mint (optional)

1 Begin with the hard part, cleaning the artichokes as directed on page 14, but instead of scooping the choke out, slice the bottom third of the artichoke off, revealing choke and heart. Remove the choke and trim the bottom. Slice across the width of the tender trimmed leaf cone to produce thin strips of artichoke. Soak heart, stem, and strips in acidulated water.

(continued)

2 Poach the clean hearts and peeled stems of artichokes in simmering vegetable broth until tender when pierced with a knife, around 10 minutes. Remove from broth, slice hearts, chop stems.

3 While the artichokes are poaching, put the chopped shallot or onion and garlic in a cold 3-quart heavy-bottomed pot, drizzle with 2 tablespoons extra virgin olive oil, and stir with a wooden spoon or fork to coat. Cook over medium heat until tender.

4 Raise the heat, add the drained artichoke strips, and sauté to evaporate any liquid.

5 Add the rice, stir to coat with oil, and cook for a few minutes to lightly toast.

6 Add the white wine, if desired, and evaporate over high heat.

7 Add the vegetable broth, 1 cup at a time, stirring the bottom of the pot with a *long* wooden spoon or fork, over high heat, boiling rice and liquid together. Risotto attains the temperature of molten lava and it's wise to keep one's distance while stirring. Add more vegetable broth when risotto is still surrounded by liquid. After another 8-10 minutes add sliced hearts and chopped stems. Begin to taste rice, which should be firm under tooth, *al dente,* since it will still cook for a few more minutes when the cheese is added. The sauce around the rice should be a little soupy because Parmigiano cheese, oil (or butter), and final whipping will tighten up the sauce, which should be opaque, bathing individual kernels.

8 Add the cheese, herbs, and remaining 2 tablespoons extra virgin olive oil and stir energetically with a long-handled wooden spoon or fork over high heat to whip ingredients together.

9 Remove from heat, ladle into individual bowls, and let risotto rest for a minute before serving. Top with optional Parmigiano.

Giuliano's Garlicky Artichoke Spaghetti

For 4–6 Servings   **First Course**

Giuliano Gargani was a butcher with a gambling debt that had to be paid and lots of friends who loved his cooking. He opened the tiny Trattoria Garga in Florence 16 years ago with his Canadian wife, Sharon, utilizing his skills as an artist, cook, and butcher to make some money. Giuliano's cooking is based on Tuscan ingredients but it's not traditional, as would be expected of an anticonformist artist. Due to popular demand, Garga moved up the street a few years ago, enlarging to three dining rooms and adding some fantastic new dishes to the menu. My favorite is Giuliano's garlicky artichoke spaghetti, a classic garlic and extra virgin olive oil sauce with the addition of thinly sliced raw artichokes.

Giuliano likes to keep the garlic raw but I add a little water during the pasta's final cooking with artichokes to lighten up the garlicky flavor. Giuliano sharpens his knife each time he slices an artichoke but a sharp mandoline or slicer can be used. I use my Cuisinart blade like a mandoline but those who choose to follow my example should be *very careful*. Artichokes are sliced at the last minute, covered with extra virgin olive oil in a skillet so they don't turn brown.

> 2–3 artichokes, cleaned (see page 14)
> 3 cups plus 5-6 quarts water
> ½ lemon
> 2–3 tablespoons sea salt
> 14–16 ounces spaghetti
> ½ cup extra virgin olive oil
> 2 garlic cloves
> freshly ground pepper
> 2 tablespoons chopped parsley

1 Cut the cleaned artichokes in half. Soak in 3 cups of water with the juice and rind of ½ lemon.

2 Bring 5–6 quarts of water to a rolling boil. Add 2–3 tablespoons salt and the pasta.

3 While the pasta is cooking, gently heat the olive oil and the garlic in a large nonstick skillet but don't brown.

4 Place the drained artichokes, cut side down, on a cutting board and slice lengthwise, with a *sharp* knife, or slice, stem end first, with a slicer, mandoline, or Cuisinart

(continued)

1-mm blade. Immediately put the slices in the skillet with the oil and garlic, stirring to coat artichoke slices with the oil. Season with salt and pepper.

5   Cook the pasta until it still offers considerable resistance to the tooth, around three quarters of the recommended cooking time on the package. Drain, reserving 2 cups of pasta water.

6   Add the pasta to the skillet with the garlic and the artichokes and cook, over high heat, stirring 1 cup pasta cooking water to complete pasta cooking, which should take 3–4 minutes. Sprinkle with parsley and serve.

Maria's Spaghetti
with Tomato and Artichoke Sauce

For 4–6 Servings   **First Course**

*M*y housekeeper Maria di Fazio, a terrific home cook, is originally from Apulia, a southern region that takes artichokes seriously. When I come back from the market with fresh produce Maria always wants to tell me what she would do with my purchases and some of her suggestions are so tempting that I hand over my vegetables for an instant cooking lesson. Maria's accent in Italian and the food she prepares reflect her southern heritage even though she's lived in Florence for more than 30 years. She eliminates the final syllable of most words, gets gender wrong more than I do, and never uses butter or cream. Maria takes all the effort out of artichoke preparation, trimming with practiced motions. I love her pasta sauce of garlicky tomato sauce with artichokes.

> 4 artichokes, cleaned as directed on page 14
>   and cut into 8 wedges
> ¼ cup extra virgin olive oil
> 1 garlic clove, minced
> 2 tablespoons minced parsley
> 1 tablespoon plus 5-6 quarts water
> 1½ cups tomato pulp
> Sea salt and freshly ground pepper
> 14–16 ounces spaghetti
> ¼ cup grated Parmigiano (optional)

1 Place the artichoke wedges in a large nonstick skillet and drizzle with the olive oil. Stir to coat the artichokes and place over moderate heat. Cook the artichoke wedges for 5 minutes, stirring frequently, to brown lightly.

2 Add the garlic and parsley and cook for 2–3 minutes. Add 1 tablespoon of water and cover the skillet. Cook for 5 minutes or until artichokes are tender. Raise the heat and evaporate the excess water. Remove the artichokes with a slotted spoon to food processor and pulse a few times to roughly chop.

3 Put the chopped artichokes back into the skillet with the tomato pulp. Cook over moderate heat for 5 minutes or until the sauce thickens slightly and season with salt and pepper.

4 Bring 5–6 quarts of water to a rolling boil. Add 2–3 tablespoons of salt and the pasta.

5 Cook the pasta until it still offers considerable resistance to the tooth, around three quarters of the recommended cooking time on the package. Drain the pasta, reserving 2 cups of pasta water.

6 Add the pasta and 1 cup pasta water to the skillet with the artichoke sauce and cook, stirring, for 3–5 minutes over high heat until pasta is done and the sauce coats pasta. Add more pasta water if sauce becomes too dry, ¼ cup at a time, to complete cooking. Serve with grated Parmigiano if desired.

Pasta with Checchino's
Artichoke-Stem Sauce

For 4–6 Servings   **First Course**

*C*hecchino is one of my favorite restaurants in Italy, where the Mariani family serves traditional Roman food, exquisitely prepared with the finest of ingredients. During the late winter and early spring season they prepare around 50 Roman-style artichokes a day, stewed with olive oil, white wine, garlic, and wild Roman mint (*mentuccia*), served with 3 inches of stem sticking straight up on the plate. Francesco Mariani uses a shoemaker's leather cutter to trim artichokes with the skill that comes of decades of practice. Artichokes arrive at the restaurant with over a foot of stem and since nothing is thrown away in a good Italian kitchen, this recipe is the solution for what to do with stems. They're carefully peeled and cooked with garlic to make an artichoke puree that's the base of a pasta sauce. Home cooks who don't have a wealth of artichoke stems can cook hearts and stems to make the puree, and slice tender leaves into thin strips to add to the pasta.

> 2 large artichokes
> ½ lemon
> ¼ cup extra virgin olive oil
> 2 garlic cloves
> ¼ cup plus 5-6 quarts water
> 2 tablespoons chopped parsley
> Sea salt and freshly ground pepper to taste
> 14–16 ounces spaghetti or linguine

1 Remove the tough outer leaves of the artichokes and cut the artichokes to separate the cone of leaves from the bottom.

2 Remove the choke from the artichoke bottoms and rub them with the split lemon. Peel artichoke stems to eliminate tough outer portion and rub stems with lemon. Slice only the tenderest part of the artichoke leaf cones into thin strips, squeeze lemon juice over the strips, and toss to coat.

3 Place the artichoke stems and bottoms and 2 tablespoons extra virgin olive oil in a small saucepan over moderate heat and cook for 5 minutes or until lightly browned.

4 Add the garlic and cook for 2–3 minutes. Add the 1 tablespoon of water and cook until artichoke stems and bottoms are tender and water is evaporated. Add more water if necessary to complete cooking.

5 Puree the artichoke stems, bottoms, garlic, and parsley in a food processor to form a smooth paste and season with salt and pepper.

6 Put the artichoke leaf strips in a large nonstick skillet and drizzle with remaining 2 tablespoons extra virgin olive oil.

7 Cook the artichoke strips over moderate heat for 5 minutes or until barely colored.

8 Bring 5–6 quarts of water to a rolling boil. Add salt and the pasta.

9 Cook the pasta until it still offers considerable resistance to the tooth, around three quarters of the recommended cooking time. Drain the pasta, reserving 2 cups of pasta water. Add pasta, artichoke stem and bottom puree, and 1 cup pasta water to skillet with artichoke strips and cook for 3–5 minutes over high heat until pasta is done and sauce coats pasta. Add more pasta water if sauce becomes too dry, ¼ cup at a time, to complete cooking.

Florentine Artichoke *Tortino*

*F*lorentines adore artichokes. Home cooks and trattorie make this traditional *tortino*, like a creamless, pastryless, minimalist quiche of sautéed artichokes baked with eggs. Traditionalists should flour and fry artichoke slices but I prefer to eliminate the flour, which gets a little gummy.

> 3 artichokes, cleaned as directed on page 14,
>   cut into 8 wedges (lightly floured if desired)
> 4 tablespoons extra virgin olive oil
> 1 garlic clove, minced
> 4 tablespoons minced parsley
> 1 tablespoon water
> 4 eggs
> Sea salt and freshly ground pepper

1   Preheat the oven to 400 degrees. Lightly oil a 10-inch round baking dish.

2   Place artichoke wedges in a large nonstick skillet and drizzle with olive oil. Stir to coat the artichokes and place over moderate heat. Cook for 5 minutes, stirring frequently, to brown lightly.

3   Add the minced garlic and parsley and cook for 2–3 minutes. Add the water, cover the skillet, and cook for 5 minutes or until artichokes are tender. Remove the lid, raise heat, and evaporate excess water.

4   Remove the artichokes with a slotted spoon to the prepared baking dish.

5   Beat the eggs to blend, season with salt and pepper, and pour over the artichokes.

6   Bake for 10–15 minutes or until set but not brown.

Brick-Flattened Artichokes
Carciofi al Mattone

For 4 Servings   **Side Dish**

*O*ne of the great joys of spring in Rome are *carciofi alla giudia*, crisp, whole, fried artichokes done in the Roman Jewish-style. They're carefully trimmed, fried twice, producing artichokes with crunchy brown leaves and a creamy heart, wonderful to eat but not fun to make. The person who invented brick-flattened artichoke must have loved the Jewish-style artichokes but hated deep-frying, just like me. He or she used a flattened-with-heavy-weight technique for grilled chicken known as *al mattone*, "with a brick," to cook artichokes, creating *carciofi al mattone*. Artichokes are mercilessly cleaned to eliminate all tough leaves and choke, sautéed in extra virgin olive oil over low heat until tender, drained upside down, and cooled. The leaves are then gently opened and the artichokes are cooked again with a film of extra virgin instead of deep-frying, covered with a weighted plate to flatten. The result is a pan-grilled version of the Jewish-style artichokes.

> 4 artichokes, cleaned as directed on page 14
> 3 tablespoons extra virgin olive oil
> Sea salt

1   Pare the base of each artichoke so that it will stand up.

2   Heat 2 tablespoons extra virgin oil in a small pot, add the artichokes, and cook over low heat, turning often, to lightly brown on all sides, for 20–30 minutes. Stand the artichokes up and cook for 8–10 minutes to cook the bottoms. Artichokes should be tender when pierced with a toothpick.

3   Remove the artichokes from the pot and drain them upside down on paper towels until cool.

4   Gently spread the leaves of the artichokes. Turn the artichokes upside down and flatten them on the paper towels.

5   Lightly oil a large nonstick skillet with remaining 1 tablespoon extra virgin olive oil and place the artichokes on the skillet, bases facing up. Place a plate large enough to cover on top of artichokes and put a heavy weight (or a pot filled with water) on the plate to flatten the artichokes during the second cooking.

6   Cook over moderate heat for 10–12 minutes or until leaves are brown and crisp. Sprinkle with sea salt and serve immediately.

Torquato's Baked Artichoke "Erects"
Carciofi Ritti

*T*he Italian language was born in Tuscany, a region that has a way with words, a subtle biting humor, and an ancient vocabulary. This is the language of Dante and also of Torquato, who relates artichoke recipes to me in spite of the fact that he doesn't sell any. Salt and pepper-cured pork are important flavor elements for Torquato's traditional Tuscan recipe but quality *pancetta* may be almost impossible to find. It's better to use first-rate sausage than crummy *pancetta*. "Erect" artichokes are usually prepared on top of the stove, steamed with a little liquid, but Torquato recommends baking in the oven, which results in a crisper, less tender artichoke.

> 2 garlic cloves
> ¼ cup parsley leaves
> 6 ounces salt pork or sausage
> Sea salt and freshly ground pepper
> 4 large artichokes, cleaned as directed on page 14,
>   stems removed

1 Preheat the oven to 375 degrees. Lightly oil a baking dish large enough to hold the artichokes (if you will be using one).

2 Chop or process the garlic and parsley and mix with the chopped salt pork or sausage with the casing removed. Season with salt and pepper. Divide the stuffing into four parts.

3 Press down on the artichokes to separate leaves, making room for the filling. Replace the choke with some of the filling and stuff the rest between the separated bracts at random.

4 Place the artichokes standing up in the prepared baking dish, cover tightly with foil, and bake for 30 minutes. Or wrap individual artichokes in foil and bake for 30 minutes. Remove the foil and brown for 10–15 minutes or until browned and tender.

Francesco Gaudenzio's
Herb and Garlic-Stuffed Artichokes

For 4 Servings   **Side Dish**

Tuscan Oiled Bread by Francesco Gaudenzio (1705) is subtitled "a work, In which the easy way to modern economical cooking is shown." In his preface, he promises to teach the inexpert "to learn the correct way to cook so that foods are welcome and proper." Gaudenzio was a Jesuit cook, practicing his art in monasteries in Spoleto, Rome, and Arezzo, and his cookbook emphasizes meatless cooking for fast days. He suggests parboiling and frying tender artichokes but his section entitled "To Cook Artichokes in Various Ways and Methods and Roast" describes cleaning, squashing to open up bracts, and stuffing with parsley, Roman mint, garlic, salt, pepper, and oil, to be baked in the oven or on the grill. The following recipe is inspired by his advice, a minimalist vegetarian version of Torquato's Baked Artichoke "Erects" (see page 30) with extra virgin olive oil sitting in for pork.

> ⅓ cup chopped parsley
>
> 1 teaspoon chopped mint
>
> 2–3 garlic cloves, minced
>
> ½ cup extra virgin olive oil
>
> 4 whole artichokes, cleaned as directed on page 14
>
> Sea salt and freshly ground pepper

1 Preheat the oven to 375 degrees. Prepare a lightly oiled baking dish large enough to hold the artichokes.

2 Mix the herbs, garlic, and ¼ cup extra virgin oil and divide the stuffing into four parts.

3 Press down on the artichokes to separate the leaves, making room for the filling. Stuff the herb mixture between the leaves and in the central cavity of each artichoke. Place the artichokes in the prepared baking dish and drizzle with the remaining oil. Season with salt and pepper.

4 Wrap each artichoke in aluminum foil and bake for 30 minutes, uncover and brown for 10–15 minutes. Or wrap with foil and grill for 30–40 minutes, turning often.

RED, WHITE
& GREENS

Maria's Bread Crumb, Pecorino, Garlic, and Herb-Stuffed Artichokes

For 4 Servings   **Side Dish**

*M*aria di Fazio, my housekeeper from Apulia, couldn't contain herself when I was trying stuffed artichoke recipes, comparing them with her traditional method, which I liked best of all. It's just the right combination of flavors, not quite as lean as Gaudenzio's or as heavy as Torquato's.

> ½ cup unflavored bread crumbs
>
> ½ cup grated Pecorino Romano
>
> 2 garlic cloves, chopped
>
> 2 tablespoons chopped parsley
>
> ¼ cup extra virgin olive oil
>
> 4 artichokes, cleaned as directed on page 14

1 Preheat the oven to 375 degrees.

2 Combine the bread crumbs, grated cheese, garlic, parsley, and 3 tablespoons extra virgin olive oil. Divide the stuffing into four parts, one for each artichoke.

3 Press down on the artichokes to separate the leaves, making room for the filling. Stuff each artichoke with the bread crumb and cheese mixture, putting it between the leaves and in the central cavity.

4 Wrap the artichokes in aluminum foil, drizzle with remaining olive oil, and bake for 30 minutes. Remove the foil and bake for 10–15 minutes or until browned.

Roberto's Batterless
Deep-Fried Artichokes

*R*istorante Omero is a five-minute ride through the Tuscan countryside just outside Florence, complete with views of stone walls, villas, farms, olive trees, and cypress. The country-style restaurant has a grocery in the front that sells olive oil from a terra-cotta urn. Prosciutto hangs from the ceiling, a wooden rack holds loaves of saltless bread, wheels of pecorino sheep's milk cheese with orange-colored rinds sit on shelves, locals stop in for a coffee at the tiny bar or to pick up bus tickets or cigarettes. The dining room is in the back, windows with a typical Tuscan vista matched by traditional Tuscan menu. Soup, simple pasta, meat and poultry grilled or deep-fried, white beans to be dressed with extra virgin oil and deep-fried seasonal vegetables are specialties, but Roberto has a better idea for frying artichokes. Artichokes are carefully trimmed to eliminate inedible tough leaves and tips, cut into wedges, and kept in water acidulated with lemon, ready to be drained, patted dry, lightly floured, and deep-fried at 325 degrees. The resulting artichoke crisps are a big improvement over traditional batter-heavy fried artichokes and are even less messy to make. Tough globe artichokes may need to be briefly boiled, drained, and dried before deep-frying but carefully cleaned fresh artichokes shouldn't be a problem.

> 4 cups extra virgin olive oil (or corn oil if you must)
>
> 4 artichokes, cleaned as directed on page 14, cut into 8 wedges, soaked in 3 cups water and juice of ½ lemon
>
> ½ cup flour in a paper bag
>
> Sea salt to taste

1 Heat the oil to 325 degrees.

2 Drain the artichoke wedges and pat them dry with paper towels.

3 Place the artichoke wedges in a paper bag with the flour. Shake the bag to lightly flour artichoke wedges.

4 Fry the artichokes until golden brown. Drain them on paper towels and serve immediately, sprinkled with salt.

Maria's Braised Artichokes

For 4 Servings   Appetizer, Side Dish

*O*nce again Maria di Fazio had to add another recipe to my artichoke repertoire. Simply braised artichoke wedges are an easy addition to any spring meal, and can be served as an appetizer or side dish. Double the recipe to ensure leftovers, which can be used in Maria's pasta recipe on page 24 or in the Florentine Artichoke *Tortino* on page 28. If Maria isn't on hand to help, the hardest part is cleaning the artichokes. All ingredients are placed in a cold pan and cooked, covered (otherwise they'll darken, says Maria), for 10 minutes over medium heat until tender.

> 4 artichokes, cleaned as directed on page 14,
>   cut into 8 wedges
> 3–4 tablespoons extra virgin olive oil
> 1 garlic clove, minced
> 2 tablespoons minced parsley
> 1 tablespoon water
> Sea salt and freshly ground pepper

1 Place the artichoke wedges in a large nonstick skillet and drizzle with the extra virgin olive oil. Stir to coat the artichokes and place over moderate heat. Cook for 5 minutes, stirring frequently, to brown lightly.

2 Add minced garlic and parsley and cook for 2–3 minutes. Add the water, cover the skillet, and cook for 5 minutes or until artichokes are tender. Raise heat and evaporate excess water. Season with salt and pepper and serve warm or at room temperature.

ARTICHOKE

Basic Boiled Cardoons (or Hunchbacks)

I've never really understood the difference between cardoons (*cardi*) and hunch-backs (*gobbi*). *The Reader's Digest Grand Illustrated Italian Gastronomic Encyclopedia* claims in the cardoon entry that the difference is in the blanching phase, when earth is mounded around the base of cardoons and "hunchbacks" are bent and buried under dirt in lateral holes. But the "hunchback" entry defines them as a dialect for cardoons. In spite of the linguistic confusion, cardoons and "hunchbacks" are found in winter markets but rarely on restaurant menus since they demand quite a lot of work. The tough stringy outer layers of cardoon ribs must be peeled away, and cardoon pieces, like artichokes, must be soaked in acidu-lated water to avoid darkening.

Although cardoons are eaten raw in Piedmont, as an important element of a tra-ditional *bagna cauda* (see page 166), everyone else in Italy eats them cooked. They're almost always given a preliminary boil after which the fantasy of regional cooking takes over. *The Reader's Digest s*uggests boiling for 2–2 1/2 hours but I think they're exaggerating. Cook until tender.

> 7 quarts water
> 2½–3 pounds cardoons
> 1 lemon, cut in half
> 2–3 tablespoons sea salt

1   Bring a large pot with 5 quarts of water to a rolling boil.

2   Trim cardoons. Remove jagged leaves at the edges of the stalks. Cut stalks into 3-inch lengths and rub cut edges with ½ lemon. Pare away the tough outer stalk or remove the strings as with celery. Place cardoon pieces in 2 quarts of water acidu-lated with remaining ½ lemon.

3   Add drained cardoon pieces and 2–3 tablespoons salt to boiling water. Boil cardoon pieces until tender, from 10–30 minutes depending on season and variety. Remove with a slotted spoon, refresh with cold water, and drain. Proceed to one of the next two recipes.

ARTICHOKE

Cardoons Baked with Cheese

*C*lassic cardoon Parmigiano is simply boiled cardoons layered with butter and grated Parmigiano, baked in the oven. But my family finds it too mushy and Massimo hates butter. So I humor him with floured and fried cardoons, sprinkled with cheese and baked until brown.

> Basic Boiled Cardoons (see page 35)
> ½ cup flour in a paper bag
> Extra virgin olive oil for frying
> Fine sea salt and freshly ground pepper
> ½ cup grated Parmigiano-Reggiano

1 Preheat the oven to 400 degrees.

2 Blot the cooked cardoon pieces with paper towels.

3 Place the cardoons in a paper bag with flour and shake to lightly coat with flour.

4 Fry cardoons in ½-inch extra virgin olive oil over moderate heat until lightly browned. Remove with a slotted spoon and drain on paper towels.

5 Place the cardoons in a baking dish, season with salt and pepper, and sprinkle with grated cheese. Bake for 15–20 minutes or until cheese begins to brown.

ARTICHOKE

Aunt Enza's Stewed Cardoons

*A*nother side dish that crowds my husband's aunt Enza's table when we have Sunday lunch together. It's a Tuscan classic although it's a lot of work. Cardoons are cooked three times—boiled, fried, and braised. I've tried to lighten this dish and lessen labor by skipping the flouring and frying steps but my family resists any effort to change this dish, which we all love in its traditional form. And so I've decided to use aunt Enza's recipe.

> Basic Boiled Cardoons (see page 35)
> ½ cup flour in a paper bag
> Extra virgin olive oil for frying, plus 1 tablespoon
> 1–2 garlic cloves, minced
> 2 cups tomato pulp
> Sea salt and freshly ground pepper
> ¼ cup water (optional)

1 Blot the cardoon pieces with paper towels.

2 Place the cardoons in a paper bag with flour and shake to lightly coat with flour.

3 Fry the cardoons in ½-inch extra virgin olive oil over moderate heat until lightly browned. Remove the cardoons with a slotted spoon and drain on paper towels.

4 Drizzle 1 tablespoon of extra virgin olive oil over minced garlic in a large nonstick skillet. Place the skillet over moderate heat and cook until the garlic barely begins to color. Add the tomato pulp, season with salt and pepper, and cook for a few minutes. Add the cardoon pieces and cook over low heat for 10–15 minutes. Add ¼ cup water to the tomato sauce if it gets too thick.

ARTICHOKE

RED, WHITE
& GREENS

ASPARAGUS AND HIS COUSINS

*Asparagi e
Suoi Cugini*

In the Italian language nouns and adjectives have gender and most vegetables are feminine. Asparagus, in Italian, is male, considered an aphrodisiac, the bigger the better. Stalks, also known as spears, spring full-grown from the soil with no warning, no leaves or first growth to distract. Green, white, or purple asparagus appears in spring markets throughout Italy, at times joined by his cousins wild asparagus and asparagus-like hops, clematis shoots, and butcher's-broom.

Asparagus, a perennial member of the Liliaceae family, along with onion, garlic, and leek, has a language and style of its own. Underground rhizomes grow horizontally to the soil's surface, sending up turions, tender young shoots with cladophylls, scales that function as leaves. Unharvested, the shoots lignify, become tough and woody, growing to up to 5 feet in height, forming fernlike branches. Male and female flowers are on separate plants and males supposedly produce better stalks since they waste no time or effort producing fruit.

Asparagus officinalis was classified by Linnaeus as a medicinal plant, hence the *officinalis* categorization. Asparagine, one of its active components, produces distinctively scented urine, is diuretic, and stimulates the urinary tract, which may account for its aphrodisiac reputation. Asparagine is also said to eliminate "bad humours" and purify the body. According to Italian folklore, asparagus root, either worn in a small pouch or brewed as tea, was an effective form of birth control. Asparagus has plenty of potassium, great folic acid, and vitamins A, B, and C, which are mostly lost when cooked. Wild asparagus have far more vitamins and minerals than cultivated specimens.

Asparagus are thought to be of Mesopotamian origin but they grow wild throughout the Mediterranean. They were utilized by Greeks and Egyptians although early references are to wild asparagus. Romans were probably the first to domesticate it and, befitting a new, improved, bigger, better vegetable, paid it a lot of attention. After the fall of the Roman Empire labor-intensive asparagus were cultivated in monastery gardens along with medicinal herbs. Wild asparagus were gathered by people who didn't write about it. Recipe collections from this period haven't survived, although surely dozens of handwritten monastery cookbooks in Latin are tucked away in Italian libraries waiting to be discovered.

Dozens of strictly regional asparagus varieties, classified by color and cultivation zone, are grown in Italy. White asparagus are grown in Bassano and much of northern Veneto and Friuli as well as Pescia in Tuscany and Tivoli outside Rome. Asparagus are white because they've been blanched, harvested before the spears emerge from the ground, which makes them harder to pick and therefore more expensive than green asparagus. Blanching tenderizes asparagus but yields a less flavorful spear. Purple Napoli, Genova, and Milano asparagus, violet-colored stalks with white butts, are harvested just after surfacing. Green asparagus are most common, cut after spears emerge from the soil, tastier than white or purple. American and Dutch cultivars dominate Italian commercial production, preferred for high yield and disease resistance. Local cultivation of traditional varieties thrives in some areas but new hybrids and out of season imports from California, Mexico, and Israel appear in Italian markets. Wild asparagus, *officinalis* as well as *acutifolius*, grow throughout Italy, intensely flavored skinny stalks found in the spring, rarely sold in markets. Alternative wild greens with asparagus-like flavor include slightly bitter hops and wild clematis shoots, hunted by foragers in the spring, usually used in risotto or *frittate* pan-fried flans. Butcher's-broom, *ruscus aculeatus* or *hypoglossum*, called "garden asparagus" in Sicily, is actually a relative of holly but sends up shoots that resemble asparagus.

There are, in Italy, three different schools of asparagus cleaning. Two begin by trimming off the hard butt end. Parers don't waste anything and remove the tough outer layer of the lower stem with knife or peeler, yielding entirely edible spears with minimum waste. Cooks in a hurry snap off the tough stalk at the point where it's tender enough to break, yielding entirely edible asparagus. The third school, for hands-on eaters, trims off most of the really tough often dirty butt end, leaving plenty of stiff inedible stalk, which is used as a handle to up pick up asparagus, discarded when it gets too tough and fibrous to eat. I usually opt for this method when serving whole asparagus because it's quick and I enjoy picking up spears with my fingers, but when entertaining etiquette-conscious diners I snap off the tough part of the stalks.

Most of the natural sugar in asparagus is lost within hours of its harvest, as those lucky enough to grow their own are well aware. Just-picked asparagus are sweet, crisp, with a livelier flavor. To simulate super-fresh asparagus slice a layer off the butt ends, place stalks in a container with 3 inches of water sweetened with sugar for 30 minutes or more.

In Italy asparagus are customarily eaten boiled, usually prepared in the same large pot that pasta is cooked in, tall enough to hold the asparagus standing up. Save the cooking water from asparagus and use instead of broth for risotto. Extra virgin olive oil is the condiment of choice although hot asparagus are often dressed with butter. Asparagus are often paired with eggs or anchovies. In Veneto, diners make a condiment for boiled asparagus at the table (never prepared in advance in the kitchen) by mashing a medium-boiled (8-minute) egg with a fork, adding olive oil, vinegar, and salt and pepper to taste. See page 51 for details. Asparagus are tasty in a vegetarian carbonara, with eggs, grated pecorino, and extra virgin. Tame and wild asparagus, hops, clematis shoots, and butcher's-broom are traditionally boiled and served simply with extra virgin and lemon, or paired with eggs in a *frittata*. Risotto with asparagus or any of his cousins is a spring ritual in northern, rice-loving Italy. Pasta fans pair asparagus with both homemade egg and commercial hard wheat pasta. The most elementary of recipes combines chunks of asparagus, butter or oil, and pasta.

Even my favorite Italian seed catalog doesn't stock seed or crowns of traditional asparagus. Disease-resistant, high-yield hybrids have edged traditional cultivars toward extinction. Fratelli Ingegnoli, the most important Italian seed catalog, doesn't have Italian cultivars.

The canning and freezing industries have done the asparagus a great disservice, totally altering flavor and texture beyond recognition. Just say no.

History

Pliny (first century A.D.) wrote of wild and domestic asparagus in *The Natural History* and commented on the huge (three to a pound!) asparagus of Ravenna, exaggerating as usual. He considered asparagus "among the most useful of foods," laxative, diuretic, improving vision, good for chest and back pain, and, of course, aphrodisiac, especially the cooking water.

The conquering legions of Julius Caesar spread asparagus cultivation throughout the Roman Empire. And according to Plutarch, when Julius Caesar ate asparagus dressed with "aromatic grease" (most likely flavored lard) in Milan instead of his customary olive oil, fellow Roman diners ridiculed this rustic northern custom. The Romans were right because extra virgin olive oil is the perfect condiment for asparagus.

In the second century Suetonius coined an expression in his *Life of Augustus* for quick action, "*celerius quam asparagi cocuntur,*" or faster than cooking asparagus. Modern Italians who subject most vegetables to lengthy cooking should heed his advice for asparagus cooking.

Social critic Juvenal got excited about the simple things in life like "wild asparagus just harvested by the farm-wife" instead of jumbo domesticated produce preferred by sophisticated society Romans. Anyone who has ever eaten just-picked wild asparagus would probably agree with him.

One of the first cookbooks written in Italian was the anonymous Tuscan's fourteenth-century *Kitchen Book*, with vague instructions, no measurements, and no cooking times—clearly written by an Italian. The book's sketchy asparagus recipe calls for boiling asparagus, then cooking

them again with oil, onion, salt, saffron, and spice, the last two expensive imports used with abandon in many ancient cookbooks which document the foods of the wealthy.

Florentine sixteenth-century poet Luigi Alamanni's classically inspired 6-volume didactic poem *The Cultivation* includes this advice in couplet for asparagus growers. "Now of the lubricious asparagus the cultivator must take care; and if from the seed a principle he wishes to produce, the site chosen will be healthy and damp." Modern gardeners will have better results planting year-old asparagus crowns, available at many nurseries, instead of the seeds recommended by Alamanni.

Costanzo Felici, provincial doctor from the Marches, corresponded at great length with Ulisse Aldrovandi, illustrious naturalist and doctor from Bologna. Felici expanded one of his letters into a treatise entitled *Of Salad and Plants Used by Man as Food*, written in 1569. He examines all members of the vegetable kingdom, both wild and domesticated, including lots of New World imports. Felici notes that asparagus, the most prized of tender shoots, "are harvested for salads, boiled, even eaten by many raw or grilled and [are] very friendly with pepper." He also describes hops, wild clematis, and butcher's-broom, remarking on their similarity of taste to asparagus.

New-wave Protestant thinker, Continental traveler in exile Giacomo Castelvetro wrote *A Brief Account of the Fruit, Herbs & Vegetables of Italy* in 1614, a heroic attempt to introduce the joys of fresh produce to the English, who took quite a few centuries to get the message. He wrote eloquently about growing and cooking vegetables and the benefits derived from eating them. Castelvetro begins his spring chapter with hops, the first shoots of the season, boiled, "seasoned with salt, plenty of oil and a little vinegar or lemon juice and some crushed, not powdered, pepper." He tries to convince skeptical farmers to cultivate asparagus for financial gain, declaring that ". . . one acre of land would yield more income in less time than ten fields sown with wheat."

Florentine monastery cook Francesco Gaudenzio's *Panunto Toscanso* was written in 1705 for inexpert cooks, revealing "the correct rule of cooking." Befitting Gaudenzio's monastery kitchen career, he includes a soup for meatless fast days and instructs cooks to break asparagus where they are tender, parboil for the time it takes to say the Fifty-first Psalm, and finish cooking in broth.

Vincenzo Corrado's *Of Pythagorean Food*, subtitled "For the Use of Nobles and Literati," takes advantage of the eighteenth-century rage for classical philosophy and diet, proposing an easier to digest regime for intellectuals leading a sedentary life. It's a far cry from Pythagoras's fifth-century B.C. Mediterranean vegan-animal rights program (no cooking, no leather or wool garments) and includes meat and poultry broth, fish, eggs and dairy products. Corrado misquotes Pliny and erroneously attributes Suetonius's expression about quick action to someone else for a little historical inaccuracy, but his culinary comments and recipes are on target. He begins all recipes with boiled asparagus, which are then dressed with oil, lemon, and anchovy paste, floured and deep-fried, dressed with oil, parsley, garlic, anchovy, and oregano, wrapped in paper, and slowly grilled or baked. Corrado's variations include soups, stuffings, vegetable torte, *frittate*, and garnishes for cold meat or fish.

Asparagus Recipes

CASTELVETRO-INSPIRED ASPARAGUS CARPACCIO

Raw asparagus slices dressed with Parmigiano curls and extra virgin olive oil

—

PENNE WITH ASPARAGUS-LEMON SAUCE

Short pasta sauced with asparagus puree and tips and lemon zest

—

NEW-WAVE ASPARAGUS CARBONARA PASTA

Asparagus substitutes for pork in the Roman classic

—

ASPARAGUS (OR HIS COUSINS) RISOTTO

WHOLE ROAST OR GRILLED ASPARAGUS

Pan-roasted or grilled asparagus spears

—

VENETO MASHED EGG CONDIMENT FOR BOILED ASPARAGUS

—

ARTUSI'S BAKED ASPARAGUS

—

PONTORMO'S ASPARAGUS BISMARCK

Boiled asparagus topped with fried eggs and Parmigiano-Reggiano

—

ASPARAGUS (OR HIS COUSINS) *FRITTATA*

Castelvetro-Inspired Asparagus Carpaccio

For 4–6 Servings   **Appetizer**

Giacomo Castelvetro escaped to England to avoid persecution for his radical new-wave Protestant ideas. He wrote *A Brief Account of the Fruit, Herbs & Vegetables of Italy* in 1614, a heroic attempt to introduce the joys of fresh produce to the English, who took centuries to get the message. He isn't impressed by raw asparagus and cheese but I was the first time I tasted it in a northern Veneto marathon asparagus meal, with 14 courses featuring my favorite turion. It's one of the easiest appetizers to throw together, with no cooking and only five ingredients, including salt and pepper. Raw asparagus are diagonally sliced paper-thin, with a mandolin, slicer, or precision knife skills. I use a 1-mm Cuisinart slicing blade and hand-slice asparagus, holding on to the tip, using the blade like a mandoline. Anyone choosing this technique should *be careful*! For best-tasting asparagus, slice off tough butt ends and stand spears in a few inches of sweetened water for at least 30 minutes to replace some of the natural sweetness lost soon after harvest.

> 8–12 fresh asparagus spears
> 2 tablespoons extra virgin olive oil
> Sea salt and freshly ground pepper
> One 4-ounce piece of Parmigiano,
>   to make cheese shavings

1   Snap the tough ends off the asparagus at the point where they break easily.

2   Slice the stalks diagonally as thin as possible to expose maximum surface with a mandoline, slicer, handheld food processor blade, or precision knife skills. Cut the asparagus tips lengthwise in halves or quarters.

3   On a platter, dress the asparagus with the olive oil, salt, and pepper.

4   Scrape a vegetable peeler over a large piece of Parmigiano (you won't need the whole piece) directly over dressed asparagus, covering the salad with curls of cheese, and serve.

Penne with Asparagus-Lemon Sauce

For 4–6 Servings   First Course

I got hooked on lemon peel and pasta made by Countess Lisa Contini, one of my favorite home cooks in Tuscany. Lisa, her husband, Count Ugo, and their children all work at their estate, the Tenuta di Capezzana, producing wonderful wine and extra virgin olive oil. The dining room table is always set for 12. Lisa's meals are casually thrown together with ingredients from her garden, homemade cured pork products, specials from a nearby supermarket, and anything she finds in the pantry, paired with the estate's fine wines. The only oil in the kitchen is Capezzana's terrific estate-produced extra virgin olive oil, used with abandon. I added the asparagus to Lisa's recipe to take advantage of seasonal bounty and her whole family liked the results.

> 1 pound fresh asparagus
> 5–6 quarts water
> 2–3 tablespoons sea salt
> 1 teaspoon minced lemon zest
> ¼ cup quality extra virgin olive oil
> Freshly ground pepper
> 14–16 ounces penne or short pasta
> ½ cup grated Parmigiano

1 Snap the tough butt ends off the asparagus or peel to the tender core. Cut the stems into 1-inch pieces. Reserve the asparagus tips.

2 Bring 5–6 quarts of water to a rolling boil, add 2–3 tablespoons salt, and cook asparagus stems for 6–8 minutes until soft and totally tender. Remove stems with a slotted spoon, refresh in cold water, and drain.

3 Cook the tips in the boiling water for 3–5 minutes until tender, remove with a slotted spoon, refresh in cold water, and drain. Reserve asparagus cooking water.

4 Puree the stems in a food processor with lemon zest, extra virgin olive oil, ½ cup asparagus cooking water, and salt and pepper to taste: transfer the sauce to a 3-quart pot.

5 Return the remaining asparagus cooking water to a rolling boil, add the pasta, and cook until it still offers considerable resistance to the tooth, around three quarters of

the recommended cooking time. Drain, reserving 2 cups of pasta water. Add pasta, asparagus tips, and ½ cup starchy water to asparagus stem puree and cook in a 3-quart pot over highest heat, stirring for 3–5 minutes until pasta is almost cooked and sauce coats pasta. Add more pasta water, ¼ cup at a time, if sauce becomes too dry. Sauce should surround pasta but be slightly liquid since cheese will thicken it.

6 Add the grated Parmigiano, heat for an additional minute to melt the cheese, and serve immediately.

New-Wave Asparagus Carbonara Pasta

For 4–6 Servings   **First Course**

*P*asta alla carbonara is a Roman classic, made with salt-cured pork jowl (*guanciale*), eggs, and grated pecorino cheese. I like to substitute asparagus for jowl for my vegetarian friends. Getting the sauce just right takes practice since eggs, cheese, pasta, and asparagus are cooked together over low heat with a little pasta water to form a savory, lightly thickened, custardlike sauce that can easily scramble. First-time carbonara makers should be careful. Bucatini or perciatelli are the classic pastas paired with carbonara but as hard to twirl around a fork as garden hose. Spaghetti or short pasta is a better choice.

> 1 pound asparagus spears
> 5–6 quarts water
> 2–3 tablespoons sea salt
> 3–4 tablespoons extra virgin olive oil
> 4 eggs
> ¾ cup grated Pecorino Romano or Parmigiano
>   or a blend of both
> Freshly ground pepper
> 14–15 ounces pasta (spaghetti, rigatoni, or penne)

1 Snap tough butt ends off the asparagus or peel to the tender core. Cut the stems diagonally into ½-inch pieces. Reserve the tips.

2 Bring 5–6 quarts of water to a rolling boil, add 2–3 tablespoons salt, and cook the asparagus stems for 3–6 minutes or until tender. Remove the asparagus stems with a

slotted spoon, refresh in cold water, and drain. Cook the asparagus tips in the boiling water in which stems have cooked for 2–3 minutes until tender, remove with a slotted spoon, refresh and drain. Reserve asparagus cooking water.

3   Combine the extra virgin olive oil, eggs, grated cheese, salt and pepper to taste, and drained asparagus tips and stems in a small saucepan.

4   Return the asparagus cooking water to a rolling boil and cook the pasta. Add ½ cup hot pasta cooking water to the eggs and cheese in the saucepan.

5   While the pasta is cooking ladle 1 or 2 cups boiling pasta water into the bowl the pasta will be served in and place the saucepan in bowl. This improvised double boiler warms both sauce and serving bowl.

6   When the pasta is cooked *al dente*, still offering some resistance to the tooth, drain it carefully. Place the well-drained pasta in a large skillet or 3-quart pot and stir in the warm egg mixture. Sauce will appear thin.

7   Place over low heat and cook, stirring constantly with a wooden fork, until sauce thickens slightly. This step requires much attention and stirring, because too much heat will scramble the eggs.

8   Throw away the hot water warming the serving bowl, transfer pasta and sauce into the warmed bowl, and serve. Salmonella-conscious diners should take the temperature of sauced pasta in the bowl, making sure the thermometer registers 160 degrees.

Asparagus (or His Cousins) Risotto

A rite of spring in asparagus-growing and rice-loving northern Italy, risotto is prepared with cultivated or wild asparagus or any of the wild greens that resemble asparagus in taste. Butcher's-broom, wild clematis shoots, or hops make a most flavorful risotto for those lucky enough to find them but cultivated asparagus are a fine choice.

½ pound fresh asparagus

1 scallion or shallot, chopped

1 garlic clove, chopped

¼ cup extra virgin olive oil (or 2 tablespoons
    extra virgin olive oil and 2 tablespoons butter)

1 cup rice for risotto, Carnaroli or Vialone Nano
    (see page 8 for information on rice)

¼ cup dry white wine (optional)

8–10 cups water or lightly salted vegetable broth made
    with 1 onion, 1 garlic clove, 1 carrot, 1 celery rib,
    asparagus trimmings, and a few parsley stems,
    cooked for 15 minutes

½ cup grated Parmigiano (and additional cheese
    to top risotto, if desired)

1 Snap the tough butt ends off the asparagus or peel to the tender core. Chop the asparagus stems and reserve the asparagus tips.

2 Pile the chopped scallion or shallot and garlic in a heavy-bottomed 4-quart pot or saucepan and pour 2 tablespoons extra virgin olive oil over them, mixing to coat. Cook over moderate heat until translucent.

3 Add chopped asparagus stems and sauté for a minute or two.

4 Add rice, stir to coat with oil, and cook for a few minutes to lightly toast.

5 Add white wine, if desired, and evaporate over high heat.

6 Add asparagus cooking water or vegetable broth, 1 cup at a time, stirring the bottom of the pot with a *long* wooden spoon or fork, over high heat, boiling madly. Risotto attains the temperature of molten lava and it's wise to keep one's distance while stirring. Add more boiling water or broth when risotto is still surrounded by liquid.

After 15 minutes add asparagus tips and begin to add boiling liquid ½ cup at a time. Start to taste the rice after another 5 minutes: it should be firm under tooth, *al dente*, since it will still cook for a few minutes. Liquid should be a little soupy because Parmigiano cheese, oil (or butter), and final whipping will tighten up the sauce, which should be opaque, bathing individual kernels.

7   Add cheese and remaining extra virgin (or butter) and stir energetically with long-handled wooden spoon or fork, over high heat, to whip ingredients together. Remove from heat, ladle into individual bowls, and let risotto rest for a minute before serving. Top with additional Parmigiano if desired.

8   To make risotto with butcher's-broom, wild clematis, or hop shoots, parboil ½ pound greens until barely tender, drain, and substitute for asparagus in the above recipe. Since wild shoots are more intensely flavored and sometimes bitter, taste cooking water before using for risotto vegetable stock.

Whole Roast or Grilled Asparagus

I love the flavor of roast vegetables but don't often have the time or desire to turn on my oven just to cook a vegetable. Luckily home ovens aren't part of the urban Italian tradition and almost all roasting is done stove-top. So asparagus are pan-roasted with extra virgin and eaten plain. Or, inspired by Giacomo Castelvetro, author of *A Brief Account of the Fruit, Herbs & Vegetables of Italy*, grilled and dressed with bitter orange juice and extra virgin. A mixture of half lemon, half orange juice can fill in for bitter orange.

> **1 pound fresh asparagus**
>
> **2–3 tablespoons extra virgin olive oil**
>
> **Salt and freshly ground pepper**
>
> **2 tablespoons lemon juice or bitter orange juice**
> **(or 1 tablespoon lemon juice and 1 tablespoon**
> **orange juice, combined)**

1 Place the asparagus in one layer in a large nonstick skillet and drizzle with 1 tablespoon extra virgin olive oil. Shake pan to coat the asparagus with oil and place over moderate heat. Cook asparagus, shaking pan every few minutes to brown evenly.

2 Lower heat and cook asparagus (cooking time may vary widely) until tender, around 10–15 minutes. Test by poking asparagus stems with a toothpick or knife. Or grill whole asparagus, turning to brown evenly, until tender. Remove to a serving dish, sprinkle with salt and pepper, and drizzle with 1–2 tablespoons extra virgin olive oil. To approximate Castelvetro's bitter orange juice, combine lemon and orange juice and sprinkle 2 tablespoons over asparagus.

Veneto Mashed Egg
Condiment for Boiled Asparagus

*W*hite asparagus are a rite of spring in northern Veneto, a cause for celebration, and many restaurants create entire meals using local production. This condiment is rarely found as part of these meals, too humble and sloppy to present to local diners who probably eat it in the privacy of their own homes. It's never prepared in the kitchen but each diner mashes his or her boiled egg with a fork, adding vinegar, salt, pepper, and delicately flavored extra virgin olive oil to make a tasty dipping sauce for boiled room-temperature asparagus.

> ¼–½ **pound asparagus per person**
> 4–5 **quarts water**
> 2–3 **tablespoons coarse salt**
> 1–2 **eggs**
> 1 **teaspoon red wine vinegar**
> **Sea salt and freshly ground pepper**
> 2–4 **tablespoons extra virgin olive oil**

1 Slice the butt ends off asparagus spears, leaving enough of the tough stalk to use as a handle if you're planning to eat asparagus with your fingers, the way they do in the Veneto. Or snap the tough butt ends off the asparagus or peel the butt ends to the tender core.

2 Bring 4–5 quarts of water to a rolling boil. Add 2–3 tablespoons coarse salt and asparagus spears and cook for 5–8 minutes or until tender. Remove the asparagus with a slotted spoon, refresh them in cold water, and drain.

3 Boil the egg (or eggs) for 10 minutes, cool in cold water, and peel.

4 Bring all ingredients to the table. Each diner should mash the egg with a fork on a plate, adding vinegar, salt and pepper to taste. Mix well, adding extra virgin olive oil until desired consistency is obtained, using more oil for a thinner sauce. Dip room-temperature asparagus into sauce.

ASPARAGUS AND HIS COUSINS

Artusi's Baked Asparagus

*N*o one was interested in publishing Pellegrino Artusi's *Culinary Science and the Art of Eating Well,* so he did it himself in 1910. With more than 110 editions to date it's the best-selling Italian cookbook of all time, the *Fanny Farmer* of Italy. Artusi wrote from an interregional pan-Italian perspective, politically correct after the 1870 unification of the independent Italian states into one country. His culinary orientation is central Italian although there are recipes from Sicily, Naples, Rome, Germanic northern Italian desserts like *presnitz* and *krapfen,* and even a few French and English specialties. Artusi's slim vegetable chapter includes this asparagus recipe but he claims the best way to eat asparagus is simply boiled, dressed with good oil and vinegar or lemon. He recommends layering *al dente* asparagus with butter and Parmigiano (too much condiment, warns Artusi, yields "nauseating results") in a baking dish, baking to melt cheese. It's a good idea, simple, combining classic flavors, and can be prepared in advance and heated at the last minute. My Tuscan husband, who refuses to admit the existence of butter, prefers this dish with extra virgin olive oil. Born-again Tuscans and those who are watching their cholesterol can follow his example.

4–5 quarts water

2–3 tablespoons coarse salt

1½ pounds trimmed cleaned asparagus

¾ cup grated Parmigiano

Sea salt

Freshly ground pepper

3–4 tablespoons butter or extra virgin olive oil

1 Bring 4–5 quarts of water to a rolling boil. Add 2–3 tablespoons coarse salt and asparagus spears and cook for 5–8 minutes or until tender. Remove with a slotted spoon, refresh in cold water, and drain.

2 Preheat the oven to 400 degrees.

3 Place a layer of asparagus in a baking dish, sprinkle with cheese, lightly salt and pepper, and continue, making two or three layers of asparagus. Top with final layer of Parmigiano and dot with butter (or drizzle with extra virgin olive oil). Bake for 15–20 minutes or until lightly browned and cheese has melted. Serve immediately.

Pontormo's Asparagus Bismarck

For 4 Servings   **Main Course**

*A*ccording to Lotteringhi della Stufa's *Dinners and Banquets*, a Tuscan history of gastronomy from the sixteenth century to modern times, anticlassical Tuscan artist Pontormo was a late Renaissance foodie. He dined on asparagus and eggs and Lotteringhi della Stufa includes a recipe. Florentines still eat boiled asparagus topped with eggs although the modern dish is named for German statesman Bismarck instead of the Tuscan artist who first documented it.

It's an easy-to-assemble main course with a different name in each region, and is called asparagus alla Milanese by those from Milan, Florentine beyond Tuscany, and Bismarck (as are all dishes that are topped with a fried egg) in Florence. Hands-on diners will enjoy eating asparagus with their fingers, smooshing the cheese, runny egg yolk, and olive oil (or butter) together to make a sauce, coating the asparagus. Dip and bite until the stalk gets tough, then discard.

> 2 pounds fresh asparagus
> 4–5 quarts water
> 2–3 tablespoons coarse salt
> 4–8 eggs
> 4 tablespoons extra virgin olive oil (or butter if you choose)
> Sea salt and freshly ground pepper
> ¼ cup grated Parmigiano-Reggiano

1 Slice the butt ends off the asparagus spears, leaving enough of the tough stalk to use as a handle if you're planning to eat the asparagus with your fingers. Or snap the tough butt ends off the asparagus or peel the butt ends to the tender core.

2 Bring 4–5 quarts of water to a rolling boil. Add 2–3 tablespoons coarse salt and the asparagus spears, and cook for 5–8 minutes or until tender. Remove with a slotted spoon, refresh in cold water, and drain.

3 Place spears with tips in the same direction on 4 individual plates.

4 Gently fry eggs, 1 or 2 per person, in 2 tablespoons olive oil (or butter) until just set, and season with salt and pepper. Or poach the eggs in acidulated water until set.

5 Place the fried or poached eggs on top of the asparagus, drizzle with the remaining olive oil (or butter) from the pan, sprinkle with the grated cheese, and serve.

Asparagus (or His Cousins) *Frittata*

*T*he *frittata*, more like a pan-fried flan than an omelet, is a classic Italian solution for a main course with few ingredients, usually only one vegetable paired with eggs and grated cheese. It's perfect for recycling leftovers although I prefer vegetables stir-fried until tender in extra virgin. As usual in Italy there are different ways to cook a *frittata*. Liliana, the cook at Castello di Ama in the heart of Chianti is a traditionalist, and cooks one side, flips it over onto a plate, slips it back into the pan to cook the other side. Some cooks cover the *frittata* to set the top, flipping it onto a serving dish to expose the browned side. Marcella Hazan recommends cooking eggs until set, then broiling the upper surface. And flamboyant cooks flip, flapjack-style. A nonstick omelet pan makes the entire process easier.

> 4 eggs
>
> Salt and freshly ground pepper
>
> 1½ pounds fresh asparagus, trimmed
>
> 2 tablespoons extra virgin olive oil or butter
>
> ½ cup grated Parmigiano

1   Mix the eggs, salt, and pepper with a fork.

2   Slice the asparagus stems diagonally into ½-inch pieces. In a 12-inch nonstick skillet or omelet pan, cook over high heat in extra virgin olive oil for 3 or 4 minutes. Add tips and cook for a few more minutes, until both stems and tips are tender.

3   Mix grated cheese with eggs and pour over asparagus.

4   Cook over low heat until eggs are set on the bottom but still runny on the surface.

5   Put a plate over the *frittata* and invert the skillet to reverse the *frittata* onto the plate. Slide the *frittata* back into pan to cook the other side. Or cook until barely set, cover, and cook for a few more minutes to finish, reversing *frittata* onto a serving platter to expose browned surface. Or cook one side and broil the top. Or flip like a pancake.

6   Slide onto a platter and serve hot or at room temperature. Leftovers make a good sandwich.

BEANS

Fagioli

*C*an it be true that beans are the reason the Renaissance, in spite of its French name, began in Florence? A Florentine bean lover assured me that beans were the brain food that fueled the Italian artistic and intellectual rebirth. Michelangelo and Lorenzo de' Medici were wild about beans. Florentines ate cowpeas before New World white beans arrived in Europe in the sixteenth century, probably introduced in Tuscany by the Medici who got them from the Pope. In Florence beans were purchased cooked, from street-cart vendors called *fagiolai*, members of a fourteenth-century guild of bakers and cooks. My Florentine doctor-engineer husband says that beans make you smart and I'd like to believe him. Florence, like Boston, is known for its love of beans, which are served in all seasons. Dried white beans, either cannellini or toscanelli, are soaked and boiled year round. Beans shelled fresh from the pod are called *fagioli sgranati*, tender and thin-skinned, a labor-intensive seasonal treat.

Beans are high in calories and in fiber, with lots of calcium, iron, phosphorous, and potassium. They're rich in protein and therefore called "meat of the poor," although they must be combined with the amino acids in wheat to get the full effects of their protein. Beans have oligosaccharides, which aren't broken down by digestive enzymes and are fermented in the large intestine, forming gas. According to Jean Carper in *The Food Pharmacy*, beans lower cholesterol and blood pressure, regulate insulin, blood sugar, and colon functions, stimulate the production of cancer-blocking agents, and prevent constipation and hemorrhoids.

National as well as regional bean varieties are found throughout Italy. Some have local cult followings and are far more costly than commonly found beans. *Lamon* and *Saluggia*, both speckled cranberry-type beans, small white *Sorana*, and tiny pale yellow *Solfini* beans are almost impossible to find outside growing areas although many bean stores sell *Tipo Lamon*, which physically resemble the real thing. Cannellini, medium-sized white beans, are highly prized throughout Italy, although toscanelli or piattellini, smaller with a thin skin, have lots of Florentine fans. In Florence a kind of dry food specialty shop, called *civaio*, sells beans, legumes, seeds, and animal food. The farmers' stands at the market and the *civaio* in Piazza Santo Spirito are my sources for beans. The farmers grow and sell their own beans. I checked out the bean bags in the back room of my *civaio* and discovered that toscanelli come from the United States and are really Great Northern. Cannellini come from Argentina. Buy the best beans available, which should be fresh, used within a year of harvest. Look for beans in a health food or gourmet shop where there should be a better selection than most supermarkets. Don't buy beans in a package that looks old. If you can't find good beans locally, order them by mail from the source below. Don't use beans that have been sitting in a pantry for too long.

Most supermarket packaged dried beans are not worth buying. Canned or frozen beans are better. If you're going to make the effort to cook beans, purchase the best beans possible, not exactly a major investment but definitely necessary for maximum success. Domestic or even locally grown beans are the best choice. Cannellini, borlotti, or cranberry are well worth ordering by mail from Phipps Ranch, P.O. Box 349, Pescadero, California 94060, Telephone: 415–879–0787.

Dried beans should be soaked for 6–8 hours. Contrary to usual instructions, I soak beans in the morning and cook them in the evening. Or speed-soak—put the beans in a pot with plenty of water to cover, bring to a boil, boil for a minute or two, remove from heat and cover for 1 hour. Drain the beans, add fresh water, and finish cooking, which will take another 1½ hours or more, depending on bean quality. Just-shelled beans don't require advance soaking and cook faster than dried beans.

Beans are easier to digest if they're passed through a food mill, eliminating the skin and part of the fiber.

The best seed selection of beans is from B & T World Seeds, Whitnell House, Fiddington, Bridgwater, Somerset, TA5 1JE U.K. for five different types of borlotto and even hard-to-find Lamon. Shepherd's Garden Seeds, 6116 Highway 9, Felton, California 95018, Telephone: 408–335–6910, has seeds for borlotto shelling beans, Pinetree Garden Seeds, Box 300, New Gloucester, Maine 04260, Telephone: 207–926–3400, has seed for cannellini, and Fratelli Ingegnoli, Corso Buenos Aires 54, Milan 20124, has seed for borlotto, cannellini, corona, and Lamon.

Boiled beans are necessary for any of the following recipes although lazy cooks can substitute canned beans. The results won't be as wonderful but they are achieved much more quickly. And first-rate canned beans are better than most dried packaged beans sold at supermarkets. Dried beans should be fresh and cooking times will vary widely, depending upon freshness and quality.

History

Apicius, wealthy Roman gastronomer of the first century, blew his entire fortune on culinary festivities and poisoned himself when he realized that he'd have to lower his culinary standards. Apicius's legend survives in a fourth-century compilation of his recipes, *De Re Coquinaria*. Book V, *Legumes*, attests to the importance of starchy vegetables in the Roman diet of both rich and poor with chapters on lentils, peas, barley, fava beans, both fresh and dried, chick-peas, and beans. Apicius was writing about cowpeas, probably brought to Italy by Greek traders. His vague advice for beans or chick-peas is to serve with salt, cumin, oil, and a little pure wine.

In *Discussions on Material Medicine* (1557), Tuscan doctor M. Pietro Andrea Mattioli translates the Latin text of Pedacio Dioscoride Anazarbeo and comments at length on "the composition and virtues of medicaments." Mattioli writes of beans—common, white, red, yellow, and dotted with diverse colors, known to ancients although "newly brought to Italy," a clear reference to Old and New World specimens. According to Mattioli, beans "eaten in food inflate, starve the stomach, generate sperm and the urge for coitus."

Giacomo Castelvetro's 1614 *Brief Account of the Fruit, Herbs & Vegetables of Italy* attempts to convince the English to eat more vegetables the way the Italians do. He writes about broad beans in his spring chapter and "Turkish" beans, a term often applied to imports. Castelvetro describes both exotic beans, white or stained with red and black, and smaller white beans with a black spot in the middle, clearly the Old World cowpea. ". . . Turkish beans grow tall and should be planted next to a hedge, or if you want a good crop, plant them next to dry branches and train them to grow tall." Castelvetro claims that women in Italy and especially Venice plant beans in window boxes, trained up a grate of white sticks, for their green leaves, shade, and especially to peer out at passers-by without being seen.

Vincenzo Corrado wrote his best-seller *The Gallant Cook* in 1773. Capitalizing on his success, he enlarged the vegetable chapter and published *Of Pythagorean Food* in 1781, a regime for nobles and literary-minded readers of delicate digestion. Corrado doesn't take Pythagoras's orthodox vegetarian regime too seriously and recipes contain meat, poultry, prosciutto, fish, broths, dairy products, and eggs. He writes, "Beans are of various colors and forms. Florentines can attest to the fact that they're tasty because, more than all others they make great use of them, particularly dried white beans that they dress with various tasty condiments." I like Corrado's recipe for Florentine beans, boiled in salted water, dressed with anchovies fried in oil and pepper even if I've never found the dish in Florence.

Bean Recipes

THE MOTHER OF ALL BEAN RECIPES

Boiled beans with sage and garlic

FLORENTINE BEANS AND CAVIAR

Classic but expensive combo

BEAN SOUP

Minestra di Fagioli

*Winter bean and vegetable soup—
the base for* ribollita

"REBOILED"

Ribollita

*Leftover bean and vegetable soup,
"reboiled" with bread*

POLDO'S MIXED LEGUME SOUP

Chick-pea, bean, lentil, and pasta soup

**MINIMALIST LOMBARD
BUT REALLY TUSCAN SOUP**

4-ingredient soup for bean lovers

**GRAND EMMER BEAN AND GRAIN SOUP
FROM LUCCA**

Bean and wheat berry soup

TUSCAN TUNA AND BEANS WHITE OR GREEN

*White or green beans dressed
with tuna and red onions*

FRANCA'S BEANS AND SHRIMP

White beans and boiled shrimp

FABIO'S SAUSAGE AND BEANS

"PRETTY BIRD" BEANS

Fagioli all'uccelletto

*Florentine beans stewed
with garlic, sage, and tomato*

"REMADE" BEANS

Fagioli Rifatti

AUNT ENZA'S OVERSTEWED GREEN BEANS

Green beans cooked with tomato sauce

The Mother of All Bean Recipes

Makes About 7 Cups of Beans

*A*lmost all Italians eat beans but Florentines, according to an insulting taunt of neighboring cities, lick plates and ladle when beans are served. The utensil of choice is a terra-cotta bean pot although purists may insist on cooking beans in a glass *fiasco* (wine flask), straw removed, set in the embers of a fireplace. I tried a covered metal pot just to see if it worked and it did. Florentines soak beans overnight but I often use the speed-soak method (see page 57). Beans are cooked in lots of water, lightly flavored with a few sage leaves and a clove or two of garlic. Some cooks add a bay leaf. Tuscans *never, ever* salt beans during cooking, claiming it breaks the beans. Although most Tuscan recipes use cannellini beans I prefer smaller, thinner-skinned toscanelli. My nearby bean and seed shop sells toscanelli, which I've discovered are actually Great Northern beans imported from the United States. Look for quality beans in a store that sells a lot of different kinds of legumes, like a health food or fancy food shop. Or from farmers' markets or mail-ordered from the source on page 57.

> 2½ cups dried beans and 10 cups water for soaking
>
> 10 cups water
>
> 4–5 sage leaves
>
> 1 bay leaf
>
> 1–2 garlic cloves, unpeeled
>
> 1–2 tablespoons coarse sea salt
>
> Extra virgin olive oil
>
> Freshly ground pepper

1 Soak the beans all day or overnight, at least 8 hours, in 10 cups of water. Or speed-soak by placing the beans in a large pot with 10 cups water, bring to a full boil, turn off the heat, and cover. Let beans stand for 1 hour.

2 Drain and rinse the beans, cover them with 10 cups of fresh water in a 3-quart pot. Add the herbs and garlic, bring to a boil, skim off any scum that forms, cover, and simmer over lowest heat for 45–60 minutes or longer until the beans are tender. Age and variety will vary cooking time.

3 Cool the beans for at least 15 minutes in their liquid before adding salt.

4 Serve the warm beans with an ample drizzle of extra virgin olive oil and freshly ground pepper to taste.

Florentine Beans and Caviar

*I*t seems perfectly natural that Florentines would pair their favorite legume with caviar since they contrast fish and beans in many dishes. And it's said that caviar once came from sturgeon that swam in the silvery Arno river. The Arno isn't exactly silver today—rats can be spotted along the banks and the sturgeon are gone but lucky diners with a good source of caviar are still enjoying this terrific combination. Beans are a far better match for caviar than tasteless white-bread toast. And delicately flavored extra virgin olive oil from Lucca or Liguria is a more sophisticated match than butter.

> **3 cups drained cooked white beans**
> **Fine sea salt**
> **Freshly ground pepper**
> **3–4 tablespoons extra virgin olive oil**
> **2–4 ounces caviar, preferably osetra**
> **1 teaspoon lemon juice (optional)**

1 Warm the white beans. Lightly season them with salt, pepper, and extra virgin olive oil.

2 Divide the beans into 4–6 portions. Top each portion with at least 1 tablespoon of caviar. If you like lemon with caviar add a few drops of lemon juice.

THE *RIBOLLITA* "REBOILED" STORY

*W*hy does almost every Italian cookbook have a recipe for *ribollita*, a hearty vegetable bean soup thickened to the consistency of porridge with stale bread, reheated, "boiled again," as its name translates in Italian? It's rustic, home-style, on most trattoria menus during the winter, the ultimate savory Florentine comfort food. It's never the same twice and every *ribollita* fan thinks his or her mother or aunt or grandma makes it best. And Florentine *ribollita* authorities are dying to spill the beans.

The truth is that home cooks don't set out to make *ribollita*. It's the last stage in a cycle that employs leftovers of leftovers, stretching a few winter vegetables into three days of food for a crowd. It's impossible to make for two. The procedure begins with the preparation of a large pot of boiled white beans. Part of the beans are served as a side dish, drizzled with extra virgin olive oil (see page 60). Leftover beans and broth are used as the base for a bean and winter vegetable soup, made in an even bigger pot, ensuring leftovers to layer with slices of stale bread and cook again the next day until the whole mixture is as thick as oatmeal, expanding in the process. Following this progression isn't a lot of work. But cooks who set out to make *ribollita* will have to work harder to dissolve the dried bread. Fortunately, the hand mixer makes short work of this step, a tip I learned from Florentine restaurateur, Fabio Picchi of Cibreo, who cooks like a Tuscan grandma.

Tuscan kale, *cavolo nero*, is an important ingredient (see page 94 for more on this regional vegetable) but carefully cleaned kale, thick stems removed, can be substituted. Chard produces a sweeter flavor. Use twice as much cabbage if none of these vegetables is available for a more delicate soup. Traditionalists should search for a prosciutto bone to flavor their bean soup; porco-vegetarians can add salt pork or pork rind for enrichment. But both bean soup and *ribollita* work well without meat.

Bean Soup
Minestra di Fagioli

For 12 or More Servings, Around 4 Quarts   **First Course**

*T*his soup combines Tuscany's winter vegetables in a simple preparation. The recipe makes enough soup for an army, so there'll be enough left over to make *ribollita*.

1 onion or leek, chopped coarsely

2 garlic cloves, chopped coarsely

2 celery stalks, chopped coarsely

2 tablespoons extra virgin olive oil or ¼ cup diced salt
   pork plus extra virgin olive oil for garnish

½ pound Tuscan kale, cabbage, kale, or swiss chard, shredded

½ medium cabbage, shredded

3 large carrots, quartered, cut into ½-inch chunks

½ pound winter squash, peeled, cut into ½-inch chunks

1 large all-purpose potato, peeled, cut into ½-inch chunks

Fresh herbs: 1 sprig each rosemary and thyme, a few
   fresh sage leaves, 1 bay leaf

7 cups bean broth or water

Coarse sea salt and freshly ground pepper

4 cups cooked white beans

1 ¾-inch slice of toasted rustic bread rubbed with garlic,
   per person

1 Put the onion, garlic, and celery in a 5-quart pot. Pour extra virgin oil over them, toss with a wooden spoon to coat with the oil, and place over low heat. Cook, stirring occasionally, for 10 minutes or until onions are tender.

2 Add the Tuscan kale, cabbage, kale, or swiss chard, cabbage, carrots, squash, potato, fresh herbs, and broth or water and bring to a simmer.

3 Cook the soup, stirring occasionally, for 1 hour over low heat.

4 Remove the rosemary sprig and the bay leaf. Add salt and pepper to taste. Puree 5 cups of vegetables from the soup with 1 cup of beans in a food processor. Return the puree to the soup, along with the remaining three cups of whole beans.

5   Place 1 slice of toasted bread in each soup bowl and ladle soup over bread. Drizzle with extra virgin olive oil and serve.

"Reboiled"
Ribollita

*T*he final stage of the *ribollita* cycle uses up leftover bean soup. First-rate rustic bread is essential and this recipe just won't work with supermarket bread. Florentines use saltless white bread. Readers lucky enough to be able to buy saltless Tuscan-style bread and bread bakers (see Carol Field's recipe for Tuscan bread in *The Italian Baker,* HarperCollins Publishers, 1986) will make the most authentic *ribollita.* Everyone else should buy the best bread available, white or whole wheat, from an artisanal baker. Poor quality bread will produce a gummy soup. Stale dried bread is the traditional choice but bread toasted until completely dry in a slow oven works fine. *Ribollita* is always served with a drizzle of extra virgin olive oil on top and a twist of pepper, never with grated cheese. Cultists insist that *ribollita* must be eaten with a fork, never a spoon.

> 6–8½ large ½-inch slices of bread, preferably saltless
>   Tuscan-style if possible
>
> 5 cups bean soup
>
> Salt
>
> At least 1 tablespoon extra virgin olive oil per person for
>   garnish
>
> Freshly ground pepper

1   Preheat the oven to 325 degrees. Toast the bread slices for 20–25 minutes or until dry but not browned.

2   Heat the bean soup to boiling in a 2-quart pot. Remove 1 cup of beans and vegetables with a slotted spoon and set aside. Add the dried bread to the pot and submerge it in the soup. Remove the pot from heat, cover, and let stand 15–20 minutes or until bread is soft.

3   Puree the soup and bread with a hand immersion mixer directly in the pot. Or pulse in the food processor until the bread is dissolved. Return the mixture to the pot. Add the reserved beans and vegetables and heat thoroughly. If *ribollita* is too thick, add water, ¼ cup at a time, diluting to the thickness of oatmeal. Taste for salt.

4   Reheat the *ribollita,* ladle into serving bowls, and top with a serious drizzle of extra virgin olive oil and freshly ground pepper.

Poldo's Mixed Legume Soup

*I*l Biondo, "The Blond Man," was the quintessential Tuscan trattoria, hidden in the hilltop village of Sassetta, no sign out front, one dining room with five tables, walls covered with framed paintings, prints, group photos, awards, with dozens of postcards tucked into the frames. Il Biondo's son Poldo, bald, robust, in his sixties, chattered endlessly, welcoming diners, calling them "kiddo" in local dialect, urging them to eat. There was no written menu but Poldo always suggested "a little taste" that rarely varied. It always began with a few *crostini*, local prosciutto and salami, pickled shallots, followed by homemade pasta with a rich meat sauce, and the following soup. Il Biondo closed in 1994 but Poldo gave me the recipe for *cacciucco di legumi*, an "unimportant mess" of legumes and pasta soup. Poldo puts the cooked soup through a food mill, which makes it easier to digest. I use the hand immersion mixer or the food processor to achieve the right texture. Although Il Biondo served this soup with short wide strips of fresh pasta (*maltagliati*) I make it with short tubular dried pasta when I'm in a hurry.

½ medium onion, chopped

1 celery stalk, chopped

1 medium carrot, chopped

2 garlic cloves, chopped

1 fresh hot pepper or red pepper flakes to taste

1 sprig rosemary

A few fresh sage leaves

3 tablespoons extra virgin olive oil plus additional oil
    for garnish (optional)

¼ cup tomato pulp, fresh or canned

4 cups water

1½–2 cups cooked white beans or drained canned beans

1½–2 cups cooked chick-peas or drained canned
    chick-peas

½ cup uncooked lentils

Sea salt

6 ounces small tubular pasta (about 1½ cups)
    or short wide strips of fresh pasta made
    with 1 egg and ¾ cup flour

(continued)

1 Put the onion, celery, carrot, garlic, hot pepper, rosemary, and sage in a 4-quart pot and drizzle with extra virgin olive oil. Stir to coat the vegetables and cook over low heat for 10 minutes or until the vegetables are tender.

2 Add the tomato pulp and 4 cups water and bring to a simmer.

3 Add the beans, chick-peas, and lentils and simmer over low heat for 25 minutes until the lentils are barely tender. Add salt to taste.

4 While the soup is cooking prepare fresh pasta with 1 egg and ¾ cup flour and cut into *maltagliati*, "badly cut" diamond-shaped pieces. Skip this step if you plan to use tubular dry pasta.

5 Add the pasta to the soup and cook until the pasta is tender, which will take only a minute or two with fresh pasta, more than 10 minutes with dry pasta. Stir to prevent the soup from sticking. Add a little more water if soup seems too thick.

6 Soup can be garnished with a drizzle of extra virgin olive oil.

Minimalist Lombard
but Really Tuscan Soup

*I*s *zuppa Lombarda* named for Bernardino Zendrini, a Lombard who drained the Tuscan Maremma Swamps? Or is it just a regional remedy when hunger bays on an almost empty cupboard? Whatever its origins, this monovegetable soup rivals black cabbage with slices of bread (see page 99) for austerity. Bean broth is essential to this dish, which excludes the use of canned beans. But it's a perfect way to use leftover beans and their cooking water.

> 3½ cups cooked beans
>
> 2 cups bean broth
>
> Sea salt
>
> Freshly ground pepper
>
> 4 ¾-inch slices of rustic country-style bread
>
> 1 garlic clove, unpeeled
>
> ½ cup extra virgin olive oil

1 Heat the beans and broth over medium heat and add salt and pepper to taste.

2 Lightly toast the bread and rub with unpeeled garlic.

3 Place 1 slice of toast in each soup bowl and ladle one quarter of the beans and broth over the toast.

4 Drizzle the soup with extra virgin olive oil and serve.

Grand Emmer Bean
and Grain Soup from Lucca

For 6–8 Servings   First Course

*E*mmer, *triticum dicoccum, farro* in Italian, is a wheatlike grain that fueled the Roman legions. And where the Roman troops camped, grain and bean soups remain a part of the culinary tradition. Emmer and borlotti bean soup, called *gran farro,* is from the Lucca area of Tuscany but has caught on in the rest of Italy as well, part of a return to wholesome rustic eating. *Farro* used to be hard to find—I used to stock up when I went to Lucca, but now it's available at Italian supermarkets as well as grain and health food stores throughout Italy. In the United States, buy soft wheat or wheat berries, available in health food stores. Many cookbooks recommend soaking emmer overnight but none of my friends from Lucca do. Traditionalists should use prosciutto skin to flavor both beans and soup but a piece of salt pork and its skin works well. Vegetarians can simply leave out the pork.

> 3 garlic cloves, chopped
>
> 1 medium red onion, chopped
>
> 2 celery stalks, chopped
>
> 2 ounces salt pork, diced, about ⅓ cup (optional)
>
> 2 tablespoons extra virgin olive oil plus
>   additional for garnish
>
> 1 cup tomato pulp
>
> Fresh sage leaves
>
> 1 sprig rosemary
>
> 1 sprig marjoram
>
> 1 pinch allspice
>
> Sea salt
>
> Freshly ground pepper
>
> 2½ cups cooked borlotti or cranberry beans
>
> 4 cups bean broth or water or a combination of both
>
> 1 cup peeled and cubed potatoes
>
> 1 cup *farro* (emmer or wheat berries)

1 Put the chopped garlic, onion, celery, and optional salt pork in a large 4-quart pot. Pour the extra virgin olive oil over the vegetables, stir to coat, and place the pot over low heat. Cook for 10 minutes or until vegetables are soft.

2 Add the tomato pulp, sage, rosemary, marjoram, and allspice, season with salt and pepper, and cook for 10 minutes.

3 Pass 2 cups of beans through a food mill, or puree in the food processor or with a hand immersion mixer. Add bean puree to soup base.

4 Add the bean broth or water and potatoes and bring the soup to a simmer over medium heat.

5 Add the *farro,* lower heat, and simmer, stirring often, for 35–45 minutes until the *farro* is tender. Add the beans and boiling water, ¼ cup at a time, if soup gets too thick.

6 Ladle soup into bowls and garnish with a drizzle of extra virgin olive oil and freshly ground pepper.

Tuscan Tuna and Beans White or Green

*P*reserved tuna, packed in extra virgin olive oil, is paired with white beans in Tuscany, a speedy dish to assemble if you've got beans on hand. Canned beans work well and simplify this preparation—open a few cans and chop an onion. Quality tuna makes a big difference in the success of this dish. Leftover grilled or poached tuna can be used instead of canned but it should be marinated in extra virgin olive oil. All choices will work better than insipid tuna packed in water. Scallions can be used in the spring, red onions for the rest of the year.

Torquato, my farmer and muse, suggested combining green beans with tuna during his glorious green bean season, a fantastic idea.

½ medium red onion, chopped (or 2 scallions, chopped)

2 tablespoons red wine vinegar

3 cups cooked beans or 1 pound steamed or boiled green beans

¼ cup extra virgin olive oil

Fine sea salt

Freshly ground pepper

8–10 ounces canned tuna, packed in olive oil (or fresh tuna, grilled or poached, marinated in extra virgin)

1 tablespoon chopped parsley

1 Marinate the onion with vinegar for 15 minutes. Drain the onion.

2 Put the beans in a serving bowl. Mix with the onion, extra virgin olive oil, salt, and pepper.

3 Drain the tuna, break it into flakes or chunks with a fork, and scatter it on top of the beans. Sprinkle with the parsley.

Franca's Beans and Shrimp

For 4–6 Servings   Appetizer, Main Dish

*T*he fish and beans combination shines, once again, in the simplest of dishes to assemble, a specialty of Franca Franceschini of the Ristorante Romano in Viareggio on the coast of Tuscany. Franca has a wonderful way with super-fresh seafood. She lightly boils local *sparnocchi* shrimp and tosses them with warm boiled beans, dressed with extra virgin, a little diced tomato, and fresh basil. This dish can be served as an appetizer or main course. For best results all ingredients should be first-rate. Frozen shrimp and canned beans will probably be acceptable for cooks in a big hurry, improved greatly when doused with great extra virgin olive oil, preferably from the Lucca area, advises Franca.

> 3 cups cooked white beans and some
>   of their cooking liquid
> 1 pound cooked, peeled shrimp
> ½ cup diced fresh tomato (optional)
> 2 tablespoons chopped basil
> 4–6 tablespoons extra virgin olive oil
> Sea salt
> Freshly ground pepper

1   Warm the beans in their liquid and drain.

2   Combine the beans, shrimp, tomato, basil, and extra virgin olive oil. Season with salt and pepper. Serve warm or at room temperature.

Fabio's Sausage and Beans

*F*abio Picchi, chef-owner with his wife, Benedetta Vitale, of the restaurant, trattoria, and caffè Cibrèo in Florence, makes the spiciest version of this Tuscan classic that I've ever encountered. Most cooks prepare sausage and white beans just like Fabio but don't add the *peperoncino* hot pepper, which livens up this dish considerably. Fabio doesn't drain the sausage and his dish is rich with pork fat but I prefer to drain it and sauté the garlic in extra virgin olive oil. Traditionalists who want to follow Fabio's example should use fatty pork sausage and sauté the garlic in the rendered fat.

8–10 sausage links

2–3 tablespoons extra virgin olive oil

2 garlic cloves

1 small hot pepper

1 tablespoon fresh sage, minced

1 tablespoon rosemary, minced

¼ cup tomato pulp

3 cups cooked white beans

1 cup bean broth or water

Coarse sea salt

Freshly ground pepper

1 Pierce the casings of the sausages on all sides so that fat can be expelled. Put the sausages in one layer in a large nonstick skillet and cook over moderate heat, turning them, until deeply browned. Remove the sausages with a slotted spoon and drain the rendered fat from the skillet.

2 Heat the extra virgin olive oil in the skillet and sauté the garlic, hot pepper, sage, and rosemary until the garlic barely begins to color.

3 Add the tomato pulp, beans, and liquid and season with salt and pepper. Simmer for 10–15 minutes over low heat.

4 Return the sausage to the skillet and simmer for 5 minutes to amalgamate flavors. Serve hot with plenty of country-style bread.

"Pretty Bird" Beans
Fagioli all'uccelletto

For 4–6 Servings   **Side Dish**

*B*eans in the guise of little birds" is what Pellegrino Artusi calls this dish, although he says that "in Florentine trattorie I've heard these beans called *fagioli all'uccelletto*." They're still a classic, beans cooked the same way as little birds like quail, braised with garlic, sage, and a light tomato sauce.

> 2–3 garlic cloves, chopped
>
> 3 tablespoons extra virgin olive oil
>
> 6–8 fresh sage leaves, roughly chopped
>
> 3 cups cooked white beans
>
> ¼ cup tomato pulp
>
> Sea salt
>
> Freshly ground pepper
>
> 1 cup bean broth or water
>
> ¼ cup water (optional)

1 Put the garlic in a large nonstick skillet, drizzle with 1 tablespoon of extra virgin olive oil, and stir to coat the garlic.

2 Place the skillet over moderate heat. When garlic begins to sizzle add the sage leaves.

3 When garlic barely begins to color add beans, tomato, salt, pepper, and 1 cup bean broth or water. Simmer for 15 minutes or until sauce is lightly thickened and creamy. If the sauce dries out, add ¼ cup hot water.

4 Stir in the remaining extra virgin olive oil before serving. Serve hot.

"Remade" Beans
Fagioli Rifatti

*L*eftover beans are cooked here with garlic, sage, and extra virgin olive oil. My husband Massimo's aunt Enza makes them like a tomatoless version of "pretty bird" beans but Massimo doesn't like the thick creamy sauce even if it doesn't have cream in it. He cooks beans without any liquid, frying them in abundant oil with garlic and sage until lightly browned and slightly crispy.

> 2–3 garlic cloves, chopped
> 3 tablespoons extra virgin olive oil
> 5–6 fresh sage leaves
> 3 cups cooked white beans
> Sea salt
> Freshly ground pepper

1 Put the garlic in a large nonstick skillet, drizzle with 1 tablespoon extra virgin olive oil, and stir to coat the garlic.

2 Place the skillet over moderate heat. When the garlic begins to sizzle add the sage leaves.

3 When the garlic barely begins to color add the beans and season with salt and pepper.

4 Cook the beans over moderate heat, shaking the pan to prevent sticking, and lightly brown the beans. Add the remaining 2 tablespoons extra virgin olive oil and serve.

Aunt Enza's Overstewed Green Beans

I, who struggled for years to achieve perfectly cooked, lively green beans love Aunt Enza's overstewed green beans, soft, almost creamy, tasting of bean, cooked far beyond crunch. Although Aunt Enza cooks the green beans in an onion and garlic-flavored tomato sauce she pointed out that leftover green beans can be subjected to the same treatment. Aunt Enza has a heavy Tuscan hand with extra virgin. I've cut down on the oil but my husband Massimo always adds a little extra at the table.

> 1 small onion, chopped
>
> 1 garlic clove, chopped
>
> ¼ cup extra virgin olive oil
>
> 1½ cups tomato pulp
>
> 1 pound green beans, stem end snapped off
>
> Freshly ground black pepper, fresh red hot pepper,
>   or dried chili pepper flakes
>
> Coarse sea salt
>
> ¼ cup boiling water
>
> 2 tablespoons chopped basil

1 Put the onion and the garlic in a heavy-bottomed 3-quart pot, drizzle with 2 tablespoons of extra virgin olive oil, and stir to coat the vegetables.

2 Place the pot over low heat and cook the onion and garlic for 10 minutes or until tender.

3 Add the tomato, green beans, and pepper (or hot pepper) and season with salt. Bring to a simmer and cover with a tight-fitting lid. Cooking time will depend on the quality and freshness of the beans, which should be tender and soft. Check after 10 minutes to make sure that cooking liquid is sufficient. Add ¼ cup boiling water if necessary. If beans expel too much water, uncover and cook over high heat to thicken sauce.

4 Add the basil, cook for 2–3 minutes, remove from heat, and stir in remaining 2 tablespoons of extra virgin olive oil.

BEANS

BROCCOLI, CAULIFLOWER, AND BROCCOLI RABE

Broccolo,
Cavolfiore,
e Broccoletti

*B*roccoli, cauliflower, and broccoli rabe (or raab), in typical Italian style, make a fashion statement at winter markets in a wide range of colors and forms—white, chartreuse, purple, deep green heads or stalks, leafy bunches with or without flowers. Italians adore all forms of the Brassica family for more than their flashy good looks. They're the heart of Italian winter cooking.

Cauliflower comes in white, purple, or green, depending on region. Romanesco broccoli (*broccolo*) looks like a punk cauliflower, with pointed chartreuse florets that spiral to form a cone-shaped vegetable of strange appearance, more flavor than cauliflower, more delicate than broccoli. Most Italian broccoli looks like the American variety although it usually has some leaves attached and may have smaller stalks.

The vegetable called *cima di rape*, *rapini*, or *broccoletti*, often called broccoli rabe or raab in English, looks like a bunch of turnip greens trying to become full-fledged broccoli, with skinny little stalks and flowering heads. Early tender specimens without stalks, florets, or flowers are called *rapini*. Leaves and florets are both cooked and taste slightly bitter, peppery, more grown up than broccoli, which was probably a domesticated version of broccoli rabe.

Broccoli, cauliflower, and broccoli rabe are members of the Crucifere or mustard family, a prehistoric Mediterranean wild plant that diversified into Brassicas classified by form—heads, hypertrophied flowers, stems, gems, roots, and leaves. Recipes and pharmaceutical advice date from the Romans and are present in most Italian cookbooks and medical texts.

Broccoli and broccoli rabe are low in calories, loaded with vitamins A and C, calcium, potassium, phosphorus, and zinc. Cauliflower has vitamin A and minerals. Both cauliflower and broccoli are rich in cancer antidotes according to Jean Carper in *The Food Pharmacy*.

Italian broccoli cultivars include the commonly found Calabrian, in addition to the Albenga early, Calabrian stalky, and Romanesco. Cauliflower varieties include Neapolitan winter and giant, Albenga little bronze, Verona early, Jesi early, Sicilian purple, Calabrian green. Japanese hybrids crowd out the local cultivars in seed catalogs.

Since both broccoli and cauliflower are enlarged, unopened hypertrophied flowers, florets should be tightly closed, compact. Broccoli should show no signs of yellow; cauliflower should be unblemished. Those lucky enough to find broccoli or cauliflower with leaves can cook them, stripped of the tough central rib. Broccoli rabe stems should be small with crisp green leaves without a hint of yellow.

Although it's an approach that most Italians would find scandalous, I think that broccoli, Romanesco, broccoflower, and cauliflower can be used almost interchangeably in any of the following recipes. A combination of broccoli and cauliflower seems like a good substitute for Romanesco if broccoflower isn't available.

Shepherd's Garden Seeds, 6116 Highway 9, Felton, California 95018, Telephone: 408–335–6910, has seeds for broccoli raab and Romanesco broccoli. Seeds of Change, P.O. Box 15700, Santa Fe, New Mexico 87506, Telephone: 800–957–3337, has seeds for Calabrese broccoli. Pinetree Garden Seeds, Box 300, New Gloucester, Maine 04260, Telephone: 207–926–3400 has seeds for broccoli di rapa and Calabrese, and Fratelli Ingegnoli, Corso Buenos Aires 54, Milan 20124, has seeds for cauliflower, broccoli, Romanesco, and broccoli rabe.

*I*n the first century, Roman millionaire epicure Apicius hosted banquets of such delectables as flamingo tongues and camel heels. He blew his entire fortune on culinary festivities and poisoned himself at his last supper when he realized that he'd have to tone down his lifestyle. Apicius's legend survives in a fourth-century compilation of his recipes, *De Re Coquinaria*. Book III, entitled "The Greengrocer," begins with the advice to cook vegetables with bicarbonate "to give an attractive emerald green color." Chapter IX, "Tops and Cabbage Shoots," features six recipes that begin with boiled *cime,* which are dressed with oil and a wide variety of condiments including spice, old wine, cooked grape must, fresh herbs, olives, pine nuts, and raisins.

Venetian Giacomo Castelvetro wrote *A Brief Account of the Fruit, Herbs & Vegetables of Italy* in 1614 while living in England; it was an attempt to convince the English to eat more vegetables. Castelvetro writes about cauliflower and sprouting broccoli. In autumn "For beauty and goodness these take pride of place in the cabbage family. First cooked in salted water, cauliflowers are served cold, dressed with olive oil, salt and pepper." He recommends sprouting broccoli in the spring, ". . . tender shoots which grow on the stalks of cabbage or cauliflower plants left in the garden over the winter. They are cooked and served cold with oil and salt and pepper . . . Some prefer to cook them with a few cloves of garlic, which gives them a wonderful flavor."

Of Pythagorean Food (1781) by Vincenzo Corrado eliminates hunks of meat and enlarges the vegetable chapter of his previously published bestseller, *The Gallant Cook* (1773). Corrado doesn't take Pythagoras's orthodox vegetarian regime too seriously and recipes contain meat, poultry, prosciutto, fish, broths, dairy products, and eggs. He writes about both broccoli and cauliflower. "The beauty of broccolo consists of an attractive large green flower, tender, first cut. Cauliflower is similar and you can use the condiment of one for the other. They should be cooked with violent heat and boiled little so they don't lose their green and their tasty virtue. Broccoli are cleaned of all leaves and of the outer stalk." Corrado's comments on cauliflower are more detailed and include more than a dozen recipes.

Broccoli, Cauliflower, and Broccoli Rabe Recipes

PASTA SAUCED WITH BROCCOLI
OR BROCCOLI RABE AND TWO VARIATIONS

*Broccoli cooked with pasta, garlic,
and hot pepper (variations with anchovies
or cured pork)*

———

PAOLA'S PASTA AND BROCCOLI
IN SKATE BROTH

*Tomato broth, garlic, and broccoli soup,
with fish*

———

PAOLA'S SKATELESS PASTA
AND BROCCOLI BROTH

*Tomato broth, garlic, and broccoli soup,
without fish*

———

BROCCOLI OR BROCCOLI RABE "JUMPED"
WITH GARLIC AND SPICE

*Broccoli boiled and stir-fried with garlic
and hot pepper*

———

ANNA'S SICILIAN CAULIFLOWER PASTA

*Cauliflower flavored with onion, anchovies,
pine nuts, and currants*

MARIA'S BAKED PURPLE CAULIFLOWER

*Cauliflower baked with red onion, olives,
and pecorino cheese*

———

FABIO'S "UNMOLDED" CAULIFLOWER
SFORMATO

Baked cauliflower custard

———

TORQUATO'S "DROWNED" CAULIFLOWER

*Cauliflower cooked with tomato,
fennel seed, and garlic*

———

TORQUATO'S CAULIFLOWER AND SAUSAGE

*Cauliflower cooked with sausage, garlic,
and hot pepper*

———

CAULIFLOWER *FRITTATA*

Pan-fried cauliflower flan

Pasta Sauced with Broccoli or Broccoli Rabe and Two Variations

For 4–6 Servings   **First Course**

*T*his sauce is made of cooked broccoli, drained and sautéed with garlic, hot pepper and served with short pasta. Two tasty variations add either anchovies or cured pork to the garlic. And cooks with some time to spare can puree broccoli stems for a more elegant-textured sauce that combines chunky florets with smooth green stem paste.

> 1 large bunch of broccoli, about 1 pound, or 1 pound
>   broccoli rabe
> At least 5 quarts water plus 2–3 cups cold water
> 2–3 tablespoons coarse sea salt
> ¼ cup extra virgin olive oil
> 2 ounces salt pork, diced, about ⅓ cup,
>   or 4–6 anchovy fillets (optional)
> 2 garlic cloves, peeled and chopped
> 1 fresh hot red pepper, chopped, or chili pepper flakes
>   to taste
> 14–16 ounces penne or other short pasta

1   Detach the broccoli florets from the stalks and divide into bite-sized pieces. Cut a ½-inch slice off the butt end of the stalks and peel the dark tough skin on the stalks. Dice stalks into 1-inch pieces. Or carefully wash broccoli rabe in a sinkful of warm water, drain, and break off the tough stems.

2   Bring at least 5 quarts of water to a rolling boil in a large pot or pasta cooker. Add 2–3 tablespoons salt and the broccoli stems or broccoli rabe and cook until tender, at least 5 minutes. Remove with a slotted spoon, refresh in cold water, and drain. Squeeze broccoli rabe lightly to remove excess water. Cook the broccoli florets for 3–4 minutes, remove with a slotted spoon, refresh in cold water, and drain. Reserve cooking water to cook pasta.

3   Chop the broccoli rabe into bite-sized pieces. Puree the stems or one third of the broccoli rabe in the food processor for a more elegant sauce.

4   Heat 2 tablespoons extra virgin olive oil (and optional salt pork or anchovy fillets) in a 3-quart pot, add the garlic and hot pepper, and cook over moderate heat until the garlic begins to color.

(continued)

5   Add the drained broccoli stem puree or the broccoli rabe, salt lightly, and cook for 2 minutes, stirring to thoroughly coat with garlic.

6   Add 2–3 additional cups of cold water to broccoli cooking water and bring to a rolling boil.

7   Cook the pasta until it still offers considerable resistance to the tooth, around three quarters of the recommended cooking time. Drain the pasta, reserving 2 cups of pasta cooking water.

8   Add the drained pasta and 1 cup cooking water to the broccoli and cook the pasta and broccoli together to complete the pasta's cooking. Add the reserved pasta water, ¼ cup at a time, if the sauce is too dry. Serve immediately.

Paola's Pasta and Broccoli in Skate Broth

Serves 6–8   **First Course**

Wine maker Paola di Mauro is one of the great home cooks of Rome. She uses extra virgin olive oil pressed with olives from her own trees, cooks with produce out of her own garden, and creates simple home-style food that's made at the last minute with no apparent fuss. This soup is one of my favorites: a light broccoli and skate broth enriched with broccoli, skate, and pasta. When I asked Paola what to use if skate wasn't available, she thought about it and said that although any delicately flavored white fish could probably be used, she'd skip the fish. The essential ingredient in this soup is Romanesco broccoli. It looks like cauliflower from another planet, with pointy chartreuse florets that spiral to form a cone-shaped vegetable with more flavor than cauliflower but more delicate than broccoli. It used to be found at markets in Rome and southern Italy but now seems to be making its way north and is available in Florence. It's only a matter of time before it's available in American supermarkets. Cooks who can't find or grow this Roman specialty can use broccoflower, broccoli, or a combination of cauliflower and broccoli. Skate, according to Alan Davidson's *Mediterranean Seafood,* is widely available in Mediterranean as well as in North American waters, but if you can't find it and want to do this soup with fish, substitute any delicately flavored white fish, the freshest you can find.

1½ pounds Roman broccoli, broccoflower,
    or a combination of broccoli and cauliflower

At least 4 quarts plus 5 cups water

2–3 tablespoons coarse sea salt

1 whole skate, around 2 pounds, or any whole
    firm-fleshed white fish

½ onion, chopped

3 garlic cloves, minced

1 celery stalk

3 tablespoons chopped Italian parsley leaves
    (save stems for broth)

6 tablespoons extra virgin olive oil

4 tablespoons tomato pulp, fresh or canned

Freshly ground pepper

7 ounces spaghetti, broken into 1-inch pieces

1 Clean the broccoli and break into small florets. Reserve the central core or the broccoli stems and save for another use (like one of the pasta sauces in this chapter). Bring a large pot of water, at least 4 quarts, to a rolling boil. Add 2–3 tablespoons salt and the broccoli florets and cook for 3 or 4 minutes. Remove the broccoli florets with a slotted spoon, refresh in cold water, and drain. Save the cooking water.

2 Peel the skate, remove both external wings, and divide the wings into strips.

3 Make a broth with the fish head, trim, and bones, onion, 1 clove garlic, celery, parsley stems, and 5 cups water, lightly salted. Simmer for 15–20 minutes, strain, and reserve 4 cups of broth.

4 Sauté 2 tablespoons of chopped parsley and 1 clove of minced garlic in 3 tablespoons extra virgin olive oil. Add 2 tablespoons tomato pulp, 4 cups broccoli cooking water, 4 cups skate or fish broth, and simmer for 10 minutes to amalgamate flavors. Taste for salt, adding some if necessary.

5 Sauté remaining clove of minced garlic in remaining extra virgin olive oil in a wide low skillet large enough to contain fish in one layer. Add remaining 2 tablespoons tomato pulp and cook for 1 minute.

6 Add the skate strips, sprinkle with salt and pepper, cover, and cook for a few minutes over low heat. Remove from heat.

7 Add the broken pasta to the simmering broth and cook over moderate heat. After about 8 minutes, when pasta is partially cooked, add broccoli florets and cook for 3 or 4 minutes or until pasta is done. Ladle pasta and broth into soup bowls, top with the fish and pan juices, sprinkle with remaining tablespoon of parsley, and serve.

Paola's Skateless Pasta and Broccoli Broth

2 pounds Romanesco broccoli, broccoflower,
    or a combination of broccoli and cauliflower

At least 5 quarts water

2–3 tablespoons sea salt

½ onion, chopped

1 celery stalk

3 garlic cloves, minced

3 tablespoons chopped Italian parsley leaves
    (save stems for broth)

3 tablespoons extra virgin olive oil

¼ cup tomato pulp, fresh or canned

Freshly ground pepper

7 ounces spaghetti, broken into 2-inch pieces

1   Clean the broccoli or broccoflower and break into small florets. Reserve the central core or broccoli stems for use in next step. Bring a large pot with at least 5 quarts of water to a rolling boil. Add 2–3 tablespoons salt and the broccoli florets: cook for 3 or 4 minutes. Remove the broccoli florets with a slotted spoon, refresh in cold water, and drain. Save the cooking water.

2   Make a broth of 10 cups broccoli cooking water, onion, celery, 1 clove garlic, parsley stems, and broccoflower core or broccoli stems. Simmer for 15–20 minutes.

3   Sauté 2 tablespoons of chopped parsley and remaining 2 cloves of minced garlic in 3 tablespoons extra virgin olive oil. Add ¼ cup tomato pulp, 8 cups broccoli cooking water, and simmer for 10 minutes to amalgamate flavors. Taste for salt, adding some if necessary, and season with pepper.

4   Add broken pasta to simmering broccoli broth and cook over moderate heat. After about 8 minutes, when pasta is partially cooked, add broccoli florets and cook for 3–4 minutes or until pasta is done. Ladle pasta and broth into soup bowls, sprinkle with remaining tablespoon of chopped parsley, and serve. Although it's not traditional a little grated Pecorino Romano wouldn't be out of place since there's no fish in this soup.

Broccoli or Broccoli Rabe "Jumped" with Garlic and Spice

For 4–6 Servings   Side Dish

*B*roccoli, broccoflower, and broccoli rabe stand up well to the big flavors of garlic and hot pepper, which make a plate of boiled greens into a palate-tingling dish. This is a classic vegetable treatment found throughout Italy, the perfect way to use leftover boiled broccoli or broccoli rabe or an excuse to boil some. Garlic can be sautéed whole and removed before serving for a lighter flavor although garlic lovers should mince or slice garlic for more intensity.

> 1½ pounds broccoli, broccoflower, or broccoli rabe
> At least 5 quarts water
> 2–3 tablespoons salt plus fine sea salt
> ¼ cup extra virgin olive oil
> 2–3 garlic cloves, whole or minced
> Fresh hot chili pepper or dried chili pepper flakes

1   Clean the broccoli or broccoflower, cut the florets off the stems, and divide into bite-sized pieces. Split large stems in half and cut into bite-sized pieces. Alternately, carefully wash broccoli rabe in a sinkful of warm water, drain, and break off the tough stems.

2   Bring a large pot containing at least 5 quarts of water to a rolling boil. Add 2–3 tablespoons salt and broccoli stems or broccoli rabe, and cook until tender, at least 5 minutes. Remove with a slotted spoon, refresh in cold water, and drain. Add the broccoli florets and cook for 3 or 4 minutes. Remove the florets with a slotted spoon, refresh in cold water, and drain, saving ½ cup cooking water.

3   Heat 2 tablespoons of extra virgin olive oil in a large nonstick skillet. Sauté garlic and hot pepper until it begins to color.

4   Add the broccoli stems to the pan and cook for a few minutes, mashing stems. Add broccoli florets and ¼ cup cooking water and cook over high heat until water evaporates. Or add the broccoli rabe and ¼ cup cooking water to the garlic and hot pepper and cook over high heat until the water evaporates.

5   Remove skillet from heat, add remaining extra virgin olive oil, and serve.

Anna's Sicilian Cauliflower Pasta

For 4–6 Servings   **Side Dish**

*A*nna Tasca Lanza, author of *The Heart of Sicily* (Clarkson Potter, 1993), owner of the Regaleali Cookery School in Sicily, and super Sicilian home-cook introduced me to this unusual dish, a classic combination of pine nuts and dried currants, paired with cauliflower and pasta. The best version I've ever had was prepared by her father's chef, Mario Lo Menzo, one of the last cooks of the aristocratic Sicilian tradition known as *monzu'*, a corruption of monsieur, a title of respect in Francophile noble kitchens. He uses a pinch of powdered saffron, a flavor appropriated from the Arab tradition for the table of noble Sicilians. Some Sicilians garnish this pasta with bread crumbs toasted in extra virgin olive oil, others with a sprinkle of grated pecorino sheep's milk cheese. Although Sicilian cauliflower is green and has more flavor than American cauliflower, either broccoflower, cauliflower, or a combination of cauliflower and broccoli can be used with favorable results.

> At least 5 quarts water
> 1–1½ pounds cauliflower or broccoflower
> 2–3 tablespoons coarse sea salt
> 1 red onion
> ¼ cup extra virgin olive oil
> 2 anchovy fillets
> 1 pinch saffron or a few saffron threads
> ½ cup tomato pulp, fresh or canned
> 3 tablespoons pine nuts
> 3 tablespoons currants
> Freshly ground pepper
> 14–16 ounces spaghetti or perciatelli
> ¼ cup unflavored bread crumbs, lightly browned in
>   1 tablespoon extra virgin olive oil, or ¼ cup
>   grated pecorino

1   Bring a large pot containing at least 5 quarts of water to a rolling boil.

2   Detach the florets from the cauliflower at the base of their stems. Add to boiling water with 2–3 tablespoons of salt and cook for 5 minutes or until tender. Drain with a slotted spoon, refresh in cold water, drain, and reserve. Reserve the cooking water.

3　Sauté the onion in the extra virgin olive oil in a large nonstick skillet over moderate heat until golden.

4　Add the anchovies and mash them into the onion-oil mixture.

5　Dissolve a pinch of saffron or a few saffron threads in 2 cups of hot cauliflower cooking water.

6　Add the saffron water and the tomato to the skillet. Simmer for 2–3 minutes.

7　Add the cauliflower, the pine nuts, and the dried currants, and season with salt and pepper. Keep the skillet of sauce warm over low heat.

8　Bring the large pot of cauliflower cooking water back to a rolling boil, adding necessary water to refill the pot. Add the pasta.

9　Cook the pasta until it still offers considerable resistance to the tooth, around three quarters of the recommended cooking time. Drain, reserving 1 cup of pasta cooking water. Add pasta to the cauliflower sauce.

10　Cook the pasta and sauce together to complete cooking of both cauliflower and pasta. Add the reserved pasta water, ¼ cup at a time, if sauce is too dry.

11　Sprinkle with toasted bread crumbs or grated cheese and serve.

Maria's Baked Purple Cauliflower

For 4–6 Servings   Side Dish

*M*aria di Fazio, my housekeeper, thought I'd be interested in the special cauliflower of her native region, Apulia, in the heel of the Italian boot, and brought me a sample after a visit home to see her family. And she showed me how to make this baked cauliflower salad with it. But even if wild-looking purple cauliflower that turns green after cooking isn't available, Maria's recipe is a winner.

> **At least 5 quarts water**
> **2 pounds cauliflower**
> **2–3 tablespoons coarse sea salt**
> **1 garlic clove, chopped**
> **2 tablespoons chopped parsley**
> **3 tablespoons extra virgin olive oil**
> **Freshly ground pepper**
> **¾ cup grated Pecorino Romano**

1   Preheat the oven to 400 degrees. Lightly oil a large low baking dish.

2   Bring a large pot of water, at least 5 quarts, to a rolling boil.

3   Detach the florets from the cauliflower at the base of their stems. Add to the boiling water with 2–3 tablespoons of salt and cook for 5 minutes or until *al dente*. Drain with a slotted spoon, refresh in cold water, drain, and reserve.

4   Sauté the garlic and parsley with extra virgin olive oil over low heat until the garlic begins to color.

5   Put the cauliflower in the prepared baking dish, top with the garlic and oil, and sprinkle with salt, pepper, and grated cheese. Bake for 15–20 minutes or until cheese is browned and crusty. Serve immediately.

Fabio's "Unmolded" Cauliflower *Sformato*

For 8–10 Servings   **Appetizer, Side Dish**

Sformato, with an *s* prefix that means "un-" in front of the past participle of the verb "to mold," is one of the vegetable specialties of Florence. It's usually made with leftover boiled vegetables blended with cheese in a light béchamel custard, baked in a loaf pan or individual baking dishes, unmolded to serve. Almost all winter vegetables are made into "unmoldeds" but I like cauliflower the best. It's an easy dish for a crowd and Fabio Picchi of the restaurant Cibrèo in Florence always has one on the menu. Although his "unmolded" cauliflower used to be made with the classic béchamel, he's switched to ricotta and I like the results.

> At least 5 quarts water
> ½ pound cauliflower, about 1 cup
> 2–3 tablespoons fine sea salt
> 16 ounces whole milk ricotta
> 3 eggs
> ¼ cup grated Parmigiano-Reggiano
> 3 tablespoons extra virgin olive oil
> A few gratings of nutmeg
> 1 garlic clove, peeled
> 2 tablespoons chopped Italian parsley
> Plenty of freshly ground pepper

1 Preheat the oven to 375 degrees. Lightly oil an 8 x 8- inch baking dish.

2 Bring a large pot containing at least 5 quarts of water to a rolling boil.

3 Detach the florets from the cauliflower at the base of their stems. Cook the cauliflower in the boiling water with 2–3 tablespoons of salt for 6–8 minutes or until soft, no longer *al dente*. Drain with a slotted spoon, refresh in cold water, and drain.

4 Mince the cauliflower in a food processor. Add ricotta, eggs, cheese, extra virgin olive oil, nutmeg, garlic, and parsley and process until smooth. Season with salt and pepper.

5 Spoon the mixture into the prepared baking dish.

6 Place the baking dish in a roasting pan and pour in enough hot water to come halfway up the sides. Bake until the *sformato* is set, about 25–35 minutes. Remove from the oven, cool for at least 15 minutes, cut into squares, and serve warm.

Torquato's "Drowned" Cauliflower

For 4–6 Servings   **Side Dish**

*C*auliflower is "drowned" in tomato sauce spiced with fennel and garlic, a wonderful recipe recounted by Torquato, my favorite farmer at the Santo Spirito market in Florence. His recipes are a culinary sales pitch for his all-organic seasonal produce from his farm on the outskirts of the city. The recipes are easy since they have to be related while Torquato chooses, weighs, prices (no calculators or electronic scales or price bars), and bags his customers' vegetables. Torquato's recipe for drowned cauliflower eliminates the meat and wine but retains the flavorings of a classic Florentine dish called "drunken pork." Cauliflower is slowly braised until soft and creamy. *Al dente* cauliflower just won't do.

> **At least 5 quarts water**
> **1½–2 pounds cauliflower**
> **2–3 tablespoons coarse sea salt**
> **3 tablespoons extra virgin olive oil**
> **2 garlic cloves, minced**
> **½ cup tomato pulp, fresh or canned**
> **½ teaspoon fennel seeds**
> **Freshly ground pepper**

1   In a large pot, bring at least 5 quarts of water to a rolling boil.

2   Detach the florets from the cauliflower at the base of their stems. Cook the cauliflower in the boiling water with 2–3 tablespoons of salt for 5 minutes or until *al dente*. Drain with a slotted spoon, refresh in cold water, drain, and reserve. Save the cauliflower cooking water.

3   Heat the extra virgin olive oil and the garlic in a large nonstick skillet.

4   When the garlic barely begins to color add the tomato pulp and the fennel seeds and cook over moderate heat for 2–3 minutes.

5   Add the cauliflower and 1 cup of hot cauliflower cooking water. Simmer for 10–15 minutes or until cauliflower is soft and liquid has evaporated. Add more cooking water if sauce gets too dry. Season with salt and freshly ground pepper.

Torquato's Cauliflower and Sausage

For 4–6 Servings   **Side Dish**

*T*orquato has some wonderful advice for his customers about how to cook cauliflower, probably because he has a lot of first-rate cauliflower to sell, large creamy white heads with green outer leaves still attached. His recipes are always easy, often flavored with garlic and hot red peppers, and usually begin with a "big puddle" of extra virgin olive oil. Torquato's classic Tuscan cauliflower and sausage is typical. I've cut down on the oil and eliminated the excess fat from the sausage but I'm not sure that Torquato would approve.

> **At least 5 quarts water**
> **1½–2 pounds cauliflower**
> **2 tablespoons salt**
> **4–6 mild-flavored Italian sausages, casings removed**
> **2 tablespoons extra virgin olive oil (optional)**
> **2 garlic cloves, minced**
> **1 hot red pepper or chili pepper flakes to taste**
> **½ cup dry white wine**

1 Bring a large pot of water containing at least 5 quarts of water to a rolling boil.

2 Detach the florets from the cauliflower at the base of their stems. Cook the cauliflower in the boiling water with 2 tablespoons of salt for 5 minutes or until *al dente*. Drain with a slotted spoon, refresh in cold water, drain, and reserve. Save the cauliflower cooking water.

3 Remove the casings from the sausage. Cook the sausage in a large nonstick skillet over moderate heat, using a wooden fork or spoon to crumble the meat as it browns. Traditionalists don't have to drain off the fat although everyone else will probably want to eliminate it.

4 Add optional extra virgin olive oil if you've removed the sausage fat, and cook the garlic and hot pepper in oil or fat until the garlic begins to color.

5 Add the cauliflower and white wine and cook over high heat to evaporate the wine. Add 1 cup of the hot cauliflower cooking water, season lightly with salt, and simmer for 10–15 minutes or until the liquid is evaporated and the cauliflower is tender.

Cauliflower *Frittata*

I love a *frittata* made with cauliflower. I usually use leftovers. *Frittata* cooks can choose one of the following cooking methods. Traditionalists cook one side, turn the *frittata* over onto a plate, and slip it back into the pan to cook the other side. Some cooks cook the lower surface and cover the skillet to set the top, flipping the *frittata* over onto a serving dish to hide the unbrowned side. Flamboyant cooks flip their *frittata*, flapjack-style. Marcella Hazan recommends cooking the eggs until set, then broiling the upper surface. A nonstick omelet pan makes the entire process easier for everyone.

> 1½ pounds cauliflower
> 4 tablespoons extra virgin olive oil
> 1 small onion, chopped
> Sea salt
> Freshly ground pepper
> ¼ cup grated Pecorino Romano
> 4 eggs
> 2 tablespoons chopped Italian parsley

1   Detach the florets from the cauliflower at the base of their stems.

2   Drizzle 2 tablespoons of extra virgin olive oil over the chopped onions in a large non-stick skillet and stir the onions to coat with oil.

3   Place the skillet over low heat and cook until the onions are golden. Add the cauliflower florets, salt, and pepper and cover skillet. Cook over low heat for 10–15 minutes or until tender. Transfer the cauliflower to a bowl.

4   Mix the grated cheese with the eggs, parsley, and cauliflower.

5   Heat remaining 2 tablespoons of extra virgin olive oil in a large nonstick skillet and add the egg and cauliflower mixture. Cook over low heat until the eggs are set on the side of the pan but still runny on the surface.

6   Either turn the *frittata* over onto a plate and slide it back into the pan to complete cooking, or cook until barely set, cover, and cook for a few more minutes to finish, reversing the *frittata* onto a serving platter to expose the browned surface. Or cook one side and then broil the top. Or flip the *frittata* like a pancake.

7   Slide onto a platter and serve hot or at room temperature.

CABBAGE AND KALE

Cavolo e Cavolo Nero

In spite of Italian expletives that substitute the word *cavolo*, "cabbage," for off-color language, it's an important element in regional winter cooking. Italians typically take a common vegetable with a ho-hum reputation and make it seem almost new. Cabbage is stewed in soups, sauce, braised, stuffed with rice or meat. Dozens of regional cabbage varieties, tight pale green balls, curly darker green loose heads, palm-tree-like fronds of Tuscan kale, are found in most markets year during the winter months, said to be tastier after the first frost.

Cabbage is a member of the Crucifere or mustard family, a prehistoric Mediterranean wild plant that diversified into Brassicas classified by form—heads (common or Savoy cabbage), hypertrophied flowers (cauliflower and broccoli), stems (kohlrabi), gems (brussels sprouts), roots (turnips), or leaves (kale).

Cabbage has a low-life reputation, possibly because it causes what one delicate writer refers to as meteorism, a euphemism for farting. It's healthy winter food, low in calories, with some vitamin C and A, potassium, calcium, and folic acid. It's said to be a cancer fighter and to stimulate the immune system. Friar Foreteller (*Frate Indovino*), a mythical Italian Franciscan monk, provides tips on gardening, wine making, cooking, and home cures that utilize vegetables, herbs, and fruit in his almanac. The friar esteems the entire cabbage family for its decongestant, disinfectant, antidiabetic, antirheumatic, and scar-healing powers. Cabbage juice is helpful for gastric ulcers, gout, arthritis, and depressive states; blanched leaves can be applied topically to irritated skin or burns.

Italian headed cabbage cultivars are divided into two main groups. Common cabbage, called *cavolo cappuccio,* has pale green leaves in a tight head. Savoy cabbage, called *verza,* includes varieties Asti super-early, late harvest of Milano, and Iron Head and has curly dark green leaves in a looser head. International hybrids are also widely found. Tuscan kale, known as *cavolo nero,* has curly palmlike leaves growing out of a central stalk and is available in Tuscany but uncommon elsewhere.

Torquato Innocenti, my Tuscan kale connection in the Piazza Santo Spirito market, is enthusiastic about the cabbage family. Headed cabbage rarely gets a starring role in his oral recipes, which are every bit as vague as the culinary texts that I haunt, but Tuscan kale is featured in soup, paired with rice or polenta, or placed on slices of toasted garlic bread, a minimalist dish that offends cookbook author Artusi. After the central stalk of Tuscan kale is harvested, lots of gems, mini-black cabbages, appear on the stalk, which Torquato recommends eating raw in a mixed salad, or stir-fried with garlic and *peperoncino,* hot red pepper, to be used as a sauce for pasta. "Watch out," warns Torquato, "cabbage eaten in the evening produces bad dreams." Milan, Iron Head, and earliest Savoy cabbage seed varieties are available from Fratelli Ingegnoli, Corso Buenos Aires 54, 20124 Milan, but I couldn't find any American seed sources. Tuscan kale seed is available, called lacinato kale by Shepherd's Garden Seeds, 6116 Highway 9, Felton, California 95018, Telephone: 408–355–6910; called Thousand-Headed kale by Seeds of Change, P.O. Box 15700, Santa Fe, New Mexico 87506, Telephone: 800–957–3337; and called Palm Tree Cabbage by the Redwood City Seed Company, P.O. Box 361, Redwood City, California 94064, Telephone: 415–325–7333.

Romans loved cabbage despite its humble status. Apicius included it in a rustic vegetable soup with lentils, split peas, leek, fennel, and herbs but dressed his soup with garum, a sauce made of fermented fish that Romans used like ketchup, on practically everything, probably an acquired taste.

Platina's recipes in *Honest Pleasure and Health* (1474) are, as usual, the same as Maestro Martino's in *The Book of Culinary Art* (1450), an early example of cookbook plagiarism, considered flattering in those days. But Platina adds historical references, mentioning Roman Cato, who distinguishes between three kinds of cabbage, Julius Caesar's war chronicles with their three-leaf wild cabbage, and Aristotle, who claimed it the best remedy for drunkenness, a popular belief found through centuries of cabbage lore. According to Platina, cabbage augments the black bile, disturbs sleep, and is bad for the stomach, vision, and head because of its fumes. It's easier to digest in the winter, he claims.

Michele Savonarola, illustrious doctor, professor, astrologist, moralist, dietitian, and gastronome from Padua, isn't too encouraging about cabbage in his 1508 bestseller *Of All Things Commonly Eaten*. He identifies it as the base vegetable in the diet of poverty, difficult to digest, helpful for hangovers.

Bartolomeo Scappi cooked for cardinals in Rome. His 1570 *Opera* has a decidedly Roman outlook and a recipe for "untricked" cabbage, made with Milanese or Bolognese cabbage, cooked in broth, chopped fine, recooked with lard, fat broth, spice, and sprinkled before serving with cheese and cinnamon. Stuffed cabbage can be spit-roasted, adds Scappi at the end of this recipe, an interesting concept expressed in a three-word culinary hint.

Bolognese doctor Baldassare Pisanelli's 1584 *Treatise on the Nature of Food and Drink* contains his usual medical warnings, stating that cabbage is "damaging for melancholiacs and should never be eaten at the end of summer." His "remedy" is boiling cabbage, throwing away the first water, and cooking in fat meat broth with fennel and pepper.

Venetian Giacomo Castelvetro wrote *A Brief Account of the Fruit, Herbs & Vegetables of Italy* in 1614 while living in England, an attempt to convince the English to eat more vegetables. Castelvetro, complementing his host-country's cuisine, says that cabbage is nicely cooked in England but his recipes for three different varieties of cabbage, which the English aren't familiar with, sound Venetian. Cabbage can be stewed with a paste of parsley, thyme, and lard, stuffed with herbs, bread crumbs, grated cheese, and egg, cooked whole and dressed with butter and pepper. He advises that cabbage is at its best in the winter, when the frost "makes them perfect."

The anonymously written *The Piedmontese Cook Perfected in Paris* (1766) clearly reveals the influence of nearby France, using terms like *entrées*, *hors d'oeuvre*, and *surtout*. The recipe for whole "surprise" cabbage is tempting, stuffed with chestnuts and sausage, tied, braised with broth, onion, and herbs, dressed with a buttery sauce.

Cabbage Recipes

TUSCAN KALE PESTO

Pureed kale, garlic,
and extra virgin olive oil condiment

————

FLORENTINE "CABBAGE WITH SLICES"

Cavolo con le Fette

Minimalist kale and garlic bread appetizer

————

MARIO'S "LITTLE HOODS" OF RICE

Cappuccetti di Riso

Risotto-stuffed cabbage balls

————

TORQUATO'S CABBAGE AND CORNMEAL SOUP

Farinata di Cavolo

————

**VALLE D'AOSTA CABBAGE
AND FONTINA CHEESE SOUP**

Cabbage baked with bread and cheese

TORQUATO'S RICE AND CABBAGE SOUP

————

**MASSIMO'S PENNE WITH TUSCAN KALE
AND POTATOES**

*A Florentine improvisation
on a southern Italian classic*

————

CLAUDIA'S STUFFED CABBAGE CAPUNET

*Meat-stuffed cabbage leaves
lightly breaded and sautéed*

————

**ANTONELLO'S SPICY UNMOLDED
BUT NOT REALLY CABBAGE**

Spicy, garlicky braised cabbage and salt pork

CABBAGE AND KALE

Tuscan Kale Pesto

*B*oiled Tuscan kale (*cavolo nero*) and garlic are processed with extra virgin olive oil to form a dark green paste for a strictly Tuscan-tasting pesto. It's handy to have a bowl of this easily prepared cabbage pesto in the refrigerator to spread on toasted bread, dress pasta, combine with white beans, or as an enrichment for vegetable soup. Those not lucky enough to find or grow Tuscan kale can substitute kale, which may be tougher and need more cooking, or cabbage, which produces a more delicately flavored pesto.

> 1 pound Tuscan kale, kale, or ½ cabbage
> 4–5 quarts water
> 2–3 tablespoons coarse sea salt
> 2 garlic cloves
> ½ cup or more extra virgin olive oil

1   Carefully wash the kale or cabbage in a sinkful of warm water. Remove the tough central ribs of black cabbage or kale or the cabbage core.

2   Bring 4–5 quarts of water to a rolling boil. Add 2–3 tablespoons coarse salt and the kale or cabbage and cook for 10–15 minutes or until tender. Kale will take much longer to cook than cabbage. Remove with a slotted spoon, refresh in cold water, and drain and squeeze to remove all excess moisture.

3   Puree the cabbage or kale, garlic, extra virgin olive oil, and salt to taste in the food processor to form a smooth stiff paste. Store in the refrigerator in a glass jar or bowl, covered with a layer of extra virgin olive oil, where it will keep for a few days.

Florentine "Cabbage with Slices"
Cavolo con le Fette

For 4–6 Servings   **Appetizer, First Course**

*P*ellegrino Artusi, transplanted from his native Romagna to Tuscany, reflects the influence of both regions in his best-seller *Culinary Science and the Art of Eating Well*, self-published in 1910 with more than 110 editions to date. Artusi includes vague directions for the Florentine dish "cabbage with slices," toasted bread slices topped with boiled black cabbage and its cooking water, drizzled with extra virgin olive oil, clearly not to his taste. He describes it as "a dish for Carthusian monks or to inflict as punishment on a gourmand." Lots of people disagree with Artusi's judgment and cabbage and slices is eaten at home and in family-style restaurants in Florence. Personal taste regulates the amount of Tuscan kale broth ladled over the garlic bread, which can be lightly moistened or swimming in clear green liquid. A healthy drizzle of extra virgin olive oil is imperative.

> 1 pound Tuscan kale, kale, or ½ cabbage
>
> 4–5 quarts water
>
> 2–3 tablespoons coarse sea salt
>
> 4–6 slices coarse country-style bread, sliced ¾-inch thick
>
> 1 garlic clove, unpeeled
>
> Freshly ground pepper to taste
>
> ½ cup extra virgin olive oil

1 Carefully wash the kale or cabbage in a sinkful of warm water. Remove the tough central ribs of the black cabbage or kale or the cabbage core.

2 Bring 4–5 quarts of water to a rolling boil. Add 2–3 tablespoons coarse salt and the kale or cabbage and cook for 10–15 minutes or until tender. Kale will take much longer, up to 15 more minutes or longer to cook. Remove the kale or cabbage with a slotted spoon, refresh in cold water, drain, and press lightly to remove excess water. Reserve the cabbage cooking water. Coarsely chop the kale or cabbage and divide into 4–6 parts.

3 Lightly toast the bread, rub the slices with the garlic, and place a slice in each bowl.

4 Cover each bread slice with the cooked kale or cabbage. Ladle ¼–½ cup of cabbage cooking water over the kale or cabbage, sprinkle with salt and pepper, and drizzle with extra virgin olive oil.

Mario's "Little Hoods" of Rice
Cappuccetti di Riso

*M*ario Lo Menzo, the private chef of Count Tasca, the patriarch of Regaleali winery in Sicily, cooks the foods of the noble Sicilian tradition, rarely found outside the home. *Monzu'*, a corruption of *monsieur*, is a culinary title of respect, a leftover from the days when French chefs headed Sicilian kitchen staffs. Mario cooks both simple Sicilian peasant food and the elegant cuisine of the nobility as well as dishes he's learned in his travels with the count. His *cappuccetti di riso*, risotto-stuffed cabbage balls, are the countess's favorite dish. A *monzu'* undoubtedly had broth bubbling on a back burner and reduced demiglace in the larder but times have changed. Mario, one of the last chefs still cooking for a noble family, has converted to the *dado* or bouillon cube as have most modern Italians. I'm not among them and prefer the clean taste of water to the chemicals, hydrogenated vegetable fat, and MSG of bouillon cubes. Faithful recipe followers should look for the best quality of cubes avail.

> 4 quarts water plus 7–8 cups hot water (optional)
>
> 2 tablespoons sea salt
>
> ½ medium-sized cabbage
>
> ½ cup chopped onion
>
> 2 tablespoons extra virgin olive oil
>
> 1 cup rice for risotto, preferably Carnaroli or Vialone Nano(see page 8 for information on Italian rice)
>
> 1 pinch saffron threads or ¼ teaspoon powdered saffron
>
> Freshly ground pepper
>
> ¾ cup grated Parmigiano
>
> 1 tablespoon butter or extra virgin olive oil

1 Bring 4 quarts of water to a boil, add 2 tablespoons salt and the cabbage. Boil for 10 minutes or until tender.

2 Remove the cabbage with a slotted spoon, refresh in cold water, and drain. (If desired, save the cooking water to add to the rice later instead of plain water.)

3 Remove the central core of the cabbage and peel off the leaves. Remove the hard central stem of each leaf.

4 To prepare the risotto filling, sauté the onion in the extra virgin olive oil over low heat until tender but not browned, around 10 minutes.

5 Add the rice and sauté for 5 minutes to coat and lightly toast the rice.

6 Add 3 cups of hot water (or water that cabbage was boiled in) and the saffron and cook, stirring occasionally with a long wooden spoon or fork, over high heat until most of the liquid has evaporated.

7 Continue cooking rice over high heat, adding water or cabbage broth, 1 cup at a time, as needed, stirring well after each addition until rice is still slightly firm and barely surrounded by semi-liquid sauce.

8 You will probably need about 7 cups of liquid. If you are using water, lightly salt to taste. Add ½ cup Parmigiano and stir for a minute over high heat.

9 Remove from heat and let the risotto sit for 5 minutes. Pour out on a large platter and spread in a layer to cool.

10 Preheat oven to 375 degrees. Prepare an oiled or nonstick baking dish.

11 Place a cabbage leaf on the palm of your hand. Put a fistful, approximately ¼ cup, of risotto on the leaf and wrap up risotto with leaf. Neatness doesn't count, leaves can be patched but should totally encase rice filling.

12 Squeeze with both hands to form a ball and eliminate any excess water.

13 Place cabbage balls on the prepared baking dish in one layer. Season with salt and pepper. Sprinkle with remaining ¼ cup Parmigiano and dot with butter or drizzle with extra virgin olive oil. Bake for 30 minutes or until lightly brown. Serve immediately.

Torquato's Cabbage and Cornmeal Soup
Farinata di Cavolo

For 4–6 Servings　　　　　　　　　　　　　　　　　　　　　**First Course**

*F*arinata is a classic Tuscan dish, cornmeal cooked to a creamy consistency with or without the addition of vegetables. I love Torquato's suggestion of Tuscan kale *farinata*, flavored, as usual, with garlic since "the cabbage family marry well with garlic," according to my culinary consultant in Piazza Santo Spirito. The double boiler makes easy work of cooking cornmeal, but if you don't have one big enough for this recipe place a 3-quart pot in a larger pot or deep skillet filled with hot water. First-rate stone-ground finely milled yellow cornmeal, either domestic or imported from Italy, will produce the best results. Check imported cornmeal for an expiration date because old cornmeal will probably have bugs.

> ½ pound Tuscan kale, kale, or cabbage
> 4–5 quarts water
> 2–3 tablespoons coarse sea salt
> 1 cup polenta
> 3–4 garlic cloves, peeled and chopped
> ¼ cup extra virgin olive oil
> Freshly ground pepper

1　Carefully wash the kale or cabbage. Remove the tough central ribs of black cabbage or kale or the cabbage core.

2　Bring 4–5 quarts of water to a rolling boil. Add 2–3 tablespoons coarse salt and the kale or cabbage and cook for 10–15 minutes or until tender. Kale will take much longer, up to 30 minutes, to cook. Remove the kale or cabbage with a slotted spoon, refresh in cold water, and drain. Reserve the cabbage cooking water. Coarsely chop the kale or cabbage.

3　Measure 6 cups of the kale or cabbage cooking water into a 3-quart pot and bring to a boil. Sprinkle polenta into the water, stirring with a whisk to prevent lumping. Add kale or cabbage to the polenta and place the pot in another, larger pot of boiling water (or double boiler) and cook over low heat for 45 minutes or until creamy, not thick.

4　Sauté the garlic in 2 tablespoons extra virgin olive oil until barely colored and stir into the *farinata* before serving. Ladle the *farinata* into soup bowls and top each bowl with a drizzle of the remaining extra virgin olive oil and freshly ground pepper.

Valle d'Aosta Cabbage
and Fontina Soup

*V*alle d'Aosta, a tiny region on the southern side of the French Alps, is mountainous; farming is difficult, the growing season short. Potatoes and cabbage turn up in winter dishes. This dish is called a soup but it's more like a savory bread pudding. If Italian fontina from Valle d'Aosta isn't available, don't use Scandinavian—substitute Gruyère or Swiss cheese.

> ½ cabbage (about 1 pound)
> 2–3 ounces sausage or salt pork, cubed, about ¼–⅓ cup
> 2 garlic cloves
> 4½ cups boiling water or light broth
> Sea salt and freshly ground pepper
> 1 pinch ground allspice
> 6 slices of stale country-style whole wheat bread
> 5–6 ounces fontina, thinly sliced

1 Remove the core of the cabbage. Slice the cabbage into thin strips.

2 Sauté the sausage or salt pork in a 3-quart pot over high heat to render some of its fat. Lower the heat and add garlic.

3 When the garlic barely begins to color, add the cabbage strips and cook, stirring occasionally, over low heat until cabbage wilts, around 10 minutes.

4 Add 4½ cups boiling water or broth, salt (quantity will depend on the saltiness of pork or sausage), pepper, and allspice, and simmer over low heat for 25–30 minutes.

5 Preheat the oven to 375 degrees.

6 Toast the bread on a rack in the oven to dry and lightly brown, about 10–15 minutes.

7 Place 2 slices of bread on the bottom of a 2-quart casserole. With a slotted spoon, remove one third of the cabbage from the soup and place it over the bread. Top with one third of the sliced fontina. Repeat with another two layers and ladle cabbage broth over the final layer, to almost cover.

8 Bake for 1 hour or until cheese topping is browned and most liquid has been absorbed. Remove from the oven, cool for 5 minutes, and serve.

CABBAGE AND KALE

Torquato's Rice and Cabbage Soup

*L*ooser than a risotto, easier to make since it doesn't demand almost constant stirring, a tasty answer for a hearty winter dish when the cupboard is practically bare. Outer cabbage leaves are used to make a vegetable broth, inner leaves are chopped and cooked with onions, rice, and broth, and enriched with grated Parmigiano-Reggiano cheese, one of the few non-Tuscan ingredients that Torquato ever mentions. First-rate rice will remain firm under tooth, the desired texture.

½ medium-sized cabbage

1 medium-sized carrot

A few parsley leaves and stems

1 garlic clove

6 cups boiling water

Coarse sea salt

Freshly ground pepper

1 red onion, chopped

2 tablespoons extra virgin olive oil

¾ cup rice for risotto, preferably Carnaroli or Vialone
    Nano (see page 8 for information on rice)

½ cup grated Parmigiano

1   Rinse the tough outer cabbage leaves. Make a light vegetable broth with the other cabbage leaves, carrot, parsley leaves and stems, garlic clove, 6 cups of boiling water, salt, and pepper. Simmer for 15–20 minutes.

2   Wash the rest of the cabbage, remove the core, and cut the leaves into strips.

3   Put the onion in a 3-quart heavy-bottomed pot, drizzle with the extra virgin olive oil, and stir to coat the onion with oil. Cook over moderate heat until tender but not colored.

4   Add the cabbage strips and sauté over low heat, stirring occasionally, until wilted. Add 5 cups of the vegetable broth and bring to a simmer. Add the rice and cook, stirring occasionally, for 15–25 minutes or until rice is cooked, firm under the tooth but not raw-tasting. This soup is more liquid than a risotto. Add more broth if soup is too dry.

5   Serve with grated Parmigiano cheese.

Massimo's Penne with
Tuscan Kale and Potatoes

For 4–6 Servings   **First Course**

*M*assimo was inspired by all my southern Italian potato and vegetable pastas and suggested that I try a version with Tuscan kale. As usual, his culinary judgment was right on target and his Florentine version of a classic from Apulia has become a family favorite.

½ pound Tuscan kale, kale, or cabbage

5–6 quarts water

2–3 tablespoons coarse sea salt

1 large yellow-fleshed potato, peeled and cut
    into ¾-inch cubes

14–16 ounces spaghetti

1–2 garlic cloves, chopped

3–4 tablespoons extra virgin olive oil

Freshly grated pepper

1 Carefully clean the kale, removing tough central ribs and washing carefully to remove all dirt. Cut the kale or cabbage into thin strips.

2 Bring 5–6 quarts of water to a rolling boil. Add the kale and 2–3 tablespoons salt and cook at a rolling boil for 5 minutes.

3 Add the potato to the pot and cook for 5 minutes. Add the pasta and cook until it offers considerable resistance to the tooth, around three quarters of the cooking time.

4 While the pasta is cooking put the garlic in a large nonstick skillet and drizzle with 1 tablespoon extra virgin olive oil. Place the skillet over moderate heat and when garlic begins to sizzle remove from heat.

5 Drain the pasta and the vegetables, reserving 2 cups of the cooking water.

6 Put the drained pasta and vegetables in the skillet with the garlic and add 1 cup pasta cooking water. Cook over highest heat until the pasta is cooked, surrounded by a creamy sauce. Add more cooking water if sauce dries out.

7 Serve pasta in bowls, topped with a drizzle of the remaining extra virgin olive oil and freshly grated pepper.

Claudia's Stuffed Cabbage *Capunet*

*C*ourt cook Cristoforo di Messisbugo's 1549 *Banquets, Food Composition and General Apparatus* includes almost every variety of the cabbage family in his list of requirements for a well-supplied palace kitchen, and two interesting cabbage recipes follow. Leaves are stuffed with grated cheese, eggs, lard, herbs, walnuts, pepper, and spice, tied closed with string, cooked in a rich broth with a hunk of prosciutto and lard, served with minced parsley, a fine example of precholesterol-consciousness cooking. I prefer the stuffing that Claudia Verro makes, rolled into a cabbage leaf in the winter, piped into a squash blossom in the summer, rolled in bread crumbs and sautéed. Claudia cooks home-style traditional food at La Contea in the village of Neive in Piedmont, one of Italy's great restaurants. White truffles used with abandon overwhelm and distract from the simpler dishes on the menu. Claudia serves her *capunet* stuffed cabbage sauced with *bagna cauda* or tomato sauce although they're fine without any sauce at all.

4 quarts water

2–3 tablespoons coarse sea salt

¼ pound spinach, cooked and chopped

8 large cabbage leaves

1 garlic clove, chopped

1 teaspoon chopped fresh rosemary

1 tablespoon extra virgin olive oil plus oil
    to sauté stuffed cabbage

6 ounces veal, cubed

2 ounces sausage, casing removed

3 tablespoons grated Parmigiano

¼ cup squeezed soaked bread (soaked in cold water
    and squeezed to remove excess moisture)

1 tablespoon chopped Italian parsley

1 egg yolk plus 1 egg

Freshly ground pepper

A few gratings of fresh nutmeg

1 teaspoon fresh thyme

About 1 cup unflavored bread crumbs

1 Bring 4 quarts of water to a rolling boil. Add 2–3 tablespoons coarse salt and the spinach and cook for 3–4 minutes. Remove the spinach with a slotted spoon, refresh in cold water, and drain.

2 Cook the cabbage leaves in the same water for 3–4 minutes or until wilted. Remove the cabbage leaves with a slotted spoon, refresh in cold water, and drain. Remove the central rib of the cabbage leaves.

3 Sauté the garlic and 1 teaspoon chopped fresh rosemary in 1 tablespoon extra virgin olive oil in a medium nonstick skillet. Add the veal cubes and crumbled sausage and brown the meat well.

4 Transfer the contents of the skillet to the bowl of a food processor. Add the spinach, Parmigiano, soaked and squeezed bread, parsley, egg yolk, salt and pepper to taste, and nutmeg and process to a smooth paste.

5 Divide cabbage leaves in half. Place 2 tablespoons of the meat filling in each leaf and roll the cabbage leaf around the filling.

6 Beat the whole egg with salt, pepper, and thyme. Dip stuffed cabbage in the beaten egg and roll in the bread crumbs to coat.

7 Sauté the stuffed cabbage in extra virgin olive oil in a large nonstick skillet until brown on all sides. Remove the stuffed cabbage from the pan and drain on paper towels.

8 Serve the stuffed cabbage plain or sauced.

Antonello's Spicy Unmolded
but Not Really Cabbage

For 4–6 Servings   Side Dish

I thought I'd hate this dish when Antonello Colonna proposed it as part of a tasting menu at his restaurant in the village of Labico, outside Rome. He called it a *sformato di verza*, unmolded cabbage, but lots of innovative cooks serve wimpy little unmolded timbales elegantly pureed into tastelessness, artfully arranged on a large white plate sitting in a puddle of sauce, and call them *sformati*. I decided to trust Antonello and was presented with a mound of spicy, garlicky braised cabbage topped with a few melted slices of salt-cured pork jowl. Since I don't have a machine to slice pork wafer-thin I cut it into chunks and sauté it with the garlic and hot pepper. And instead of making individual "unmoldeds" I serve this dish mounded on a platter. I'm sure that Antonello wouldn't mind.

    4 quarts water
    2 tablespoons salt
    ½ medium-sized cabbage
    2 ounces salt pork, diced, about ¼–⅓ cup
    2–3 garlic cloves, minced
    1 fresh hot red pepper or dried chili pepper flakes
    2 tablespoons extra virgin olive oil

1 Bring a pot with 4 quarts of water to the boil, add 2 tablespoons salt and the cabbage, and boil for 10 minutes or until the cabbage is tender.

2 Remove the cabbage with a slotted spoon, refresh in cold water, drain, and gently squeeze to remove excess moisture. Reserve 2 cups of the cooking water.

3 Remove the central core of the cabbage and cut the cabbage into strips.

4 Sauté the salt pork in a large nonstick skillet over moderate heat until lightly colored. Add the garlic, hot pepper, and olive oil. Lower the heat, and cook until the garlic barely begins to color.

5 Add the cabbage strips, 1 cup cabbage cooking water, lightly season with salt, and simmer for 10–15 minutes or until liquid has evaporated.

CAPERS

Capperi

I was never impressed by capers when I lived in the United States and even
when I moved to Italy I didn't understand what the big deal was about.
Tiny olive green balls that looked like droppings, packed in crummy vinegar and tasting of little else, a mushy garnish that could easily be eliminated
from any recipe with no ill effects. But once I traveled to Sicily and tasted the
world's greatest capers, cured in sea salt, I was hooked. I discovered that capers
have a big flavor of their own, floral, so intense that their scent can be smelled
through a plastic package. Sicilian capers are produced on two tiny islands in
small quantities and globally share shelf space with tons of inferior tasteless
buds packed in vinegar that give the caper a bad reputation.

The caper, *Capparis spinosa inermis* of the Capparidaceae family, is the
most Mediterranean of plants, a perennial that grows wild in highly inhospitable
places—in walls, wedged in between rocks, amid ruins, along the coast, in clay
calcareous soil. Caper plants are hearty, disease- and pest-resistant and are often
grown organically. The caper bush has a woody base with shoots up to 3 feet in
length; it has shiny round leaves and flowers with stalks known as gynophores,
which end in ovaries. Many varieties have thorns, hence the *spinosa* genus.
Tightly closed, not even beginning to think about flowering, buds are handpicked, then salt-cured to become capers. Unharvested buds get bigger, softer,
and open to reveal flamboyant hermaphrodite flowers, four white petals with
dozens of long, purple-tipped stamens. These flowers form tender, olive-shaped
green fruits which turn purple when mature. Larger buds are less desirable
because they're closer to blooming and therefore not as compact, but smaller
does not necessarily mean better. Larger, less expensive buds are fine for chopping or for caper paste.

Caper buds, fruit, and tender first-growth shoots are all comestible but
have to undergo salt-curing to remove bitterness. Plants are hand-harvested,
examined every few days from the end of May through August for tiny buds, a
laborious, expensive process. An especially industrious picker can gather up to 40
pounds a day but most work part time and pick less than 10 pounds daily. Once
harvested, capers are mixed with coarse sea salt, which forms a brine with the
water given off by the capers, stirred every day for 10 days. The brine is drained

off, and the capers are salted again for another 10 days. They are then separated by size, put in barrels, and aged for 2 months before being packaged. Capers are unlisted in all my nutritional texts, both Italian and English, ignored in the literature of the U.S. Department of Agriculture. An Italian book on caper production doesn't include information on calories but credits them with vitamin A, B_1, B_2, and C and lots of minerals. Capers contain a bitter irritant glucoside, capparinetine, said to have tonic, diuretic, and antiarthritic effects. They're often reputed to be aphrodisiac, probably due to their diuretic action. The caper may be an antioxidant and a circulatory stimulant. According to an Italian pharmacology text, they're also rich in bioflavonoids rutin and quercitin, which help to assimilate vitamin C, and pectins, which have protective and moisturizing benefits.

Capers grow wild and are harvested throughout the Mediterranean but are cultivated commercially only in Italy, Spain, Turkey, and Morocco. Color, texture, flavor, size, and shape vary with caper cultivars. The finest capers are make from the *nocellara* from Pantelleria and the *nocella* from Salina. Is it the volcanic soil or the salty sea breeze that makes them the best in the world? Although capers grow wild in France they aren't cultivated or grown commercially. And cultivated capers are better than wild, with more sepals and stamens and therefore more flavor.

Capers are graded by caliber, ranging from tiny 7 mm to oversize 14 mm, although traditional sizing names like "partridge-eyes," "super buttonholes," and "tiny teardrops" are sometimes used. Bottles of tiny, expensive nonpareil (7 mm or less) French capers are from North Africa where labor costs are far lower, imported tax-free under a European Union program to aid developing nations, packaged by the clever French under vinegar, which turns them into mush and overwhelms flavors. Few self-respecting Sicilian caper growers would consider packing buds in vinegar. Sea salt is the only way to go. Brine, favored by the Spanish, is a distant second.

Wild capers were mentioned in the Bible, known to Greek and Roman physicians, viewed as dangerous by Pliny in his *Natural History*. Roman agricultural expert Columella carefully describes first-century cultivation techniques although millionaire epicure Apicius doesn't call for them in his cookbook

Culinary Arts. They were considered medicinal plants with slight gastronomic implications and therefore barely mentioned in most culinary texts.

In modern Italian kitchens capers are often paired with oregano, used to flavor dishes with fresh fish, anchovies, and cured tuna, added to tomato sauce for the *pizzaiola* or *ghiotta* treatment, or topping the tuna-flavored mayonnaise sauce on cold veal (*vitello tonnato*). Sicilian islanders make a paste of capers, pureed plain, with chili peppers or sun-dried tomatoes that I can't live without. Thinned down with extra virgin olive oil it's a perfect sauce for grilled fish or pasta.

Salt-cured capers should be rinsed off before using, although if they're still too salty they can be soaked in water for at least 15 minutes. More water and time will remove more salt but too long a bath may make them soggy. Capers that appear dried out will need a good soak.

Capers grow well in poor soil in a hot, arid Mediterranean climate. Seeds are available from B & T World Seeds, Whitnell House, Fiddington, Bridgwater, Somerset TA5 1JE, United Kingdom, but I haven't found any American sources.

Salt-cured capers can last for years and are worth mail-ordering if they're not available in your area. The following all sell first-rate capers: Balducci's, Telephone: 800–225–3833, Dean & Deluca, Telephone: 800–221–7714, extension 270, and Todaro Brothers, Telephone: 212–679–7766, all in New York; Sutton Place Gourmet, Telephone: 301–564–0006 in Washington, DC; Zingerman's Delicatessen, Telephone: 313–663–3400 in Ann Arbor, Michigan; and Vivande, Telephone: 415–346–4430 in San Francisco. Capers can be ordered in 2.2 pound bags from Manicaretti, Telephone: 800–799–9830 in Oakland, California.

CAPERS

*M*edical tracts by physician Pedacio Dioscoride Anazarbeo, translated from Latin into Italian with modern sixteenth-century commentary by M. Pietro Andrea Mattioli, a doctor from Siena, consider the caper in detail. The original text describes the curing of capers in salt and their medicinal effects. They "excite the body, make thirst" and are known to benefit sciatica, purge phlegm from the head, and are good for toothache. Mattioli expounds at length on the caper plant and fruit as used in Tuscany, conserved in brine or in strong vinegar, well known in Italy, with fruit used more as medicine than food. Preserved, they have little nutriment but stimulate the appetite, open obstructions of the liver and spleen, but must be eaten before other foods, dressed with oil and vinegar.

Bartolomeo Sacchi wrote under the Latin pen name Platina. His 1474 *Honest Pleasure and Health* credits mentor Maestro Martino and proceeds to utilize all the recipes from Martino's 1450 *The Book of Culinary Art*. Bread and *focaccia*, fruit, vegetables, sauce, comestible birds, and game are examined and Platina throws around a lot of classical references. Book IV, Chapter 107, deals with capers. Egyptian and Apulian capers are best, according to Platina; good for the spleen and liver, they prevent paralysis, are diuretic, aphrodisiac, eliminate worms, and are effective against poison. Capers are cured in salt, eaten dressed with oil and very little vinegar, and possibly some mint, which makes them tastier and healthier.

Domenico Romoli, known as Panunto (literally "oily bread," Tuscan dialect for grilled, olive-oiled bread) was a Florentine gentleman and expert on culinary court behavior. He wrote *The Singular Doctrine* in 1560, flowery prose describing table service, diet, employer-employee relationships, and the obligations of the *scalco*, a kind of food and beverage manager to the nobility. One of the book's thirteen sections is dedicated to herbs, vegetables, and cooking suggestions and includes a chapter on capers. Romoli rightly claims that cultivated capers have better flavor than wild. He describes the salt-curing process and warns that they must be carefully washed before using because of their saltiness. Eaten with parsley and tender salad herbs with oil, vinegar, and sugar, capers are an appetite stimulant, aphrodisiac, antidepressant, and diuretic. Romoli also includes advice on the medicinal properties of caper roots, juice, infusions, and oil.

Bestselling cookbook author Vincenzo Corrado's 1781 *Of Pythagorean Food* presents a dietary regime for high-minded readers of delicate digestion that includes meat and fish broth, dairy products, and eggs, all strictly forbidden on what was probably the first Mediterranean diet, Pythagoras's fifth-century B.C. animal-rights vegan approach. Corrado is from Naples, a city that takes capers seriously, utilizing them in many dishes. He finds capers a "grand condiment, not only for salads, salumi but with cold foods, sauce, in meat ragù, in both stuffings with or without meat." He advises readers to preserve capers in vinegar flavored with fennel both wild and cultivated, tarragon, mint, thyme, chervil, parsley, and sorrel, a whole herb garden of aromas.

Caper Recipes

ROLANDO'S DEEP-FRIED CAPERS

Batterless crispy caper buds

———

CAPER PASTE, "CILENO" STYLE

Spicy paste for bread and fish and as an accent for tomato sauce

———

CAPER PASTE WITH SUN-DRIED TOMATOES

PANTELLERIA POTATO SALAD

Potato, tomato, onion, olive, and caper salad

———

PIZZAIOLA FOR MEAT, GHIOTTA FOR FISH

Tomatoes, oregano, and caper sauce for meat or fish

Rolando's Deep-Fried Capers

For 3–4 Servings   **Snack or Topping**

*H*elp! A nontraditional recipe never prepared in Italy is sneaking into this book, a creation of Italo-Argentino Rolando Beramendi, fantastic Italian home cook and founder of Manicaretti, a quality Italian food import company. Rolando deep-fries caper buds and serves them with a glass of wine or as a topping for simply cooked fish. Those who don't mind the mess of deep-frying will enjoy these batterless crispy, salty bites.

> ½ cup capers, packed in salt
> 3 cups extra virgin olive oil for deep-frying

1 Rinse the salt off the capers and pat dry with paper towels.

2 Heat the extra virgin olive oil to 350 degrees in a deep fryer.

3 Fry the capers for a few minutes or until they puff up. Watch out for spattering!

4 Drain the capers on paper towels and serve at once.

Caper Paste, "Cileno" Style

Makes About ⅔ Cup   **Condiment**

*N*atives on the island of Pantelleria usually have a nickname and Antonio Belvisi, who spent twenty years away from home in Chile is called *Il Cileno*. He and his wife, Silvia, sell wild oregano, capers packed in salt, caper paste, *zibibbo* (sun-dried raisins), and the raisiny dessert wine Moscato di Pantelleria out of their cluttered living room. The Italian sanitary bureaucrats who insist on food production in tiled, screened kitchens with separate changing rooms for workers have had no effect on *Il Cileno*, who makes his caper paste in one of the least hygienic environments I've ever seen. It's sold in label-less jars or spooned into plastic bags from a bowl covered with a dirty napkin, protection against insects. *Il Cileno* also ignores fiscal laws that require receipts but the military police officer who was tasting wine and caper paste canapés when I was there didn't seem to mind. *Il Cileno* brought a few South American customs back to Pantelleria. His garden is traditional, with high walls of volcanic rock to protect it from the island's fierce winds but he's got a nontraditional avocado tree growing in the middle. And he's got a spicy palate and adds chili pepper to his caper paste, livening it up considerably. During a one-week stay on Pantelleria I bought lots of caper products but *Il Cileno*'s caper paste was the best. Use it spread on bread, thinned down with olive oil on grilled fish, or to liven up tomato sauce.

> ½ cup capers, preferably packed in salt
>
> 3 cups water (optional, for salt-packed capers)
>
> 1 fresh hot chili pepper or dried flakes to taste
>
> ¼ cup extra virgin olive oil

1 Soak the salt-packed capers for 30 minutes in 3 cups water, drain, and pat dry with paper towels. Or rinse brine-packed capers and pat dry with paper towels.

2 Process the capers with chili pepper and extra virgin olive oil to make a fine-textured paste. Pack into a jar and cover caper paste with a thin layer of extra virgin. Store in the refrigerator where it will keep forever.

Caper Paste with Sun-Dried Tomatoes

Make About 1 Cup   **Condiment**

*T*hose with delicate palates will prefer this caper paste, milder than the preceding recipe, that I found on a foraging trip on Pantelleria with Anna Tasca Lanza, Sicilian Marchesa and gastronome, author of *The Heart of Sicily* (Clarkson Potter, 1993).

> ½ cup capers, preferably packed in salt
>
> 3 cups water (optional, for salt-packed capers)
>
> ¼ cup sun-dried tomatoes
>
> ¼ cup extra virgin olive oil
>
> 2 teaspoons dried Sicilian oregano

1 Soak the salt-packed capers for 30 minutes in 3 cups water, drain, and pat dry with paper towels. Or rinse brine-packed capers and pat dry with paper towels.

2 Process the capers with the sun-dried tomatoes, extra virgin olive oil, and oregano to make a fine-textured paste. Pack into a jar and cover caper paste with a thin layer of extra virgin. Store in the refrigerator where it will keep forever.

Pantelleria Potato Salad
Insalata Pantesca

For 4–6 Servings   **Side Dish**

*T*racking down recipes on the island of Pantelleria isn't easy. Everyone I spoke to had a slightly different version of the same dish and *insalata pantesca* is no exception. It's found with green or black olives or sometimes with no olives at all, with or without tuna. I like to cut the tomatoes and potatoes into chunks although most island cooks prefer them sliced. And although it's usually assembled at the last minute I like to prepare this salad at least 30 minutes before serving so that the vegetables marinate in the extra virgin, wine vinegar, and oregano dressing. Don't bother with jars of supermarket oregano. Fresh oregano is a better choice.

> 1 pound potatoes
> 1 tablespoon sea salt
> 1 pound tomatoes
> 1 large red onion
> 2–3 tablespoons capers
> ¼ cup black or green olives (optional)
> 1 tablespoon wine vinegar
> ¼ cup extra virgin olive oil
> 1 teaspoon dried Sicilian oregano (or fresh if you can't
>   find quality dried oregano)
> Freshly ground pepper

1   Place the potatoes in a large pot and add water to completely cover. Add 1 table-spoon salt and boil potatoes for 20–30 minutes or until tender when pierced with a toothpick. Drain the potatoes, peel while still warm, and cool.

2   Cut the tomatoes in half and squeeze into a sieve over a small bowl, pressing con-tents to extract juice. Save juice for another purpose. Cut seeded, juiced tomatoes into chunks.

3   Cut the onion in half, then into ¼-inch-thick slices.

4   Slice the potatoes ½ inch thick or into chunks.

5   Rinse the capers to eliminate excess salt. Toss the potatoes, onions, tomatoes, olives, capers, vinegar, extra virgin olive oil, oregano, and salt and freshly ground pepper to taste and serve.

CAPERS

RED, WHITE
& GREENS

117

Pizzaiola for Meat, *Ghiotta* for Fish

*T*omato sauce zapped with capers, garlic, and oregano is used to cook both fish and meat in southern Italy. When it surrounds beef the sauce is called *pizzaiola,* "of the pizza-cook." But practically the same sauce, when paired with fish, is called *ghiotta,* "delicious." It also goes well with pork, poultry, or pasta. The idea is to lightly cook meat or fish with garlic and extra virgin, add tomato pulp and herbs, and finish cooking the meat or fish in the sauce. Vegetarians can skip the protein and use the sauce on pasta.

> 2 tablespoons extra virgin olive oil
>
> 1 pound thinly sliced and pounded beef round, chicken breasts, or fish fillets
>
> 1–2 garlic cloves
>
> 2 cups tomato pulp, fresh or canned
>
> 3–4 tablespoons capers, rinsed
>
> 1 teaspoon dried Sicilian oregano (or fresh if you can't find quality dried oregano)
>
> **Coarse sea salt**
>
> **Freshly ground pepper**

1 Heat 1 tablespoon extra virgin olive oil in a large nonstick skillet until hot and sear the meat, poultry, or fish on both sides, browning well. Remove from the skillet and reserve.

2 Heat 1 tablespoon extra virgin olive oil in the skillet and sauté the garlic over moderate heat until it barely begins to color. Add the tomato pulp, capers, and oregano and season with salt and pepper.

3 Bring the sauce to a simmer and cook for 5 minutes to amalgamate flavors. Add the meat, poultry, or fish and simmer for a few minutes. Timing will depend on the thickness of the meat. Fish will cook quickly. Meat will take longer to cook. Serve when meat or fish is done.

CELERY

Sedano

ew food lovers take celery seriously. And it's no wonder, since most of us grew up crunching celery stalks stuffed with peanut butter or cream cheese, progressing to blue cheese, and on to a dietetic dipping vehicle or an edible swizzle stick. Supermarket celery sheathed in a plastic bag, decapitated, almost leafless, rates little attention. But in Italy although celery is eaten raw, as part of the *pinzimonio* medley of raw vegetables dipped in fruity extra virgin olive oil (see page 153), it's far more important cooked, as a subtle base of many sauces or starring in appetizers and side dishes.

Celery, like parsley, is a member of the Ombelliferae or Apiaceae family, low in calories, with moderate amounts of vitamin A, calcium, potassium, and phosphorus. It's diuretic, stimulates digestion and the production of bile, said to help cure kidney stones, catarrh, and chronic bronchitis. Celery is also said to cause slight congestion of the pelvic organs, which may be how it got its aphrodisiac reputation. Medieval apothecaries included celery juice in their love potions. Friar Foreteller (*Frate Indovino*), a mythical Italian Franciscan monk, concurs about the sexually stimulating effects of celery leaves but also claims that it's a great tonic, capable of eliminating intestinal gas. Sweet celery stalks are less interesting from a therapeutic aspect, according to the friar.

Apium graveolens was a wild Mediterranean swamp plant with an unpleasant acrid scent. It still grows wild in the fifth-century B.C. Sicilian ruins of Selinunte, a city of Greek origins, its name derived from the Greek "selinon," wild celery. Celery leaves on the colony's coinage depict the important part of this vegetable because before this wild herb was domesticated its stalks were hard and stringy, and only leaves and seeds were used in cooking.

Although Romans used many herbs and flowers to decorate the table they never utilized celery because it was used for funeral wreaths. Apicius employed celery seed in many of his sauces and even has a recipe for celery puree, with leaves boiled with a pinch of bicarbonate, minced, then cooked in a pot with herbs, pepper, onion, wine, olive oil, and *garum* (fermented anchovy sauce).

Full White, Full Stalk Green Giant, Giant of Castelnuovo, Golden Asti, Arezzo, and Cutting Celery are some Italian cultivars. White or golden-stalked varieties are customarily eaten raw, in the *pinzimonio* style, dipped by diners into individual bowls of extra virgin olive oil, sea salt, and pepper. Green celery is used cooked, braised, or as part of the classic *battuto* of chopped celery, onion, and carrot that begins many recipes.

Torquato, my favorite farmer in Florence's Santo Spirito daily market, is a major source of information and recipes utilizing celery. He sells two varieties—*sedano*, sweet celery stalks topped with a few leaves to be eaten cooked or raw, and *sedanino*, "little celery," tough stalks with leaves to be used for flavoring. Clients frequently ask him to cut off the tops, which he sells to the nearby trattoria La Casalinga. See page 128 for a recipe inspired by their dish.

Italian celery cultivars seem to be unavailable in American seed catalogs but they can be ordered from Italy's oldest mail-order seed catalog, Fratelli Ingegnoli, Corso Buenos Aires 54, Milan 20124.

*T*uscan doctor M. Pietro Andrea Mattioli's *Discussions on Material Medicine*, a translation of an ancient Latin text with modern (1557) commentary on "the composition and virtues of medicaments," expounds at length about different kinds of *apio, hipposelino,* and *smirnio,* which all resemble celery in the elegant etchings that illustrate the text. Mattioli points out lots of classification errors in classical references, concluding with Greek, Latin, Arab, German, Spanish, and French terminology for all celery-related plants, differentiating between domestic, swamp, and mountain celery, parsley, and impossible to translate *hipposelino* and *smirnio.* Mattioli recommends using stems in broth and leaves as a condiment, "not unpleasant" in his opinion.

Celery gets more culinary attention after its seventeenth-century domestication, which utilized the blanching technique, with soil banked to cover the stalks, producing a tender-textured, delicately flavored edible stalk instead of intensely flavored leaves. Giacomo Castelvetro, in his 1614 *A Brief Account of the Fruit, Herbs, & Vegetables of Italy*, describes the process of mounding earth around stalks, leaving "four fingers above the earth, and left for fifteen to twenty days. They will then have blanched and become good to eat." He recommends serving celery raw, with salt and pepper, as a digestive after meals and adds that "young wives often serve celery to their elderly or impotent husbands."

Author-cook Vincenzo Corrado wrote *The Gallant Cook* in 1773, proudly declaring his Apulian origins on the title page. Recipes reveal a southern Italian influence, and tomato is frequently used. Corrado's commentary is fascinating, and cooking terms, befitting a chef to the nobility, are sometimes in French, but spelled in Italian. Hence *gattó* (*gâteau* or cake), *coli* (*coulis* or sauce), and *budin* (pudding). A later edition with the subtitle *Of various capricious foods and of spirited thoughts, bigger and adorned* was published in 1778, followed by my favorite of Corrado's works, *Of Pythagorean Food*, subtitled *For the Use of Nobles and Literati*, published in 1781. It's an amplified rehash of a chunk of his previous work, expanded, probably written because Pythagorean philosophy and dietary regime were the rage among European nobility in the eighteenth century. He calls celery *sellari* and informs readers that although ancient cooks didn't eat celery, modern knowledge has made it a requirement in the kitchen and tasty to the palate. More than a dozen recipes transform celery into soups and side dishes—it's boiled, stuffed, battered, fried, and cooked in flans. And his raw celery salad sounds tasty, dressed with anchovy, mint, tarragon, and pistachio nuts, pounded fine, blended with olive oil, lemon, and vinegar.

Pellegrino Artusi's *Culinary Science and the Art of Eating Well* was self-published in 1910 since no publishers were interested. It went on to become a classic, the best-selling Italian cookbook of all time, with over 110 printings to date. Artusi's blend of advice, folklore, and classic recipes are influenced by his Romagna-Tuscan culinary background. He informs readers that celery adorned the heads of diners at ancient banquets, worn for its ability to neutralize the effects of wine. Artusi appreciates celery for its scent and since "it's not windy deserves a place among salubrious vegetables." He employs celery in its customary role, finely chopped, as part of a *battuto* (literally "beaten") along with carrot and onion, a frequent flavor base for stewed meats and sauces. But he includes side dish treatments, all parboiled, then sautéed and sauced, battered, or breaded, and deep-fried.

Celery Recipes

TORQUATO'S PENNE WITH LEEKS AND CELERY

——

PASTA WITH MOCK MEAT SAUCE
Pasta con Sugo Finto
Pasta sauced with meatless meat sauce

——

STAFF LUNCH LENTIL AND RICE SOUP

——

LA CASALINGA'S BRAISED CELERY STALKS WITH GARLIC
Inspired by a Florentine restaurant's stewed celery leaves

MASCARON'S OCTOPUS AND CELERY SALAD
Boiled octopus, celery, and tomato salad

——

CHECCHINO'S COWMEN'S OXTAIL AND CELERY
Coda alla Vaccinara

——

NATALE'S "DEALT-WITH" TALEGGIO
Taleggio Trattato
Taleggio cheese dressed with minced celery

Torquato's Penne with Leeks and Celery

For 4–6 Servings   First Course

*T*orquato's winter selection of vegetables looks miserable compared to nearby stands supplied by the wholesale market outside Florence. They've got lemons, bananas, out-of-season produce like zucchini and tomatoes, imports from the south and abroad. He's got vegetables from his own garden, members of the cabbage, chicory, and garlic-onion family displayed on his trestle table. An entire vegetable crate is devoted to celery, another to leeks. "Have you ever had pasta with leeks and celery sauce?" Torquato asked me, with a crowd of impatient shoppers in no mood to listen to culinary advice. Luckily he ignored them and continued with his recipe. Torquato uses *rigatino*, a local rolled-up variety of salt-cured pork similar to *pancetta*; salt pork, sausage, or *pancetta* can substitute for this impossible-to-find ingredient. Porco-vegetarians will enjoy the hearty flavor of cured pork but vegetarians can leave it out, sautéing vegetables in extra virgin olive.

The same base can be used to prepare a leek and celery risotto.

2–3 ounces salt-cured pork, diced, about ¼–⅓ cup,
    or 2 tablespoons extra virgin olive oil

1 cup chopped leeks

2 cups chopped celery

2 cups hot water plus 5–6 quarts

2 tablespoons chopped Italian parsley

1 teaspoon fresh thyme

Sea salt

Freshly ground pepper

14 ounces penne or other short pasta

½ cup freshly grated Parmigiano-Reggiano

1   Sauté the salt-cured pork in a 3-quart pot over moderate heat to melt slightly. Add the leeks and celery and cook till the leeks barely begin to color. Add 2 cups of hot water and simmer for 15 minutes until celery is tender.

2   Transfer one third of the contents of the pot to the food processor, puree and return it to the pot. Add parsley, thyme, and season with salt and pepper.

3   Bring 5–6 quarts of water to a rolling boil, add the pasta, and cook until it still offers considerable resistance to the tooth, around three quarters of the recommended cooking time. Drain, reserving 2 cups of pasta water.

4   Add the pasta to the sauce with ½ cup pasta cooking water and cook over highest heat for 3–5 minutes, stirring so pasta doesn't stick, until it is almost cooked and the sauce coats pasta. Add more pasta water, ¼ cup at a time, if the sauce gets too dry. The sauce should surround the pasta but be slightly liquid since grated cheese will thicken it.

5   Add grated Parmigiano-Reggiano, cook for an additional minute to melt cheese, and serve immediately.

Pasta with Mock Meat Sauce
Pasta con Sugo Finto

For 4–6 Servings   **First Course**

At the height of medieval Italian religious regulation there were over 200 fast-days a year for observant Catholics. Mock meat sauce must have replaced real meat *ragù* for both fasters and farmers looking for extra flavor from vegetable-garden ingredients. I prepare a speedy, 10-minute broth with the vegetable trimmings but stock makers and bouillon cube and canned broth users won't have to bother.

1 cup plus 5–6 quarts water

Onion, celery, and carrot trimmings
    and parsley stems (from chopped parsley)

½ cup minced onion

½ cup minced celery

½ cup minced carrot

1 teaspoon minced fresh rosemary

1 teaspoon minced fresh sage

2 tablespoons chopped Italian parsley

¼ cup extra virgin olive oil

1 cup tomato pulp, canned or fresh

Sea salt

Freshly ground pepper

14 ounces penne or short pasta

½–¾ cup grated Parmigiano-Reggiano

(continued)

1. Make a vegetable broth with 1 cup of water, onion, celery, and carrot trimmings and parsley stems, simmering for 10–15 minutes.

2. Place the minced onion, celery, and carrots and the rosemary, sage, and parsley in a 3-quart pot, add olive oil, and stir to coat vegetables. Sauté the vegetables over low heat until the onion is lightly browned.

3. Add the tomato pulp and ½ cup vegetable broth. Season with salt and pepper and simmer over low heat for 25 minutes to amalgamate flavors. Add more broth if sauce dries out.

4. Bring 5–6 quarts of water to a rolling boil, add the pasta, and cook until it still offers considerable resistance to the tooth, around three quarters of the recommended cooking time. Drain, reserving 2 cups of pasta water.

5. Add the pasta to the sauce with ½ cup pasta cooking water and cook over highest heat for 3–5 minutes, stirring so pasta doesn't stick, until it is almost cooked and the sauce coats the pasta. Add more pasta water, ¼ cup at a time, if the sauce gets too dry. The sauce should surround pasta but be slightly liquid since cheese will thicken it.

6. Add grated Parmigiano-Reggiano, heat for an additional minute to melt cheese, and serve immediately.

Staff Lunch Lentil and Rice Soup

I first encountered this soup in Rome over 20 years ago. I learned the basic techniques of Italian cooking at Ristorante Silvano Paris, where I apprenticed when I first came to Italy. Classic Italian and Roman *cucina* were beautifully prepared but my favorite recipes were always from the staff meals, food considered too humble to appear on the menu. Restaurant owner Silvano Paris had lunch daily in the dining room with a few regular clients but never failed to ask what the staff had eaten, often preferring the simple dishes to the classic fare offered on the daily menu.

½ cup chopped red onion

¾ cup chopped celery

2 tablespoons extra virgin olive oil

1 garlic clove, chopped

1 cup lentils, picked over and washed

¼ cup canned tomato sauce

8 cups hot water or light broth

Sea salt

¾ cup rice for risotto (Vialone Nano or Carnaroli)

Freshly ground black pepper

2 tablespoons chopped celery or parsley leaves

½–¾ cup grated Parmigiano-Reggiano or Pecorino
    Romano (optional)

1 Place the chopped onion and celery in a 3-quart pot, add olive oil, and stir to coat vegetables. Cook over medium heat until the onion is soft.

2 Add the garlic, and cook for a minute or two. Add the lentils, tomato sauce, and hot water and salt lightly. Bring to a simmer and cook for around 35 minutes or until the lentils are almost cooked. (This dish can be prepared in advance up to this point.)

3 Add the rice to the lentils, bring to a simmer, and cook for 20 minutes, stirring occasionally to prevent sticking, especially during the final minutes of cooking. Add more water if the soup seems too dry.

4 Taste for salt and season with pepper. When the rice is cooked but is still firm under tooth and not mushy remove the pot from the heat and let the soup rest for 5 minutes. Garnish with celery or parsley leaves and serve plain or garnished with grated Parmigiano-Reggiano or Pecorino Romano cheese.

La Casalinga's Braised Celery Stalks
with Garlic

*T*his dish was inspired by the stir-fried celery leaves served at the trattoria La Casalinga, "the housewife" in Italian, my favorite local excuse for not cooking. Inexpensive, with paper tablecloths, terrible house wine, friendly service, aproned, ample, and smiling Paolo at the bar, and home-style food prepared by Graziella and Ferruccio. La Casalinga utilizes celery leaves that most greengrocers throw away, boiling them until they're tender, then stir-frying the leaves with garlic. Those lucky enough to have access to lots of celery leaves can try this recipe the way it's prepared at La Casalinga but should cook the leaves until they're tender, around 20 minutes, and use a pinch of bicarbonate in the water, according to Graziella. If you don't have celery leaves, you can taste the same flavors with tender celery stalks. Torquato, who gives his celery leaves to La Casalinga, suggests a variation that adds 1/2 cup tomato pulp and is served with a sprinkle of Parmigiano-Reggiano.

> 1 pound celery, tough outer stalks removed (and leaves if
>   you've got them)
> 5–6 quarts water
> 2–3 tablespoons sea salt
> 2 tablespoons extra virgin olive oil
> 2 garlic cloves, chopped
> ½ cup tomato pulp (optional)
> Freshly ground black pepper
> ½ cup grated Parmigiano-Reggiano (optional)

1 Cut the celery stalks into 2-inch lengths and split wide stalks in halves or quarters.

2 Bring 5–6 quarts of water to a rolling boil, add 2–3 tablespoons salt, and cook the celery for 5 minutes or until tender. Remove the celery with a slotted spoon, refresh in cold water, and drain. Reserve the celery cooking water.

3 Put the celery in a large nonstick skillet, drizzle with extra virgin olive oil, shake the skillet to coat the celery with oil, and place over high heat to lightly brown.

4 Add garlic, sauté briefly, and add ¼ cup celery cooking water and optional tomato pulp. Cook over moderate heat until liquid is almost evaporated.

5 Serve hot sprinkled with cheese or at room temperature without.

Mascaron's Octopus and Celery Salad

For 4–6 Servings   **Main Course, Appetizer**

*C*elery adds a lively crunch to this unrubbery octopus salad prepared at Mascaron, a wine bar-trattoria in Venice. Small snacks known as *cicchetti*, like Venetian tapas, are served in traditional wine bars called *bacari* since Italians rarely drink without eating something. Mascaron's octopus salad is a little fancier than the classic version of simply boiled octopus, extra virgin olive oil, lemon, and parsley. They add raw celery and tomatoes for a nice contrast in textures and substitute balsamic vinegar for the lemon juice. I always add a wine cork or two to the water in which the octopus cooks; it's said to tenderize the octopus.

1½ pounds octopus

½ onion

1 carrot

1 stalk plus 2 cups sliced celery (½-inch slices)

1 bay leaf

A few parsley stems plus 2 tablespoons chopped Italian
     parsley

1–2 corks from bottle(s) of wine (optional)

1 cup cherry tomatoes, quartered (optional)

¼ cup extra virgin olive oil

1 tablespoon balsamic vinegar

Sea salt

Freshly ground black pepper

1   Bring a large pot with enough water to cover the octopus to a rolling boil. Add the onion, carrot, celery stalk, herbs, octopus, and cork. Simmer over low heat for 45 minutes.

2   Turn off the heat and let the octopus cool in the water for at least 30 minutes or up to an hour.

3   Slice the octopus into ½-inch chunks, and toss with the sliced celery, the tomatoes, olive oil, balsamic vinegar, chopped parsley, and salt and pepper to taste. Serve hot or at room temperature but don't refrigerate.

Checchino's Cowmen's Oxtail and Celery
Coda alla Vaccinara

*C*owmen, *vaccinari* in dialect, were the butchers of Rome. They were paid for their labors with the hide, tail, and cheeks of the cows they butchered. Although it doesn't sound like a great deal, the hides were tanned to be sold, and the tail turned into this oxtail dish that's still popular in the slaughterhouse district restaurants of Rome. My favorite version is from the Ristorante Checchino, where traditional Roman fare is prepared better than anywhere else. Checchino's cowmen's oxtail is fantastic, best made a day in advance so that excess fat can be removed, a modern touch that makes Checchino's *coda alla vaccinara* far more digestible than most. Blanched celery is cooked with oxtail sauce, raisins, pine nuts, and a hint of bittersweet chocolate (the secret ingredient) and is added to the stewed oxtail before serving. Leftover sauce is great with pasta and is often served with tonarelli, thick, squared-off spaghetti.

2 tablespoons extra virgin olive oil

2 tablespoons lard or minced pork fat (optional)

3 pounds oxtail, severed at the joints

1 small onion, minced

2 garlic cloves, minced

2–3 cloves

Sea salt

Freshly ground pepper

½ cup dry white wine

3 cups canned tomatoes

5 quarts water

1 pound celery, cut into 2-inch lengths,
    sliced into ¼-inch sticks

1 tablespoon pine nuts

2 tablespoons raisins

1 teaspoon grated bittersweet chocolate

1 Heat the extra virgin olive oil (and optional lard or pork fat) in a 4-quart heavy-bottomed pot and add the oxtail. Brown the meat over moderate heat, turning often.

2 Add the onion, garlic, and cloves and lightly season with salt and pepper. Cook for 3–4 minutes over moderate heat.

3 Add white wine, bring to a simmer, cover the pot, and cook for 15 minutes over low heat.

4 Add the tomatoes and cook, uncovered, over low heat for 1 hour.

5 Add hot water to cover the meat and cook, tightly covered, for 3 hours or until the meat falls off the bones.

6 Cool the oxtail stew and refrigerate until the fat has congealed, overnight or until ready to serve.

7 Remove all the hardened fat at the top of the pot.

8 In a large pot bring 5 quarts of water to a rolling boil. Add the celery sticks, season with salt, and cook for 5 minutes or until tender. Remove with a slotted spoon, refresh in cold water, and drain.

9 Heat 1 cup of the oxtail sauce and add the cooked celery, pine nuts, raisins, and chocolate. Cook for 5 minutes to amalgamate flavors.

10 Heat the oxtail and the remaining sauce and combine with the celery mixture and serve.

Natale's "Dealt with" Taleggio
Taleggio Trattato

For 4–6 Servings   **Appetizer, Cheese Course**

*R*aw celery plays a minor role in this easy to prepare recipe, learned in the home kitchen of Italy's greatest hotelier and one of my favorite cooks in Venice, Natale Rusconi, managing director of the Hotel Cipriani. He deserves a monument in the Gastronomic Hall of Fame for introducing regional Italian *cucina* to luxury hotel dining rooms, previously the dominion of Continental cuisine with menus in French. Taleggio *trattato* (treated or dealt with) takes only a minute to make but finding a decent piece of Taleggio, a soft cow's milk cheese from Lombardy may not be as simple. First-rate Stracchino or even French Camembert or Brie are better options than a weary or overripe Taleggio. Another difficulty may be the decision to remove the rind, which many cheese mavens feel is the best part. Check rind carefully for dirt or sand if you don't remove it.

> ½–¾ pound Taleggio at room temperature
>
> 2–3 tablespoons minced celery
>
> 2–3 tablespoons extra virgin olive oil
>
> Freshly ground black pepper

1   Slice the cheese ¼-inch thick, place in a layer on a serving dish.

2   Sprinkle the cheese with celery, extra virgin olive oil, and pepper. Serve promptly.

EGGPLANT

Melanzana

Eggplant, another spooky member of the Solanaceae or nightshade family, is a fleshy berry with a bad reputation, called *mela insana*, unhealthy or mad apple, in early citations. It was used as an ornamental for its attractive leaves, white or purple flowers, and deeply colored glossy fruit, and considered dangerous to eat, inducing insanity.

Eggplant, *Solanum melongena*, was originally from India, unmentioned by Romans, possibly introduced into Italy by Saracens or Jews, probably encountered by the Crusaders during their Holy War travels, mentioned by Boccaccio in 1355. Its first cookbook appearance is at the end of the fifteenth century, in a recipe of an anonymous Neapolitan who submits eggplant to an early example of culinary overkill—peel, blanch, flour, and fry eggplant, dress with garlic, oregano, anchovies, bread crumbs, pepper, saffron, and *agresto*, lightly acidic wine vinegar, then stir-fry the whole mess and top with spice.

Eggplant is grown as an annual, a bushy plant with a woody base, tough gray prickly leaves, and attractive purple flowers. Fruit should be harvested before skin toughens, seeds ripen, and it increases in bitterness.

Eggplant is low in calories and nutritional content, with good potassium, fiber, and folic acid. Eaten in moderate quantities, eggplant is said to improve digestion and induce a state of well-being, although excessive consumption may result in digestive and nervous disorders. It was called *petonciano*, from the Italian word for fart, for its "meteoristic" or gas-producing attributes. Folk medicine utilized eggplant, applied topically for burns and hemorrhoids. Eating eggplant may lower cholesterol and stimulate metabolism, according to Giovanni Ballarini's *Risks and Virtues of Foods* (Calderini, 1989).

Regional archaic dialect calls eggplant *mollegnane*, *marignani*, *petonciani*, *mulignani*, *melanciane*, *mele isdegnose*, *meli di giano*, and *mela insana* but it is currently called *melanzana* throughout Italy. Varieties are divided by shape and skin color, long dark-skinned Long Violet of Naples, dark-skinned oval Black Beauty, lighter purple and white Florentine Violet. Many of the best recipes come from the southern Italian regions, especially Sicily and Campania.

Everyone I spoke to had different ideas about how to eliminate eggplant's bitterness. Some cooks never salt, some soak sliced eggplant in salted water, most recommended salting and pressing in a colander. Paula Wolfert and Suzanne Hamlin, both incredible sources of culinary advice, agree that salting depends on the recipe, variety, and ripeness. Eggplant is capable of initially absorbing enormous amounts of oil, which are later expelled during subsequent cooking. I like to brush slices with oil before pan-frying, or grill thick slices without any oil as Torquato, a constant source of wisdom, recommends.

Eggplants should be firm, with glossy, taut, smooth skin without any hint of blemish or bruise. Smaller (but not dwarf) specimens will be more tender. Purchase eggplants that feel light in weight, which will have fewer seeds.

Italian eggplant cultivars are available from Seeds of Change, P.O. Box 15700, Santa Fe, New Mexico 87506, Telephone: 800–957–3337; Pinetree Garden Seeds, Box 300, New Gloucester, Maine 04260, Telephone: 207–926–3400; The Cook's Garden, P.O. Box 535, Londonderry, Vermont 05148, Telephone: 802–824–3400; and Shepherd's Garden Seeds, 6116 Highway 9, Felton, California 95018, Telephone: 408–335–6910.

History

*I*n *Discussions on Material Medicine* (1557) Tuscan doctor M. Pietro Andrea Mattioli translates the Latin text of Pedacio Dioscoride Anazarbeo and comments at length on "the composition and virtues of medicaments." Members of the animal, mineral, and plant kingdom are described, often illustrated, traced through classical writing, and medical properties are thoroughly examined. Mattioli's notes briefly mention eggplant, unknown by ancients, in the mandrake chapter. He recommends frying eggplant in oil with salt and pepper, "like mushrooms," and says many Italians eat eggplant to "arouse lust."

Costanzo Felici, provincial doctor from the Marches, corresponded frequently with Ulisse Aldrovandi, illustrious naturalist and doctor from Bologna, author of an entire library of handwritten volumes on minerals, medicine, plants, fossils, insects, birds, fish, rare fruit, snakes, sonnets, expenses, general observations, lots of letters to druggists, and botanical seed and plant swapping. Felici's lengthy letter entitled *Of Salad and Plants Used by Man as Food*, written in 1569, carefully documents vegetables, although Felici isn't terribly impressed by produce without classical references. He feels that eggplant is decorative and looks good on a windowsill, but admits that many people eat it with gusto, grilled, stuffed, fried, floured, and stewed like mushrooms. Felici describes two kinds of eggplants—one with a larger, more handsome fruit—but skirts his usual historical discussion, citing unresolved questions about ancient knowledge.

Giacomo Castelvetro, continental traveler, intellectual, target of the Venetian Inquisition for his new-wave Protestant, anti-Papal thinking, tutor of James VI of Scotland, wrote *A Brief Account of the Fruit, Herbs & Vegetables of Italy* in 1614 while living in England, an attempt to convince the English to eat something fresh. He lovingly describes the seasonal produce of his homeland, with simple cooking hints and medical implications. Eggplant appears at the end of spring, "the size of apples, but oval, with a shiny skin like a gourd." Castelvetro suggests stuffing, grilling, stewing, or frying, dressed with salt, pepper, and bitter orange juice, but warns against eating too much eggplant.

Bartolomeo Stefani, chef of the wealthy worldly Gonzaga Duke of Mantua, in his 1662 *The Art of Cooking Well*, informs readers that eggplant can be found in monastery gardens, and suggests soaking in cool water to eliminate natural bitterness.

Pellegrino Artusi, in his classic bestseller *Culinary Science and the Art of Eating Well*, first published in 1910, with more than 110 printings to date, claims that eggplant is a newcomer to the Florentine markets, previously scorned as "food for Jews who demonstrate with this, as in other more important matters, that they have more taste than Christians."

Eggplant Recipes

Ezio's Eggplant Caviar

*Roast eggplant chopped with garlic,
herbs, and tomato*

Torquato's Thick Grilled Eggplant

*Grilled eggplant, dressed with garlic,
herbs, extra virgin olive oil*

Sergio's Fresh-Fried Eggplant

Sicilian *Caponata*

Spaghetti with Eggplant

*Garlic, herbs, and eggplant cubes
lightly dress spaghetti*

New-Wave Eggplant Parmigiano

Lightly sauced and cheesed eggplant sticks

Sicilian Warbler-Style Eggplant

*Baked with dried currants, pine nuts,
bread crumbs, and bay leaves*

Dora's Stuffed Eggplant

*Pan-roasted eggplant stuffed
with pecorino cheese, garlic, and herbs*

Ezio's Eggplant Caviar

*E*zio Santin is one of the great chefs of Italy and prepares sophisticated, elegant food at his restaurant Antica Osteria del Ponte in Cassinetta di Lugagnano outside Milan. Ezio's cooking is totally unlike the home-style cooking that I almost always prefer but a few years ago I asked for a simple appetizer for a special dinner and he gave me this recipe. Ezio bakes his eggplant in the oven, easy for a restaurant chef who's always got an oven on, but I wrap whole eggplant in aluminum foil and roast it on a stove-top grid, *tostapane*, a common kitchen tool in Italy. Those who aren't lucky enough to have a *tostapane* can roast on a wire rack over a low gas flame. Ezio, as befitting a Michelin 3-star chef, shapes his eggplant caviar into quenelles, served on a puddle of tomato sauce, but I don't bother, and serve the caviar in a bowl and pass the sauce separately.

2 pounds eggplants

1 garlic clove

1–2 tablespoons chopped fresh basil plus leaves
      for garnish

Sea salt

Freshly ground black pepper

½ cup extra virgin olive oil

10 ripe plum tomatoes, peeled, seeded, and juiced

1 Preheat the oven to 400 degrees.

2 Cut the eggplants in half lengthwise, score their cut surfaces with a sharp knife, and bake for 20–30 minutes on a cookie sheet or until the pulp is soft. Alternately, wrap each eggplant in a double layer of aluminum foil and grill the eggplant over a low gas flame on a wire rack or gas grill for 20 minutes or until the pulp is soft. Cool the eggplant.

3 Scoop out the eggplant pulp with a spoon and drain it in a mesh strainer for 15 minutes. Reserve half of the eggplant skin.

4 Cut the reserved eggplant skin into large pieces and mince with the garlic and basil in a food processor. Add the drained eggplant pulp, salt and pepper to taste, and ¼ cup extra virgin olive oil and pulse to mix well but not puree. Chill the eggplant caviar.

5   Puree tomato pulp and juice with ¼ cup extra virgin olive oil and add salt and pepper to taste.

6   Form the eggplant caviar into quenelles using 2 spoons and place 3–4 quenelles on a puddle of tomato sauce at room temperature. Or serve the eggplant caviar in a bowl, accompanied by the sauce. Serve the same day.

Torquato's Thick Grilled Eggplant

For 4–6 Servings   **Appetizer, Side Dish**

*T*orquato Innocenti's recipes, related at his Santo Spirito farmers' market stall, are a low-key sales pitch delivered while weighing and wrapping produce from his garden outside Florence. They are always simple, hyper-Tuscan, dressed with extra virgin olive oil. He sells two varieties of eggplant, dark-purple Neapolitan, which need no salting when small and tender (larger specimens do require salting). His milder-flavored violet and white Florentine eggplant doesn't need salting. Torquato's recipe for grilled eggplant slices can be prepared on a charcoal or gas grill, or in a cast-iron ridged stove-top grill. Basil or arugula can substitute for parsley. Torquato's son Valerio likes to dress grilled eggplant with pesto, a fine idea.

> **2 pounds eggplants, unpeeled, in ¾-inch slices**
> **¼ cup extra virgin olive oil plus additional for garnish**
> **2 garlic cloves, minced**
> **2–3 tablespoons chopped fresh parsley, basil, or arugula**
> **Sea salt**
> **Freshly ground black pepper**

1   Heat a cast-iron grill or pan over high heat.

2   Brush the eggplant slices with extra virgin olive oil. Or pour extra virgin on a plate and dip the eggplant slices into the oil, scraping off excess with a spatula.

3   Grill the slices over high heat, turning once, until well browned.

4   Transfer the grilled eggplant slices to a platter, sprinkle with garlic, herbs, season with salt and pepper, and drizzle with a little extra virgin olive oil. Serve warm or at room temperature.

Sergio's Fresh-Fried Eggplant

For 4 Servings   Side Dish

A Venetian friend took me to the outskirts of an area known as Malamocco near the island of Lido in the Venetian lagoon, known for its vegetable gardens. We visited Sergio Maggion, who grows organic fruits and vegetables for his son's first-rate pastry shop on Lido, a Venetian sea resort. Sergio spoke about the need to respect the earth, the importance of the lagoon and its fertile soil and salt air, and we toured the garden where he pointed out vegetables and fruit and picked choice samples along the way. We then proceeded to a simple hut with an outdoor kitchen-dining area-veranda with a well. Sergio lit a camp stove under a large black skillet filled with olive oil, then thickly sliced just-picked eggplant, slipped them into the skillet, fried them till dark brown, drained the slices on paper towels, and sprinkled them with salt. My skepticism—no salting, pressing, flouring, or batter, and what looked like serious overcooking— disappeared with my first bite. The inside of the eggplant had turned into a creamy filling.

> **2 pounds eggplants, unpeeled**
> **3–4 cups extra virgin olive oil**
> **Fine sea salt**

1   Cut the freshest seasonal eggplants you can find into 1-inch slices.

2   Heat the oil in a large skillet or deep-fryer to 375 degrees.

3   Slip 3 or 4 eggplant slices into the oil and fry until dark brown. Turn slices to brown the other side. Remove the eggplant with a slotted spoon and drain on paper towels. Cook all the eggplant slices in the same manner, taking care not to crowd the pan.

4   Lightly sprinkle the eggplant with salt and serve at once.

Sicilian *Caponata*

I've eaten *caponata* dozens of times in Sicily and each version varies slightly
 although the basic ingredients are usually the same. Fried eggplant and
blanched celery are mixed with a sweet-and-sour tomato sauce flavored with capers
and green olives, topped with a sprinkle of chopped almonds at times. It must have
been prepared without tomatoes for centuries since all the other ingredients are
typically Sicilian. Most recipes call for tomato paste instead of the more traditional
Sicilian *estratto,* tomato sauce dried to a paste in the sun. But since *caponata* is a
summer dish it was probably made with fresh tomatoes and no paste.

> **At least 5 quarts water**
>
> **2–3 tablespoons sea salt**
>
> **3 celery stalks, cut into ½-inch pieces**
>
> **1½–2 pounds eggplants, peeled and cut into 1-inch cubes**
>
> **1 large onion, coarsely chopped**
>
> **2 tablespoons extra virgin olive oil plus 4 tablespoons oil
>   for frying eggplant**
>
> **1½ cups tomato pulp**
>
> **½ cup pitted green olives, cut into pieces**
>
> **3 tablespoons capers (preferably salt-packed),
>   rinsed and drained**
>
> **3 tablespoons sugar**
>
> **¼ cup wine vinegar**
>
> **Freshly ground pepper**

1 Bring at least 5 quarts of water to a rolling boil in a large pot. Add 2–3 tablespoons
   salt and the celery and cook until just tender, around 5 minutes. Remove the celery
   with a slotted spoon, refresh in cold water, and drain.

2 Salt the eggplant cubes and place in a colander topped with a weight to eliminate
   excess water while preparing the sauce.

3 Put the onion in a large nonstick skillet, drizzle with the 2 tablespoons extra virgin
   olive oil, and stir to coat the onion with the oil. Cook over moderate heat until the
   onion is tender.

4 Add the celery and tomato pulp and simmer until the sauce thickens slightly. Add
   the olives, capers, sugar, vinegar, and season with salt and pepper.

(continued)

EGGPLANT

RED, WHITE
& GREENS

5   Squeeze the eggplant cubes to remove excess water, rinse, and pat dry with paper towels.

6   Place a large nonstick skillet over high heat and add 2 tablespoons extra virgin olive oil. When oil is hot add half the of the eggplant cubes and cook until they are soft and golden brown. Remove with a slotted spoon and drain on paper towels. Cook remaining eggplant in the same manner.

7   Combine drained eggplant with the tomato sauce. Serve at room temperature within a day or two.

Spaghetti with Eggplant

For 4–6 Servings   **First Course**

*E*ggplant is rarely paired with pasta in Italy. But in Sicily it's easy to find pasta sauced with tomato sauce and salted ricotta and garnished with fried eggplant slices or sticks. In Catania it's called pasta alla Norma, said to be in honor of native son Vincenzo Bellini's greatest opera. I'd like to think it has something to do with Giuditta Pasta, who sang the role of Norma when it was first performed. Adding the eggplant at the last minute is a great idea because it doesn't get mushy. Taking a hint from the classic recipe, I often make a simple garlic and herb dressing for pasta and toss in pan-fried eggplant cubes at the last minute. Fresh parsley combined with basil, oregano, or mint are the herbs of choice. Sicilians top their pasta with ricotta salata, a dried grating cheese made with sheep's milk, which may be hard to find and not worth the search. Substitute grated Pecorino Romano cheese.

Sea salt plus 2–3 tablespoons salt

1 pound eggplant, peeled and cubed into 1-inch chunks

5 tablespoons extra virgin olive oil

5–6 quarts water

14–16 ounces spaghetti

2 garlic cloves, minced

2 cups tomato pulp, fresh or canned

Freshly ground black pepper (or fresh hot red pepper or
    chili pepper flakes for readers with a spicy palate)

2 tablespoons chopped Italian parsley

1 tablespoon chopped fresh basil, oregano, or mint

½ cup grated dry ricotta salata or Pecorino Romano

1   Salt and drain the eggplant chunks if necessary.

2   Place a large nonstick skillet over high heat. Toss half of the eggplant cubes with 2 tablespoons extra virgin and place in hot pan. Cook, shaking the pan, until the eggplant is soft and brown. Remove the eggplant with a slotted spoon and drain on paper towels. Cook the remaining eggplant cubes in the same manner. Lightly salt the eggplant chunks.

3   Bring 5–6 quarts of water to a rolling boil, add 2–3 tablespoons salt and the pasta. Stir occasionally with a wooden fork or spoon.

4   While pasta is cooking sauté garlic with remaining 1 tablespoon extra virgin olive oil in a large nonstick skillet until it barely begins to color. Add the tomato pulp, season with salt and pepper to taste, and cook over high heat for 2–3 minutes to evaporate excess liquid. Add the herbs and remove from the heat.

5   When the pasta is cooked but still offers considerable resistance to the tooth, around three quarters of the recommended cooking time, drain the pasta, reserving 2 cups of pasta water.

6   Add the pasta and ½ cup pasta cooking water to the sauce in the skillet. Cook over highest heat for 3–5 minutes until pasta is almost cooked and sauce coats pasta. Add more pasta water, ¼ cup at a time, if sauce gets too dry.

7   Add the eggplant cubes, stir to mix well, and serve, topping pasta with grated cheese.

EGGPLANT

New-Wave Eggplant Parmigiano

*T*hree different areas of Italy claim the creation of eggplant Parmigiano, known as *la parmigiana di melanzane* or *melanzane alla parmigiana*. Parma's claims are weak since vegetable dishes called *parmigiana* are simply baked with butter and grated Parmigiano-Reggiano cheese. Food historian Mary Taylor Simeti, in *Pomp and Sustenance* (Knopf, 1989), claims that the name comes from the Sicilian pronunciation of *palmigiana*, louvered shutters, since overlapped eggplant slices resemble this window treatment. But Sicilians use caciocavallo cheese, not mozzarella, which appears in the classic version. It's most probably from Campania as Jeanne Carola Francesconi claims in *La Cucina Napoletana* since mozzarella wasn't really found elsewhere. The dish seems typical of the Baroque style of Neapolitan cooking, transforming a couple of eggplants, a little cheese, some tomato sauce, and herbs into something that looks far more important. But no matter where eggplant Parmigiano comes from it's a terrific dish although it involves lots of work. Traditionally eggplant is salted, pressed, drained, dried, floured, deep-fried, layered with tomato sauce, sliced mozzarella, grated Parmigiano cheese (Sicilians substitute caciocavallo cheese), and baked. Fabio Picchi of the restaurant Cibrèo in Florence says that this was the first dish he ever prepared, when he was seven, and he's been modifying it ever since. His most recent revision substitutes raw tomato for cooked sauce and cuts down on cheese. He doesn't salt eggplant, a custom I immediately adopted. Fabio layers eggplant, barely dressed with tomato and mozzarella, in individual stacks, sprinkling grated Parmigiano on top after baking. I've changed his recipe slightly, pan-roasting slices of eggplant coated with extra virgin olive oil instead of frying in 2 inches of oil; this technique lightens the dish a little since eggplant seems capable of absorbing enormous quantities of oil. Leftover grilled eggplant (see page 139) can also be used. Large eggplant slices should be stacked in three layers, smaller eggplants in four.

2 large eggplants, about 2 pounds

½ cup extra virgin olive oil

½ cup fresh tomatoes, peeled, seeded, and juiced, or quality canned diced tomato

1 tablespoon fresh basil leaves

1 garlic clove

Sea salt

Freshly ground black pepper

4 ounces mozzarella, thinly sliced, broken into pieces

3 tablespoons grated Parmigiano

1 Cut the eggplant into twenty-four ½-inch slices.

2 Place a large nonstick skillet over high heat.

3 Paint the eggplant slices with extra virgin olive oil. Or pour extra virgin on a plate and dip the eggplant into the oil, scraping off excess with a spatula.

4 Brown the eggplant slices in one layer in a hot skillet, 3 or 4 minutes per side, and transfer to a plate as they are done.

5 Blend the tomatoes, basil, and garlic in a food processor until smooth. Season with salt and pepper.

6 Cut the mozzarella into 4 slices and divide each slice in four.

7 Place 8 slices of eggplant on a nonstick baking pan and top each slice with 1 teaspoon tomato puree, spread in a thin layer. Place a piece of mozzarella in the center. Cover the mozzarella with another eggplant slice, 1 teaspoon tomato sauce, and another piece of mozzarella. Cover with a third eggplant slice and top with remaining tomato sauce. Let the stacks rest for 30 minutes. Don't worry if some liquid begins to ooze from eggplant.

8 Preheat the oven to 400 degrees. Bake eggplant stacks for 15–20 minutes until bubbling and well browned. Remove from oven and sprinkle each stack with 1 teaspoon grated Parmigiano.

9 Let the stacks rest for 2–3 minutes before serving.

Sicilian Warbler-Style Eggplant

*E*nrico Alliata (1879–1946), the Sicilian Duke of Salaparuta, was a fervent theosophist, vegetarian, Milan Conservatory-trained baritone, enologist, and director of the Salaparuta winery, founded by his grandfather in 1824. The duke expounds his erudite dietary philosophy (eliminating "degenerate necrophagistic appetites" in favor of a "regime in harmony with the laws of nature") in *Vegetarian Cooking and Raw Naturism*, a "manual of naturistic gastrophy," with 909 recipes "chosen from every country." An appendix on "raw naturism" calls for the elimination of all animal products and cooking. The *cucina* is aristocratic Sicilian with a worldly outlook—"booklets" (sandwiches) of tomato, cress, truffles, mushrooms or pseudo-foie gras, Yorkshire pudding, vegetarian haggis, and 39 pureed soups. But traditional Sicilian dishes like couscous, *salmoriglio* lemon, olive oil and oregano marinade, pasta timbales, pseudo-tripe in tomato sauce, and *sfincione* pizza creep into the duke's recipe collection. One of my favorites substitutes slices of eggplant for fresh sardines in the *beccafico* or warbler style. The pine nut-currant-bread crumb stuffing is a perfect example of Arab-influenced Sicilian flavors.

> ¾ cup fine bread crumbs
>
> 2 pounds eggplants, sliced ½ inch thick
>   into 3 to 4 inch rounds
>
> ¼ cup plus 2 tablespoons extra virgin olive oil
>
> Sea salt
>
> 2 tablespoons dried currants
>
> 2 tablespoons pine nuts
>
> 1 teaspoon chopped parsley
>
> Freshly ground black pepper
>
> Bay leaves

1   Toast the bread crumbs in a medium-sized nonstick pan until lightly browned.

2   Place a large nonstick skillet over high heat. Brush 3–4 eggplant slices with extra virgin olive oil and cook for 2–3 minutes until browned; turn and cook the other side. Remove from the skillet and drain on paper towels. Repeat with remaining eggplant slices. Lightly salt the eggplant slices.

3   Combine the bread crumbs, 2 tablespoons extra virgin olive oil, dried currants, pine nuts, parsley, and salt and pepper to taste.

4   Preheat the oven to 350 degrees.

5   Place 2 teaspoons bread crumb stuffing along the middle of each eggplant slice, fold the slices in half lengthwise, pressing to close. Place the eggplant, folded edge down, in a baking dish with a bay leaf between each piece. Sprinkle with any remaining stuffing.

6   Bake for 20–30 minutes or until lightly browned. Serve immediately.

Dora's Stuffed Eggplant

For 4–6 Servings   **Appetizer, Side Dish**

*D*ora and Angelo Ricci's restaurant Il Fornello is a fantastic reason to head for Apulia and Ceglie Messapico, a town without any architectural, artistic, or archaeological claim to fame. It's starred on the Michelin map but almost impossible to find. Dora's cooking is home-style, casual, produced with the finest local ingredients. I love her cheese and herb-stuffed eggplant. Use small seasonal purple eggplants for best results.

> 3 eggplants, ½ pound each (or 6 eggplants, each ¼ pound)
>
> Sea salt
>
> 3 garlic cloves
>
> 3 tablespoons capers, rinsed and chopped
>
> Freshly ground black pepper
>
> 1 tablespoon parsley leaves
>
> ¾ cup diced fresh sheep's milk pecorino, about 4 ounces
>
> 3 tablespoons extra virgin olive oil
>
> ¼ cup red wine
>
> 2 tablespoons red wine vinegar
>
> 1 teaspoon dried oregano (use fresh if you can't get decent dried oregano)

1   Cut the stem and base ends off each eggplant. Slice each eggplant in half lengthwise and cut 2 incisions, about 1 ½ inches deep, lengthwise in the skin of each eggplant half. Sprinkle the incisions and cut side of the eggplant halves with salt and place in a colander to drain for 30 minutes.

(continued)

2 Mince the garlic, capers, pepper, and parsley in a food processor. Add the diced cheese and pulse to combine well.

3 Rinse the eggplant halves of salt and dry with paper towels.

4 Push some of the cheese mixture into the eggplant incisions.

5 Heat the extra virgin olive oil in a large nonstick skillet over high heat and place the eggplants, skin side up, in the skillet. Lower the heat to medium and cook for 5–8 minutes or until golden brown. Turn the eggplant halves over and cook for 5 minutes. Larger eggplants will take longer and should be cooked until tender.

6 Turn the eggplant halves over again, add the red wine, vinegar, and oregano, and cook over highest heat until liquid is almost all absorbed. Serve immediately.

FENNEL

Finocchio

Fennel, *finocchio* in Italian, is a Mediterranean native with anise-flavored white bulbs, seeds that are actually fruits, and green fernlike fronds. According to a sixteenth-century medical text *finocchio*, "fine eye," was named for its vision-improving properties. It's also slang for homosexual, although no one could tell me why. Fennel is a natural flavor enhancer and almost anything eaten after fennel tastes better. The verb *infinocchiare*, "to fennel up," means to deceive, derived from a clever marketing technique of Tuscan farmers. They offered a slice of bread and *finocchiona*, a fennel-seed-studded salami as a snack to prospective clients before sampling wine for purchase, obscuring any defects in the wine.

Fennel, *Foeniculum vulgare*, is a member of the Umbelliferae or carrot family, with swollen white basal leaves that form bulbs topped with stalks ending in green fernlike fronds. Wild fennel, *Foeniculum officinale,* produces an insignificant bulb, is used for its fruit, pollen, and fronds, and has a long history of medicinal applications.

Fennel is low in calories with good potassium, some calcium, vitamins C and E. It's said to have antibiotic and antibacterial properties. Friar Foreteller (*Frate Indovino*), a mythical Italian Franciscan monk who provided tips on gardening, wine making, cooking, and health benefits of vegetables in his almanac, claimed that fennel improved vision, stimulated digestion, was diuretic, and calmed coughs and asthma. A bag of fennel seeds, applied to a child's temples, would ensure deep sleep according to the friar.

In the medieval era, fennel was a symbol of pain and falsity and therefore never offered to guests. Caterina de' Medici may have brought fennel to France, known there as Florence Fennel, when she married the future King Henry II. She was a heavy packer and brought cooks, pastry chefs, olive oil, beans, 100 trunks, and her jewelry cases but I couldn't find any mention of fennel in her luggage.

Modern Italians eat fennel raw in salads and in *pinzimonio*, dipped in seasoned extra virgin olive oil (see page 153). Fennel is also boiled, then braised or baked with sauce or grated Parmigiano. Italian fennel varieties include Neapolitan Giant, Romanesque, Sicilian or Bolognese Big, Florentine Sweet, Mantuan and Parma, Domino, Latina, and Montebianco.

Fresh fennel is at its best in the fall through the spring, and should be firm, white, without brown spots or bruises, topped with green fernlike fronds. Peel off the tough outer leaves, trim the butt end, and slice fennel into wedges to serve. Wild fennel fronds are utilized in many Sicilian dishes but cultivated fennel fronds can be substituted. In parts of Tuscany, wild fennel flowers are picked, dried, and crumbled to produce fennel pollen, used to flavor pork dishes but equally wonderful with fish (see page 156 for more information). If the flowers aren't picked they develop into seeds, which according to a botanical text, are actually fruits. Fennel fruits or seeds are frequently paired with pork or fish. Both my husband and son love raw fennel but dislike it cooked and I tend to agree, which is why this chapter doesn't have any cooked fennel recipes.

Seeds for fennel can be purchased from Shepherd's Garden Seeds, 6116 Highway 9, Felton, California 95018, Telephone: 408–335–6910; Nichols Garden Nursery, 1190 North Pacific Highway, Albany, Oregon 97321–4598, Telephone: 503–928–9280; Pinetree Garden Seeds, Box 300, New Gloucester, Maine 04260, Telephone: 207–926–3400.

History

Michele Savonarola, noted doctor from Padua, wrote *The Little Book of All the Things Which Are Eaten* in 1452 but gave little importance to his work, writing in the vernacular instead of Latin, which he used for his more important publications. Dr. Savonarola classifies foods as hot, cold, wet, or dry, as prescribed by the eleventh-century Salerno regimen, an attempt to balance the nature of food and man, used to heal returning Crusaders. Fennel is hot and dry to the second degree, wild fennel even hotter, and improves vision.

Provincial doctor Costanzo Felici, in a March 10, 1572, letter to his botanical pen pal Ulisse Aldrovandi, writes about domestic fennel, noted for the sweetness of its flower, seeds, and leaves. Domesticated fennel bulbs are eaten raw or pickled in salted vinegar for use all year round, tender leaves are used in salad or soups. According to Felici, wild fennel flowers flavor many foods, especially roasted fish, while seeds are paired with sausage.

New-wave Protestant thinker, Continental traveler in exile Giacomo Castelvetro wrote *A Brief Account of the Fruit, Herbs & Vegetables of Italy* in 1614, a heroic effort to introduce the joys of produce to the English. Castelvetro places fennel in his summer chapter and says that ". . . sweet fennel bulbs appear, which we eat raw with salt after meals." He relates that "villainous Venetian wine-sellers solicitously offer innocent or simple-minded customers a piece of nice fennel to eat with their wine . . . insisting that otherwise they might do themselves harm by drinking wine on an empty stomach . . ." Castelvetro recommends preserving fennel in vinegar to eat in the winter and harvesting the seeds in the autumn.

Fennel Recipes

RAW FENNEL *PINZIMONIO*

*Raw fennel wedges dipped
in extra virgin olive oil*

———

SICILIAN PASTA WITH SARDINES AT SEA

*Sardineless version of the classic Sicilian
pasta with tomato sauce, pine nuts,
and dried currants*

———

FENNEL AND CITRON (OR ORANGE) SALAD

*Raw sliced fennel and citron or orange
dressed with extra virgin olive oil*

FENNEL POLLEN

An almost unknown but incredible ingredient

———

CARMIGNANO FENNEL SEED-SPICED DRIED FIGS

Picci di Carmignano

*Dried figs stuffed with walnuts
and fennel seeds*

Raw Fennel *Pinzimonio*

*R*estaurants throughout Italy serve a full-fledged *pinzimonio* in the winter as an appetizer, a still life of raw vegetables like celery, radishes, scallions, endive, artichokes, carrots, and fennel, accompanied by a little bowl of extra virgin olive oil for each diner, to be salted and peppered to taste and used as a dipping sauce for the vegetables. But at home Italians often serve a single vegetable in the same way. For years my son Max wouldn't eat most vegetables unless they were disguised with pasta or hidden in soup. One of the few exceptions was raw fennel *pinzimonio*. The ritual of dipping and the noisy crunch of raw fennel are part of the fun of this Tuscan approach to raw vegetables. Traditionalists can dispense with the little bowl and place a fork, tines down, under the far side of a plate, pour the extra virgin oil onto the near side of the plate, dress with salt and pepper, and dip.

> **2–4 fennel bulbs**
> **2–3 tablespoons extra virgin olive oil per person**
> **Fine sea salt**
> **Freshly ground pepper**

1   Cut the fennel stalks off where they meet the bulb. Discard any bruised or tough outer layers. Slice off a thin piece of the butt end of the bulb. Cut the fennel bulb in half lengthwise and cut each half into 3 or 4 wedges.

2   Place the wedges on a platter. Pour extra virgin olive oil into individual ramekins or very small bowls. Each diner should add salt and pepper to taste, then dip fennel wedges in oil.

FENNEL

RED, WHITE
& GREENS

Sicilian Pasta with Sardines at Sea

*T*he sardines are at sea, not in the sauce for this vegetarian version of a classic Sicilian pasta that combines the traditional flavors of pine nuts, raisins, spice, and wild fennel greens. Cultivated fennel greens can substitute for the wild if they're not available. Marchesa Anna Tasca Lanza, Sicilian culinary expert, author of *The Heart of Sicily* (Clarkson Potter, 1993), was horrified by the idea of using fennel bulbs but I think it's not such a bad choice if no other form of fennel is available. Bear in mind that the texture and color of the dish will be different, without the herby flavors and dark green color of fennel fronds. The pasta of choice is perciatelli, long, hollow strands that can be twirled on a fork with the ease of winding up garden hose. I prefer spaghetti.

> 5–6 quarts water
> 2–3 tablespoons coarse sea salt
> ½ pound wild fennel fronds, tough stalks removed
>   (see Note)
> 1 large onion, chopped
> 3 tablespoons extra virgin olive oil
> 1½ cups tomato pulp, fresh or canned
> 3 tablespoons pine nuts
> 3 tablespoons dried currants
> A few gratings of fresh nutmeg
> Freshly ground pepper
> 1 pinch powdered saffron or a few saffron threads
> 14–16 ounces perciatelli or spaghetti

1   In a pot, bring 5–6 quarts of water to a rolling boil, add 2–3 tablespoons salt, and cook the fennel fronds for 6–8 minutes or until tender. Remove the fennel from the pot with a slotted spoon, refresh in cold water, and drain. Chop coarsely. Reserve the cooking water.

2   Put the chopped onion in a large nonstick skillet, drizzle with extra virgin olive oil, and stir to coat the onion. Sauté over low heat until the onion is soft.

3   Add the tomato, pine nuts, currants, nutmeg, chopped fennel, and salt and pepper to taste and cook until the sauce thickens.

4 Dissolve the saffron in 2 tablespoons of pasta cooking water.

5 Return the fennel cooking water to a rolling boil, add the pasta, and cook until it still offers considerable resistance to the tooth, around three quarters of the recommended cooking time. Drain, reserving 2 cups of pasta water.

6 Add the pasta, saffron water, and ½ cup pasta cooking water to the sauce and cook over highest heat for 3–5 minutes until pasta is cooked and sauce coats pasta. Add more pasta water, ¼ cup at a time, if sauce gets too dry.

Note: If wild or cultivated fennel greens aren't available, cut the fennel bulbs into thin slices and proceed as directed for the greens. But don't serve it to a Sicilian marchesa.

Fennel and Citron (or Orange) Salad

For 3–4 Servings   **Side Dish**

*I*n Sicily, fennel is greatly appreciated and the fronds of wild fennel often flavor many dishes. This simple salad pairs raw fennel with fresh citron, dressed with extra virgin olive oil, salt, and pepper. Citrons can sometimes be found in the fall for the Jewish holiday of Succoth. Citrons should be peeled of their zest to reveal the edible thick white pith and fruit. Tart oranges can be used if citrons aren't available.

> **1 large citron or tart orange**
> **2 fennel bulbs, quartered and thinly sliced**
> **2–3 tablespoons extra virgin olive oil**
> **Sea salt**
> **Freshly ground pepper**

1 Peel the citron of the yellow zest. Cut the citron into quarters and cut each quarter into thin slices.

2 Combine the sliced fennel and citron with the extra virgin olive oil and the salt and pepper to taste.

FENNEL POLLEN

*F*ennel pollen is one of the most exciting flavors of central Italian cooking and a well-kept secret. It's used to flavor pork and poultry by Dario Cecchini, my favorite butcher in the world, located in the village of Panzano. Dario is a true *Chiantigiano*, "a man of Chianti country," who revels in anything from his home turf. His meat is local, organic, flavored with wild herbs and spice. Strands of dried red peppers, chains of purple onions, and braids of garlic decorate Dario's shop, and music from a super hi-fi system resonates off white-tiled walls as Dario carves meat with the skill of a gifted surgeon, a pleasure to observe. Dario picks wild fennel flowers before they go to seed, then dries the flowers and rubs them to remove the golden pollen. Fennel pollen is never sold commercially, which is why almost no one knows about it. Even in Sicily, where wild fennel grows with abandon and the green fronds are used in many dishes, no one has ever heard of using fennel pollen. Those lucky enough to have a source of wild fennel can follow Dario's example and pick and dry the flowers to be used to flavor pork, poultry, or fish. Everyone else can hope that someone in California, where fennel grows wild in great abundance, will start to sell the fennel as well as the pollen.

Carmignano Fennel
Seed-Spiced Dried Figs
Picci Di Carmignano

Picci are a hard-to-find specialty of the Carmignano area west of Florence, not to be confused with the hand-rolled pasta called *pici* found in southern Tuscany. Split, dried figs are sandwiched with a few fennel seeds and a walnut half, then layered with bay leaves. They're served as part of the fruit course during the winter when palates are bored with apples and oranges and need a taste of the summer sun. *Picci* should be prepared at least a week or two before serving and will last for months stored in an airtight container. Quality dried figs will yield best results in this almost effortless preparation, as close as I come to making dessert.

> 18 dried figs
> 1 tablespoon fennel seeds
> 18 walnut halves
> 18 bay leaves

1   Split each fig in half, leaving it attached at the bottom.

2   Open each fig, insert a few fennel seeds and a walnut half and press the fig closed.

3   Layer the figs with the bay leaves in an airtight container.

4   Discard the bay leaves before serving.

FENNEL

GARLIC

Aglio

Garlic plays a starring role in the Italian kitchen. It's been a Mediterranean classic since the Neolithic era but its origins are probably Asian. Ancient Greeks, Egyptians, and Romans cultivated garlic, considered it stimulating, magical, antiseptic. Romans exported garlic throughout their empire as the expression *Ubi Roma ibi allium,* "where there is Rome there is garlic," attests. Gladiators, soldiers, laborers, and galley rowers ate garlic for its strength, resistance, and courage-building powers but gave it a low-life reputation.

Garlic, *Allium sativum, aglio* in Italian, is a strongly scented bulb of the lily family, planted in the winter in Italy. Those who want a beautiful garlic patch, according to a rhyming maxim, should sow garlic in January (*chi vuole un bel'agliaio lo semina a Gennaio*), single cloves set in the ground which form bulbs with six to fourteen cloves, harvested in the summer and dried, to be utilized all year long. Tender immature garlic heads that haven't formed skins are pulled up in the spring and add a delicate flavor to many dishes.

Garlic's distinct scent is due to the crystalline amino acid alliin, converted to allicin by enzymes. Popular medicine attributes decongestive, antibiotic, and antiparasitic powers to garlic, confirmed by modern science. Large quantities of raw garlic may lower blood pressure and block the aggregation of platelets in the blood with anticoagulant powers equal to aspirin. Raw garlic may lower LDL and raise HDL cholesterol according to Giovanni Ballarini's *Risks and Virtues of Foods* (Calderini, 1989). But eating half a pound of raw garlic daily may seem unrealistic to all but the most devoted garlic lovers.

Friar Foreteller (*Frate Indovino*), a mythical Italian Franciscan monk, councils readers of his almanac on gardening, wine making, cooking, lunar cycles, and home cures effected with vegetables. He claims that garlic stimulates the digestive, respiratory, and circulatory systems and was once called the panacea of the poor. The friar writes about the "four thieves' vinegar," steeped with garlic, herbs, and spice, created by four prisoners who had to bury plague victims. The thieves claimed their immunity was due to their vinegar and went into the home-cure business.

Italians use both white- and pink-skinned garlic varieties, Piacenza or common white, Sulmona, Neapolitan, or Aquila pink and cultivars. Garlic dominates or subtly flavors many dishes throughout Italy.

Torquato Innocenti, my favorite farmer at the Santo Spirito outdoor market, is my major garlic source and doesn't believe in moderation. Most of his recipes begin with a "puddle" of oil and a "little wedge" of garlic. Garlic bunches and braids plaited by his wife Lina hang in the Innocenti garage. Torquato harvests on the eve of June 24, "The Night of the Garlic," he calls it, also the feast of San Giovanni, patron saint of Florence. Torquato's son Valerio recommends pressing a peeled garlic clove under a glass and running the clove under cold water for 10 seconds to make garlic more digestible.

Garlic heads should be large, firm, with tight blemishless skins. Old garlic will form a green sprout, known in Italian as the *anima* or soul, which should be removed. Yellowed, dried-out garlic cloves should be discarded. Keep garlic in a cool, dry place but never in the refrigerator. And never use prepared minced garlic, garlic powder, or flavored oils, which never equal the flavor of fresh garlic.

The degree of intensity of garlic can be moderated by using whole cloves instead of chopped, sliced, or mashed garlic. Don't use a garlic press, which wastes most of the garlic. Garlic is cooked until it begins to color and is never browned.

Red-skinned Italian garlic sets are sold by Shepherd's Garden Seeds, 6116 Highway 9, Felton, California 95018, Telephone: 408–335–6910.

*B*artolomeo Sacchi, a classicist inspired by Epicurus, wrote in Latin and adopted the pen name Platina. His *Honest Pleasure and Health*, first published 1474, is a compendium of knowledge on diet, hygiene, alimentary ethics, and the pleasures of the table. Platina writes about garlic's ability to "fight dangerous infirmities and makes snakes, serpents and other small beasts hide. Together with honey it is useful against dog bites, mixed with oil it heals poisoned wounds and ulcerations" and snobbishly states that although many foods are prepared with garlic, it's used rarely by city dwellers, frequently by peasants.

Michele Savonarola, illustrious doctor, professor, astrologist, moralist, dietitian, and gastronomer from Padua, wrote the best-seller *Of All Things Commonly Eaten* in 1508. Garlic is found in his citrus fruit chapter, along with onions and leeks. Savonarola claims that garlic darkens vision, provokes headaches, and is used instead of ginger by peasants. He includes a recipe for *agliata* (see page 165), pounding garlic in a wooden mortar for 15 minutes, throwing away the paste, then adding almonds, bread, cooked wine, and fennel seeds for the mildest of garlic sauces.

Castor Durante's *The Treasure of Health*, an agricultural tract with medical implications written in 1586, claims that garlic causes headaches, "stimulates Venus," and is useful as a remedy for all poison, worms, and lice.

Bolognese doctor Baldassare Pisanelli's 1584 *Treatise on the Nature of Food and Drink* recommends garlic as a remedy for poison, frigidity, to clear the voice, rid the body of worms, provoke coitus and urine, good for old people in the winter, bad for pregnant women.

Francesco Gaudenzio's 1705 *Panunto Toscana* states that "You can use garlic in all dishes, it goes well everywhere, but be careful to use small amounts except with legumes, otherwise finely chopped and at the beginning of cooking." His recipe for clams sounds delicious, sautéed in oil with garlic, chopped onion, herbs, salt and pepper, white wine, served over toasted bread to absorb clam juices, the best part of this dish according to Gaudenzio.

Best-selling author Vincenzo Corrado's 1781 *Of Pythagorean Food* includes garlic extensively even though Pythagoras himself excluded it. Corrado warns that garlic should be used with parsimony but he enthusiastically claims that it's a necessity in the kitchen, excites appetite, and should be used in sauce and with meat. According to Corrado, the French eat garlic in the spring with butter, Italians roast garlic whole, and dress with oil, salt, and pepper.

Garlic Recipes

GARLIC BREAD *FETTUNTA*

―――

FABIO'S WALNUT, PECORINO,
AND GARLIC SALAD

―――

GARLICKED SAUCE

Agliata

―――

"HOT BATH" GARLIC DIP

Bagna Cauda

―――

TORQUATO'S COLD PASTA WITH
MISUNDERSTOOD GARLIC SAUCE

*An error of interpretation results
in a summery cold pasta*

"TUNA" OF CHICKEN

*Chicken is poached like tuna and flavored
with garlic, sage, and extra virgin olive oil*

―――

ENZA'S 10 CLOVE "LEAN" *MAGRO*

Stove-top roast beef with garlic

―――

ROMAN GARLIC ANCHOVY SALAD DRESSING
FOR CATALAN CHICORY OR BELGIAN ENDIVE

Garlic Bread *Fettunta*

For 4 Servings   Appetizer

*T*his is, without a doubt, my favorite recipe in the world. It's fast, simple, calls for no special equipment or skills, has no cholesterol, and is open to seasonal adaptation with the addition of numerous toppings. Diners always seem to be impressed. *Fettunta,* a contraction of the words *fetta,* "slice," and *unta,* "oily," is prepared by olive oil millers on a heater/stove while working at the cold, damp, oily-aired mill. Bread is lightly toasted, rubbed with garlic, dipped in newly pressed, bright green, peppery-flavored olive oil, sprinkled with salt and pepper. It's meatless, milkless, effortless, pleasing to even the most jaded palates, and involves none of the fuss usually associated with garlic bread—peeling and chopping garlic, brushing oil on the bread. Traditionalists will need a wood fire, although a charcoal or gas grill or a toaster will do. And Scouts can skewer their bread on a stick.

Unsalted rustic Tuscan bread, white or whole wheat, sliced about 3/4-inch thick is the bread of choice for olive oil millers. Do-it-yourself bread bakers should refer to Carol Field's *The Italian Baker* (HarperCollins, 1986). But almost any basic, water-based, butterless, country-style bread will do. A friend favors rye. Day-old bread is okay. And 1 slice per person may be only a beginning.

First-rate extra virgin olive oil is a must, otherwise you'll wind up with greasy bread instead of *fettunta.* Newly pressed oil, called *olio nuovo,* easily recognizable by its bright green color, cloudy with chlorophyll, found from late November through January in Italy, yields spectacular results but any quality extra virgin olive oil will do. See page 4 for more information about extra virgin.

> **4 slices of country-style bread, sliced ¾ inch thick**
> **1 garlic clove, unpeeled**
> **½ cup or more extra virgin olive oil**
> **Fine sea salt**
> **Freshly ground black pepper**

1   Toast, grill, or broil the bread slices until lightly colored on both sides.

2   Rub the garlic clove over the bread's surface. The garlic will grate itself on the hardened toast and the peel will disintegrate. Garlic lovers should press hard.

3   Drizzle at least 2 tablespoons extra virgin olive oil, barely enough for any self-respecting Tuscan, over each slice of toasted bread, sprinkle with salt and pepper, and serve immediately.

Fabio's Walnut, Pecorino, and Garlic Salad

For 4–6 Servings   Appetizer

*F*abio Picchi, chef-owner with his wife Benedetta Vitale of the restaurant Cibrèo in Florence, is one of my favorite home-style cooks. He absolutely adores garlic and uses around 50 heads of garlic daily. Vampires steer clear of Cibrèo but almost everyone else is wild about the food. Fabio has a spicy palate and uses red hot peppers, *peperoncini,* together with pepper in many of his dishes. In the winter he often serves a little bowl of this salad of walnuts and pecorino sheep's milk cheese zapped with garlic, herbs, extra virgin olive oil, and wine vinegar at the beginning of the meal along with his usual seasonal appetizers.

> ½ cup shelled walnuts
>
> 1 cup diced fresh pecorino, about 4 ounces
>
> 1 garlic clove, minced
>
> 1 tablespoon minced parsley
>
> ½ teaspoon dried marjoram
>
> ½ teaspoon dried oregano (use fresh if you can't get good dried oregano)
>
> 1 teaspoon white wine vinegar
>
> 1 teaspoon dry white wine
>
> 3–4 tablespoons extra virgin olive oil
>
> Fresh hot red pepper or dried chili pepper flakes
>
> Sea salt
>
> Freshly ground black pepper

1   Combine all the ingredients in a ceramic or glass bowl and marinate for at least 30 minutes or up to 1 day.

Garlicked Sauce
Agliata

For 1½ Cups Sauce   **Condiment**

*G*iacomo Castelvetro, in his 1614 *A Brief Account of the Fruit, Herbs & Vegetables of Italy* writes about garlic but doesn't make any side remarks about bad breath or peasant food, probably to avoid scaring the English about its lively flavor. He includes garlic in all four seasonal chapters of his lovely, still current book and his version for *agliata* combines walnuts, garlic, and pepper pounded to a paste with soaked stale bread, thinned down with broth, used to sauce pork, goose, pasta, or mushrooms. It's a typically medieval recipe, acid and fatless. The more modern Tuscan rendition of this sauce leaves out the walnuts, and substitutes extra virgin olive oil for the broth. But I like to combine the recipes and use both walnuts and extra virgin olive oil, thinning down the paste with a little vegetable broth.

1–2 slices of stale bread

1 cup water

2 tablespoons wine vinegar

4 garlic cloves, peeled

¼ cup walnuts (optional)

½ cup extra virgin olive oil

2–4 tablespoons vegetable or meat broth

Fine sea salt

Freshly ground pepper

1   Soak the bread with 1 cup of cold water and the vinegar until the bread can be easily crumbled.

2   Squeeze the liquid out of the bread and measure ½ cup damp bread.

3   Blend the damp bread with the garlic, walnuts, and extra virgin olive oil. Add the broth to thin the sauce to the consistency of heavy cream. Season with salt and pepper to taste. Use to sauce roast or grilled pork, goose, mushrooms, or even pasta.

"Hot Bath" Garlic Dip
Bagna Cauda

For 4–6 Servings   **Main Dish**

*G*arlic is used with abandon in Piedmont, a region of big red wines matched by big, flavorful cooking. A local expression states that you can take the wife from a Piedmont man but not his garlic. In the late fall, friends gather to drink just-made wines, young and grapy, paired with *bagna cauda*, "hot bath" in local dialect, a garlic and anchovy dip that's kept hot in a terra-cotta pot over a burner like fondue, eaten with bread and a raw vegetable medley. Everyone I spoke to from Piedmont had important advice for me about *bagna cauda,* focusing on digestion, breath, ingredients, and technique. Eat it with friends. Scramble eggs in the pot when most of the dip is gone and top with a grating of white truffle. Finish the meal with a bowl of broth to aid digestion. Sleep with the window open! One expert insisted on three-year-old anchovies, melted unboned into the dip, but told me I'd never find any and I didn't. Most recipes stuck to the formula of 1 head of garlic per person, peeled and cooked whole, sliced, or minced, in milk, cream, or even wine. Extra virgin olive oil was used alone or combined with butter. A few walnuts were added to the dip. I tried them all and we ate *bagna cauda* at home with friends for a week. And slept with the window open. The following recipe combines elements from dozens of suggestions. Leftover *bagna cauda* can be used to dress pasta.

Raw vegetables like celery, fennel, radicchio or endive, and peppers are dipped into *bagna cauda*. Some cooks serve boiled potatoes, cooked beets, and baked onions as well. In Piedmont, red peppers are pickled in layers of grape pomace and are my favorite vegetable on the platter.

NOTE: Anchovy quality may vary widely. The best are usually packed in salt in large tins, purchased by weight, to be cleaned and filleted at home. First-rate anchovy fillets (usually packed in jars) are a better choice than poor-quality salted whole anchovies. Forget about anchovy paste made of smashed-up scraps of inferior quality.

3–4 garlic heads, broken into cloves and peeled (about ⅔ cup)

½ cup water or milk

⅓ cup anchovy fillets

1 cup extra virgin olive oil

2–3 walnuts, shelled, nuts broken into pieces (optional)

Raw vegetables for dipping: celery stalks, carrots, fennel, Belgian endive, red or yellow peppers, kohlrabi, cut into sticks or wedges—quantities will depend on how many vegetables you use

1 large loaf of country-style bread

1 Cook the garlic in the water or milk in a small pot, uncovered, over low heat for 15–20 minutes or until garlic is tender and liquid is absorbed.

2 Mash up garlic and anchovy fillets with a fork, food processor, or immersion blender to thoroughly blend. Add extra virgin olive oil. Mixture may resemble separated mayonnaise although an immersion blender will emulsify the dipping sauce.

3 Heat mixture in a saucepan until hot and pour into an earthenware fondue dish. (Hasn't everyone in the world been gifted with a fondue set?) Substitute a flame-proof casserole for a metal fondue dish. Ignore the forks. *Bagna cauda* fans can get out their terra-cotta *bagna cauda* set.

4 Before serving add optional walnut pieces.

5 To serve: Dunk raw vegetables into anchovy-garlic hot bath, scooping up some of sauce. Hold a piece of bread under the dipped vegetable so you don't dribble the dip on the table. Eat the vegetable and then the bread. Drink a young red—Barbera or Dolcetto from Piedmont are the traditional choices.

Torquato's Cold Pasta
with Misunderstood Garlic Sauce

For 4–6 Servings   **First Course**

Florentine summers are hot and sticky, too torrid to even think about eating a plate of hot pasta. Super home-cook Countess Lisa Contini of the wine- and olive-oil producing estate of Tenuta di Capezzana feeds summertime visitors non-traditional chilled pasta dressed with traditional sauce and I often follow her example. So when Torquato mentioned cold garlic pasta I raced home with his vague hints and produced the following dish. When we discussed the results the next day I realized that Torquato's garlic sauce, and not the pasta, was cold. But no one at my table complained.

> 5–6 quarts water
>
> 2–3 tablespoons fine sea salt
>
> 14–16 ounces spaghetti
>
> 2–4 garlic cloves, sliced
>
> 3–4 tablespoons or more extra virgin olive oil
>
> 2 tablespoons chopped Italian parsley
>
> Freshly ground black pepper

1   Bring 5–6 quarts of water to a rolling boil, add 2–3 tablespoons salt and the pasta. Stir occasionally with a wooden fork or spoon.

2   While the pasta is cooking sauté the garlic with 1 tablespoon extra virgin olive oil until it barely begins to color. Add the parsley, remove from the heat, and season with salt and pepper.

3   When the pasta is cooked al dente, still offering some resistance to the tooth, drain the pasta, reserving ¼ cup of the pasta water.

4   Run cold water over the pasta in a colander in the sink until the pasta has cooled.

5   Place the pasta in a bowl and toss with 2–3 tablespoons extra virgin olive oil, the cooked garlic and parsley, and 2 tablespoons pasta cooking water. Chill in the refrigerator for up to 2 hours before serving.

"Tuna" of Chicken

*W*hen tuna was preserved at home in Italy, before the days of canned tuna, it was poached and packed in extra virgin olive. The same procedure was applied to rabbit but I decided to try it with chicken since so many people are worried about eating "bunny." I discovered that skinned chicken behaves more like lean rabbit and recommend removing the chicken skin before cooking. Those lucky cooks who think of rabbit as food instead of pet can substitute it for the chicken in this recipe. In either case it must be prepared a day or two in advance. Marinating chicken or rabbit in olive oil gives it a velvety rich texture; whole garlic cloves, sage leaves, and black pepper add delicate flavor. I like to serve this dish with tender salad greens, dressing the salad with the garlic-sage-flavored marinade.

> 1 chicken, about 3–4 pounds, skin removed
>
> 1 carrot, peeled
>
> 1 medium onion
>
> 2 garlic cloves
>
> Sea salt
>
> Freshly ground black pepper

For the marinade:

> Extra virgin olive oil
>
> ⅓ cup packed fresh sage
>
> 10 garlic cloves, peeled
>
> Whole black peppercorns
>
> Sea salt
>
> ½ pound tender salad greens

1 Place the chicken in a large pot, add the carrot, onion, garlic cloves, sea salt and pepper to taste, and enough water to cover the chicken. Bring to a boil over low heat, spooning off any scum that rises to the surface. Simmer for 2 ½ hours, remove from the heat, and let the chicken cool completely in the broth at room temperature.

2 Remove the chicken from the broth, remove the bones, and rip or chop chicken into bite-sized pieces.

(continued)

3 Drizzle a little extra virgin olive oil in a glass or ceramic terrine. Cover with a layer of chicken pieces, a few sage leaves, a few garlic cloves, a few peppercorns, and lightly season with salt. Drizzle with more extra virgin olive oil. Make at least three layers.

4 Add enough extra virgin olive oil to cover the chicken and marinate in the refrigerator, covered with plastic wrap, for at least 1 day (or up to 3 days). Remove from refrigerator for 2 hours before serving.

5 To serve: Toss tender salad greens with a few spoonfuls of the extra virgin olive oil marinade and place chicken pieces and a few of the marinated sage leaves on top of the salad.

Enza's 10 Clove "Lean" Magro

*M*assimo's Aunt Enza has played an important role in my life as a born-again Tuscan. We often dine at her home on Sunday, for a traditional family lunch, prefaced by Enza's statement that she hasn't prepared anything. This means that there's nothing new on the table and that we're in for our usual treat of a Florentine meal. The main course will probably be what Enza calls *magro*, literally lean or fatless, a choice cut of beef used for roast beef, sliced thin, lightly sauced with meat juices, topped with whole brown cloves of garlic. Since Italian home cooks in the city rarely had ovens, meat is often roasted on top of the stove. It's faster than oven-roasting, perfect for those who love rare roast beef. Turning the meat is the hardest part.

> 2 pounds beef loin roast at room temperature
> Freshly ground pepper
> 2 tablespoons extra virgin olive oil
> 1 bay leaf
> 10 garlic cloves, peeled
> Sea salt

1   Rub the beef with freshly ground pepper, and place in a heavy-bottomed pot large enough to hold the meat. Drizzle the extra virgin olive oil over the meat and turn the meat over to coat with the oil. Add the bay leaf and garlic cloves and marinate for 15 minutes.

2   Remove the bay leaf. Brown the meat over medium-high heat, turning to brown evenly. This step will take about 15–20 minutes, depending on the size of the roast. When the garlic begins to color remove it with a slotted spoon.

3   When the roast is well browned on all sides and ends return the browned garlic cloves to the pot, remove the pot from the heat, and cover. Let the meat rest for 15–30 minutes. The internal temperature will be 140 degrees. Season the pan juices with salt after meat has rested.

4   Cut the meat into thin slices, sprinkle with salt, and serve with the garlic and pan juices.

GARLIC

Roman Garlic Anchovy Salad Dressing
for Catalan Chicory or Belgian Endive

For 4–6 Servings   **Side Dish**

*R*oman cooking is flashy, with big bold flavor combinations that have worked for centuries. Romans spread the use of garlic through their empire. Roman naturalist Pliny utilizes garlic in 71 medical prescriptions although Apicius, in *De Re Coquinaria*, an elitist gastronomic manual, ignores garlic as vulgar. He'd probably refuse to eat salad dressed with the garlic, anchovy, extra virgin olive oil, and vinegar that modern Romans adore. Catalan chicory, *puntarelle,* is the green of choice, although Belgian endive, sliced into thin strips, can be substituted with success. Arugula and most full-flavored salad greens will also pair well with this sauce. Home gardeners can get *puntarelle* seeds from B & T World Seeds, Whitnell House, Fiddington, Bridgwater, Somerset, TA5 1JE, UK.

> 3 whole anchovies packed under salt or 3 tablespoons
>   anchovy fillets (see Note)
>
> ¼ cup plus 2 teaspoons red wine vinegar
>
> 2–3 garlic cloves, peeled
>
> ½ cup extra virgin olive oil
>
> Freshly ground black pepper
>
> Sea salt (if necessary)
>
> 1 head of Catalan chicory, central core cut into thin strips
>   or 4–6 Belgian endive, cut into thin strips, or an equal
>   amount of arugula or other robust salad green

1   Marinate whole salt-packed anchovies in ¼ cup red wine vinegar for 6 hours. Drain, rinse, and debone. Or marinate canned or jarred anchovy fillets in ¼ cup vinegar for 1–2 hours. Drain the anchovies and pat dry with paper towels.

2   Mince the anchovy fillets and the garlic in the food processor or with a hand immersion mixer. Add the extra virgin olive oil, 2 teaspoons vinegar, and pepper to taste and blend until smooth. Bland anchovies may require the addition of salt. Dressing can be stored in the refrigerator for a week at least.

3   Dress the salad before serving.

Note: Anchovies packed under salt are more work but taste best. Jarred in glass anchovies are a good second choice, canned (and therefore hidden from inspection) the last decent choice. Anchovy paste is made from leftovers. Avoid it.

GREENS: SPINACH, WILD AND DOMESTICATED GREENS

Spinaci e Verdure del Campo

*I*t must have been easy for the Italians to accept spinach, an import from Persia, probably brought by Arab traders around 1000, because they were already eating plenty of foraged greens. Spinach and swiss chard are sold raw at Italian vegetable markets in the winter, spring, and fall, to be washed and cooked at home. Many produce shops and bread bakeries sell spinach and chard cooked, pressed into balls that are sold by weight, taking all the pain out of preparation. When I moved to Italy not only did I find ready-cooked spinach and chard but a whole world of wild greens with wild flavors that I'd never encountered before.

Italians often stalk greens in the countryside, to be eaten raw in salad when young and tender, cooked when leaves are tough. Wild greens were considered peasant food but are now quite chic, expensive, sold by fancy greengrocers to urban vegetable fans without the time or knowledge to forage.

Popeye, or *Braccio di Ferro* as he's called in Italian, was on to a good thing. Spinach is loaded with calcium, iron, potassium, magnesium, vitamins A and C, and folic acid. Wild greens are usually even richer in vitamins and minerals although it's difficult to find their nutritional contents. The calendar of Friar Foreteller (*Frate Indovino*), a mythical Italian Franciscan monk, contains useful advice on the health benefits of vegetables as well as gardening tips, recipes, lunar cycles, folk wisdom, state and religious holidays. Spinach, according to *Frate Indovino*, helps anemia, rheumatism, diabetes, liver and kidney ailments, problems of the digestive and urinary tracts, physical and psychic depression. Spinach leaves, cooked in olive oil, applied topically, are used to heal burns, dermatosis, and boils. The friar quotes the ancients on the virtues of spinach— "Good humor, clean air and spinach—you'll live one hundred years in holy peace."

Salsola soda, called *agretti* or *barba di Cappuccino* (monk's beard) in Italian, is known as barilla in English. It's a slightly sour spring vegetable, not found in all regions, boiled until tender, drained, dressed with extra virgin olive oil and a squeeze of lemon. Barilla isn't grown in the United States yet but it's only a matter of time since Ingegnoli sells the seed for export even though it's not in their catalog.

Carletti (*Silene vulgaris*) bladder campion, tender poppy greens (*Papaver strigosum*) from plants that haven't yet flowered, and many greens too tough to eat raw are usually boiled, then sautéed with garlic, cooked into a *frittata* or risotto. Cooked wild greens were sold as street food in Florence in the fourteenth century by *cialdonai*, who topped slices of toasted bread with the greens. They belonged to the Florentine bakers' guild, which may be why cooked greens are sometimes found at bread bakeries.

Tender wild greens like *raperonzolo* (*Campanula rapunculus*) rampion, *terracrepolo* (*Reichardia picroides*) French scorzonera, *cicerbita* (*Sonchus oleraceus*) sow's thistle and *salvastrella* (*Sanguisorba minor*) salad burnet, *portulaca* (*Portulaca oleracea*) purslane, and dozens of other varieties change name from region to region (I've given the Florentine dialect) and are eaten raw in salad. *Valeriana* (*Valerianella eriocarpa*), also called *soncino* or *gallinella*, corn salad in English, is usually cultivated and said to have sedative effects. Everyone knows domesticated arugula (*Eruca sativa*) but southern Italians eat a wild version (*Diplotaxis muralis*)with a sharper flavor called wall rocket in English. *Misticanza* is a term for mixed small unheaded leaf lettuce and herbs, cultivated or wild.

Spinach, swiss chard, and wild greens are cooked the same way, boiled in a large pot of salted water, drained, refreshed in cold water or spread out on a counter to cool, then pressed to eliminate excess water.

Supposedly dishes with spinach are called "*à la Florentine*" because Caterina de' Medici brought spinach to France when she married the future King Henry. But don't look for this phrase in Florence on Italian menus.

Seeds for many of the wild greens mentioned in this chapter are sold by B & T World Seeds, Whitnell House, Fiddington, Bridgwater, Somerset, TA5 1JE, UK.

History

Roman millionaire epicure Apicius hosted banquets of delectables like flamingo tongues and camel heels in the first century, blew his entire fortune on culinary festivities, and poisoned himself when he realized that he'd have to change his lifestyle. Apicius's legend survives in a fourth-century compilation of his recipes, *De Re Coquinaria*. Book III, entitled "The Greengrocer," begins with the advice to cook vegetables with bicarbonate "to give an attractive emerald green color." Apicius writes about rustic herbs, eaten raw with *garum*—essence of fermented anchovy—oil, and vinegar or cooked, with pepper, cumin, and lentisk kernels, translated as mastic in my dictionary.

Vincenzo Corrado's 1781 *Of Pythagorean Food* devotes a chapter to spinach, always boiled, then utilized in dumplings, stuffed with grated cheese and eggs, deep-fried, in savory tarts, and *frittate*.

Tuscan doctor M. Pietro Andrea Mattioli of Siena's 1557 translation (from Latin to Italian) of Greek physician Dioscoride's *Discussions on Material Medicine* includes Mattioli's modern sixteenth-century commentary on the Greek physician's work. Dioscoride writes about raw arugula and its aphrodisiac properties; Mattioli goes into greater detail, claiming it ". . . augments sperm and provokes men to coitus."

Greens Recipes

CLAUDIA'S GREEN *SUBRICH*
WILD OR TAME GREEN FLANLETS

Mini pancakes of wild greens, herbs, garlic, and Parmigiano

———

GIOVANNI'S RICOTTA AND WILD GREENS (OR SPINACH) PASTA

Tomato sauce, ricotta, and wild greens with pasta

———

NUDIES

Greens and ricotta dumplings

———

WILD GREENS RISOTTO

———

WILD OR TAME GREENS FRITTATA

FAVA BEANS AND CHICORY

Dried fava bean and potato puree, paired with chicory, served with condiments

———

FABIO'S SQUID (OR CUTTLEFISH), SWISS CHARD, AND SPINACH STEW

Calamari (o Seppie) in Inzimino

Spicy greens, tomato, red wine, and cuttlefish stew

———

"JUMPED" GREENS

Boiled, stir-fried greens with garlic and hot pepper

———

CATERINA'S SALAD

Claudia's Green *Subrich*
Wild or Tame Green Flanlets

For 4–6 Servings   **Appetizer**

*C*laudia Verro, one of the great home-style cooks of Piedmont, prepares some amazing traditional dishes rarely found elsewhere in her restaurant La Contea in the village of Neive. She taught me to make these green *frittatine*, mini *frittate*, a cross between mini flans and savory silver-dollar pancakes, called *subrich* (su-BRICK) in local dialect. Claudia serves them with a glass of spumante as an appetizer, made with wild herbs like poppy greens or nettles in the spring and with broccoli rabe or spinach in the fall. I like the way she livens up the flavor of cooked greens with garlic, a hint of Parmigiano, and plenty of fresh herbs from her garden. These flanlets are the green version of Claudia's potato *subrich* (see page 250). In typically frugal Italian style, stale bread, soaked in water and squeezed, is used to stretch 2 eggs into an appetizer for 4–6.

> 1 pound wild greens, nettles, swiss chard, broccoli rabe,
>   or spinach, cooked and squeezed dry to make ⅔ cup
>
> 4 quarts water
>
> Fine sea salt
>
> 2 large slices of stale bread
>
> 2 scallions
>
> 1 garlic clove
>
> 2 tablespoons chopped fresh herbs—a mixture of at least
>   2 of the following: rosemary, sage, thyme, bay,
>   marjoram, mint
>
> 1 tablespoon chopped Italian parsley
>
> 2 eggs
>
> ¼ cup grated Parmigiano
>
> Fine sea salt
>
> Freshly ground black pepper
>
> Extra virgin olive oil for frying

1 Toss the greens in a sinkful of warm water to clean. Rinse the greens well until all grit and sand are removed. Dirty spinach may need more than one change of water. Lift the greens from the water and drain them in a colander. Remove the bruised leaves and thick stems.

(continued)

2 Bring 4 quarts of water to a boil in a large pot. Salt the water, immerse the greens in the boiling water, and cook, 3–5 minutes, or until tender. Wild greens may need to cook longer. Remove the greens with a slotted spoon, place in a colander, and run under cold water to cool the greens. Divide the cooked greens in two parts and squeeze between both hands to form balls and remove all excess water. Squeeze hard!

3 Soak the stale bread in a bowl of cold water until soft. Crumble the bread and squeeze to remove excess water. Measure ½ cup damp bread.

4 Chop the scallions, garlic, herbs, and parsley in the food processor.

5 Measure ⅔ cup of the cooked greens. Untangle the greens after measuring. Add the greens to the herbs in the food processor and chop.

6 Add the eggs, soaked bread, Parmigiano, and salt and pepper to taste to the greens and process to a smooth paste.

7 Heat 1 tablespoon extra virgin olive oil in a large nonstick skillet over moderate heat. Place 1-tablespoon mounds of the egg-greens mixture in the skillet and flatten lightly. Rounds should be the size of a silver dollar. Cook for 3 minutes to lightly brown, turn the *subrich* over and brown the other side. Remove them from the skillet, place on a paper towel, and keep warm while cooking remaining *subrich*. Add more olive oil to the pan when necessary.

8 Serve the *subrich* warm.

Giovanni's Ricotta and Wild Greens (or Spinach) Pasta

For 4–6 Servings   **First Course**

During a winter visit to Sicily I visited the unheated country home of a four-teenth-generation Sicilian baron with culinary inclinations. His kitchen was low-tech with almost no modern equipment but plenty of style. When the famous modern Sicilian artist Renato Guttuso was the baron's houseguest he painted a door panel with a brightly colored still life of Sicilian vegetables. Baron Giovanni made some interesting regional dishes, including his legendary (and complicated) pasta timbale over the course of a weekend spent mostly in the kitchen, the only room that managed to warm up. My favorite dish of the weekend was this pasta, dressed with tomato sauce, ricotta, and wild greens from the vineyard, a kind of wild broccoli rabe called *cavoluzzi di vigna*, literally "little ugly vineyard cabbage." Broccoli rabe, tender mustard greens, swiss chard, or even spinach can be substituted with satisfying results. Tender greens will need to cook less than the baron's wild greens.

½ pound greens (broccoli rabe, mustard or wild greens,
    swiss chard, or spinach)

1 small onion, chopped

1 garlic clove, chopped

2 tablespoons extra virgin olive oil

1½ cups canned tomato pulp

1 teaspoon sugar

Coarse sea salt

Freshly ground black pepper

5–6 quarts water

14 ounces short pasta (penne, rigatoni, macaroni)

¾ cup whole milk ricotta

¼ cup grated Parmigiano

1   Toss the greens in a sinkful of warm water to clean. Masochists can use cold. Rinse the greens until all grit and sand are removed. Dirty spinach may need more than one change of water. Lift the greens from water and drain them in a colander. Remove any bruised leaves and thick stems. Chop the greens into 2-inch pieces.

2   Put the chopped onion and garlic in a large pot, drizzle with extra virgin olive oil, stir to coat the vegetables, and place over low heat. Cook for 10 minutes or until the onions are tender. Add the tomatoes and cook over moderate heat for 5 minutes to evaporate excess water. Add sugar and season with salt and pepper.

3   Bring 5–6 quarts of water to a rolling boil. Salt the water and add the chopped greens. When the water returns to a boil add the pasta.

4   When the pasta is cooked but still offers considerable resistance to the tooth, around three quarters of the recommended cooking time, drain the pasta and greens, reserving 2 cups of pasta water.

5   Add the greens and pasta to the tomato sauce along with 1 cup of cooking water and turn the heat to high. Cook over highest heat for 3–5 minutes, stirring, until pasta is cooked and sauce coats pasta. Add more pasta water, ¼ cup at a time, if sauce gets too dry. Add ricotta and Parmigiano, stirring to mix and heat thoroughly.

Nudies

*N*udies? In Florentine dialect they're called *gnudi*, nudies, poking fun at a
dish from the Casentino, a neighboring area that makes their greens and
ricotta gnocchi with the same filling Florentines use for ravioli. Nudies because
they're not wearing pasta. Pronounced YNOO-dees. Spinach is used in Florence
but wild greens are common in the mountainous Casentino. And ravioli are stuffed
with wild greens in many regional recipes. Use wild greens if you can get them, otherwise use chard or spinach, whichever is fresh and tender. Traditionalists may want
to search for sheep's milk ricotta, which yields richer results, but everyone else can
get by with whole cow's milk ricotta. Drain watery ricotta in a metal sieve for 30
minutes if necessary. Cooks in search of a labor-intensive experience can form nudies by hand, one at a time, or use the 2-spoon French quenelle method. I prefer to
pipe the mixture from a plastic bag onto a floured countertop, sprinkle the blobs
with flour, and lightly roll to form walnut-sized, roughly shaped balls. Serve the
nudies with melted butter or tomato or meat sauce, sprinkled with Parmigiano, and
baked in the oven to melt the cheese.

> 1 pound wild greens, swiss chard, or spinach
>   to make 1⅓ cups squeezed cooked greens
>
> 5 quarts water
>
> Salt plus 1 teaspoon fine sea salt
>
> 1 cup ricotta, drained in a metal sieve if watery
>
> ½ cup grated Parmigiano
>
> 1 egg
>
> A few gratings of nutmeg
>
> Flour to lightly coat nudies

For the sauce:

> ¼ cup melted butter or ½ cup tomato sauce
>   (see page 289) or ½ cup homemade meat sauce
>   (check out another Italian cookbook)
>
> ¼ cup grated Parmigiano-Reggiano

1 Toss the greens in a sinkful of warm water to clean. Rinse the greens until all grit and sand are removed. Dirty spinach may need more than one change of water. Lift the greens from the water and drain them in a colander. Remove any bruised leaves and thick stems.

2 Bring 5 quarts of water to a boil in a large pot. Salt the water, immerse the greens in boiling water, and cook, 3–5 minutes, or longer for some wild greens, until tender. Remove the greens with a slotted spoon, reserving water for poaching the nudies. Place the greens in a colander and run them under cold water to cool. Divide the cooked greens in three parts and squeeze between both hands to form balls and remove all excess water. Squeeze hard!

3 Measure 1⅓ cups of the cooked greens. Untangle the greens after measuring; they'll be easier to process. Roughly chop the greens in a food processor. Add the ricotta, Parmigiano, egg, 1 teaspoon sea salt, and nutmeg and process to form a smooth paste.

4 Transfer the paste to a pastry bag with a large tip or a medium-sized plastic bag with a ½-inch corner cut off.

5 Sift a layer of flour onto a large clean surface and pipe the paste in blobs the size of a walnut, 2 inches apart. Sift another layer of flour over the blobs and delicately roll in the flour. Carefully toss each nudie from hand to hand to remove the excess flour.

6 Bring the reserved cooking water to a boil and poach 8–9 nudies at a time, for 2–3 minutes or until they float to the surface of the water. Transfer with a slotted spoon to a large baking dish.

7 Preheat the oven to 400 degrees. Drizzle the nudies with melted butter, or tomato or meat sauce, and sprinkle with grated cheese. Bake for 10–15 minutes or until lightly browned and cheese has melted and serve.

Note: Nudies can be made a day in advance, up to step 6, and heated with the melted butter or sauce and cheese before serving.

Wild Greens Risotto

*W*ild greens are often paired with rice in Veneto, a region that takes risotto seriously. Hops *bruscandoli*, silene *carletti*, nettles *ortica*, wild clematis shoots *vitalba*, and practically anything edible from the fields are cooked with rice and broth over high heat, enriched with cheese and butter. But Cesare Benelli, chef-owner of Ristorante Al Covo in Venice, who has a wonderful way with risotto, uses extra virgin olive oil instead of butter. And I love the results.

> ½ pound wild or cultivated fresh greens
>
> 4 scallions, chopped
>
> ¼ cup extra virgin olive oil or 2 tablespoons
>   extra virgin olive oil and 2 tablespoons butter
>
> 1 cup Italian rice for risotto, preferably Vialone Nano
>   or Carnaroli
>
> ¼ cup dry white wine (optional)
>
> 8–10 cups boiling water or lightly salted vegetable broth
>   (made with 1 spring onion, 1 garlic clove, 1 carrot,
>   1 celery stalk, stems and tough leaves of
>   picked-over greens)
>
> Coarse sea salt
>
> ½ cup grated Parmigiano-Reggiano (and additional
>   cheese to top risotto, if desired)

1 Toss the greens in a sinkful of warm water to clean. Rinse the greens until all grit and sand are removed. Dirty spinach may need more than one change of water. Lift the greens from the water and drain in a colander. Remove any bruised leaves and thick stems. Chop the greens.

2 Put the chopped scallions in a 4-quart pot, drizzle with 2 tablespoons of extra virgin olive oil, stir to coat the scallions with oil, and place over low heat. Cook for 5–10 minutes, until scallions are tender but not browned. Add the rice, stir to coat with oil, and cook for a few minutes to lightly toast but not brown the rice.

3 Add the chopped greens and the white wine, if you are using it, to the rice, stir to mix well, and raise the heat to high to evaporate the wine. Add the boiling water and lightly salt (or vegetable stock, which should be lightly salted), 1 cup at a time, stirring the bottom of the pot with a *long* wooden spoon or fork, over highest heat, boil-

ing madly. Risotto attains the temperature of molten lava! Add more water or broth when risotto is still surrounded by liquid, not dried out. After risotto has cooked for 10 minutes begin to add water or broth ½ cup at a time, until rice is almost cooked.

4   Taste rice after another 5 minutes of cooking; it should be firm under tooth since it will continue to cook for a few more minutes. Liquid should be a little soupy because Parmigiano, oil (or butter), and final whipping will tighten up the sauce.

5   When rice is *al dente* and still surrounded by its opaque liquid, add the Parmigiano-Reggiano and remaining extra virgin oil (or 2 tablespoons butter) and stir energetically with long-handled wooden spoon or fork over high heat for 2 minutes to whip ingredients together. Remove from the heat, ladle into individual bowls, and let the risotto rest for a minute before serving. Top with additional cheese if desired.

Wild or Tame Greens *Frittata*

*W*ild or tame greens make a fantastic *frittata*. They're used alone or combined, often simply the results of whatever a hunt in the fields turns up. There are different ways to cook a *frittata*. Liliana, the cook at Castello di Ama in the heart of Chianti, is a traditionalist, and cooks one side, flips it over onto a plate, slips it back into the pan to cook the other side. Others cover the *frittata* to set the top, flipping onto a serving dish to expose the browned side. Marcella Hazan recommends cooking eggs until set, then broiling the upper surface. And flamboyant cooks flip, flapjack-style. A nonstick omelet pan makes the entire process easier.

> 1½ pounds wild greens, swiss chard, or spinach
>
> 4 quarts water
>
> Fine sea salt
>
> 4 eggs
>
> Freshly ground black pepper
>
> 2–3 tablespoons extra virgin olive oil

1 Toss the greens in a sinkful of warm water to clean. Rinse the greens until all grit and sand are removed. Dirty spinach may need more than one change of water. Lift the greens from the water and drain in a colander. Remove any bruised leaves and thick stems. Chop the greens.

2 Bring 4 quarts of water to boil. Salt the water, immerse the greens in the boiling water, and cook, 3–5 minutes, or longer for some wild greens, until tender. Remove the greens with a slotted spoon. Place the greens in a colander and run them under cold water to cool. Divide the cooked greens in three parts and squeeze between both hands to form balls and remove all excess water. Squeeze hard! Chop the greens.

3 Mix the eggs and salt and pepper to taste with a fork and combine with the greens.

4 Heat the extra virgin olive oil in a medium-sized nonstick skillet. Add the eggs and greens and cook over low heat until eggs are well set on the bottom but still slightly runny on the surface. Shake the pan to loosen the *frittata*, running a spatula under the *frittata* if it sticks.

5 Put a plate over the *frittata* and invert the skillet to reverse the *frittata* onto the plate. Slide the frittata back into pan to cook the other side.

6 Slide onto a platter and serve hot or at room temperature. Leftovers make a good sandwich.

Fava Beans and Chicory

For 4–6 Servings   **First Course**

*D*ried fava bean puree and simply boiled chicory paired together in a soup plate, drizzled with extra virgin olive oil, is a popular newly chic rustic first course found at home and in restaurants in the region of Apulia, heel of the Italian boot. But my favorite version was served by Camillo Guerra at Il Melograno, a spectacular hotel that takes regional cuisine seriously, in Monopoli. "Fava beans and chicory *alla Martinese,*" exclaimed Camillo, "this is the way we serve it in our area." The traditional fava bean puree was studded with chunks of toasted bread and served with bowls of condiments on the table; sun-dried tomatoes, artichoke hearts, pickled eggplant and peppers, onion and capers, all to be eaten along with the puree. Since most of these side dishes come from a jar it's an easy meal to make for a crowd. As usual with the simplest preparations, quality ingredients are a must. Split fava beans simplify this dish greatly, requiring no soaking or skin removal. I wasn't crazy about the toasted bread in the puree and list it as optional.

> 1½ cups split dried fava beans
>
> 5 cups plus 4 quarts water
>
> 1 medium potato, peeled and cubed
>
> 1 pound chicory, wild greens, or chard
>
> Salt
>
> ¼ cup extra virgin olive oil
>
> Freshly ground pepper
>
> 1 cup toasted bread cubes (optional)
>
> Some or all of the following condiments: sun-dried tomatoes, artichoke hearts, pickled eggplant packed in olive oil, roast pepper strips, and the marinated onion and caper salad on page 223.

1 Put the fava beans in a 4-quart pot, add 5 cups of water, and bring to a boil. Reduce the heat to low and simmer for 10–15 minutes. Add the potatoes and cook until the favas and potatoes are tender and most of the liquid has been absorbed. If the vegetables dry out, add hot water, ¼ cup at a time.

2 While the fava beans are cooking, toss the greens in a sinkful of warm water to wash them. Rinse the greens until all grit and sand are removed. Dirty spinach may need more than one change of water. Lift the greens from the water and drain in a colander. Remove any bruised leaves and thick stems.

(continued)

3 Bring 4 quarts of water to a boil in a large pot. Salt the water, immerse the greens in the boiling water, and cook, 3–5 minutes, or longer for some wild greens, until tender. Remove the greens with a slotted spoon. Place them in a colander and run under cold water to cool. Divide the cooked greens in three parts and squeeze between both hands to form balls and remove most excess water. Untangle the greens.

4 Puree the favas and potatoes through a food mill or potato ricer or whip with a wire whisk. Don't use a food processor.

5 Beat in 2 tablespoons extra virgin olive oil and season with salt and pepper. The puree should be the consistency of creamy mashed potatoes.

6 Spoon the fava puree into soup bowls, top with some of the cooked greens, and drizzle with the remaining extra virgin olive oil. Serve plain or with toasted bread cubes, sun-dried tomatoes, artichoke hearts, pickled eggplant, roast pepper strips, and the marinated onion and caper salad.

Fabio's Squid (or Cuttlefish), Swiss Chard, and Spinach Stew
Calamari (or Seppie) in Inzimino

For 4–6 Servings   **Main Course**

*T*his is probably my favorite Florentine fish dish, a blend of spicy greens and tender squid or cuttlefish, at its very best prepared by Fabio Picchi, chef-owner of Cibréo, a Florentine restaurant that serves spectacular home-style food. Squid or cuttlefish are stewed with greens, tomato, red wine, garlic, and hot pepper, a robust spicy dish that even fish-haters may enjoy. It's served with slices of toasted country-style bread. I use my favorite Chianti from Castello di Ama to cook *inzimino* and serve the rest of the wine with the meal.

> 1 small red onion, minced
>
> 1 small carrot, minced
>
> 1 small celery stalk, minced
>
> 1 garlic clove, minced
>
> 1 hot red pepper (*peperoncino*) or dried hot pepper flakes to taste
>
> ¼ cup extra virgin olive oil
>
> 1 pound cleaned squid, cut into ½-inch pieces and rings
>
> ½ cup canned tomato pulp
>
> ¼ cup red wine (preferably Chianti)
>
> 1 teaspoon coarse sea salt or more to taste
>
> 1 pound swiss chard, well washed and cut into 2-inch strips
>
> ½ pound spinach, well washed and cut into 2-inch strips

1 Place the onion, carrot, celery, garlic, and hot pepper in a large 4-quart pot. Pour the extra virgin olive oil over the vegetables, stir to coat them with the oil, and place over moderate heat. Cook for 5–10 minutes, stirring occasionally, until vegetables are golden.

2 Stir in the squid, add the tomatoes and red wine, and season with salt. Bring to a boil and add the swiss chard and the spinach. Cover, lower heat, and cook for 45 minutes, stirring after 15 minutes when the leafy vegetables have wilted.

3 Uncover the pot, raise the heat, and evaporate excess liquid if necessary. Serve the *inzimino* with toasted bread.

"Jumped" Greens

*T*here is really only one main cooking method and three ways to serve cooked greens like spinach, chard, chicory, broccoli rabe, or wild greens as a side dish in Italy. Greens are boiled like pasta, in salted water, then drained, cooled, and squeezed of excess water. They're served at room temperature with extra virgin olive oil and a squirt of lemon. Or warmed up, *saltate*, the past participle of the verb "to jump," given a brief stir-fry with butter for a mild-flavored dish. Or jumped with garlic, hot red pepper, and extra virgin olive oil, my favorite method.

> 1½–2 pounds spinach
> 4 quarts water
> Fine sea salt
> 2–3 garlic cloves, chopped
> 4 tablespoons extra virgin olive oil
> 1 hot red pepper, chopped, or dried hot pepper flakes
>   to taste

1 Toss the greens in a sinkful of warm water to clean. Masochists can use cold. Rinse the greens until all grit and sand are removed. Dirty spinach may need more than one change of water. Lift the greens from the water and drain in a colander. Remove any bruised leaves and thick stems.

2 Bring 4 quarts of water to a boil in a large pot. Salt the water, immerse the greens in the boiling water, and cook, 3–5 minutes, or until the greens are tender. Reserve ½ cup cooking water. Remove the greens with a slotted spoon, place in a colander, and run under cold water to cool the greens. Divide the cooked greens in three parts and squeeze between both hands to form balls and remove all excess water.

3 Untangle the cooked greens and roughly chop.

4 Place the garlic in a large nonstick pan, drizzle with 2 tablespoons extra virgin olive oil, stir to coat the garlic, and place over moderate heat. When the garlic begins to sizzle add the hot pepper. Cook until the garlic barely begins to color.

5 Add the greens and ¼ cup greens cooking water to the garlic and season with salt. Raise the heat to high and stir-fry for 3 or 4 minutes to heat the greens, amalgamate the flavors, and evaporate the water. Remove from the heat, add the remaining extra virgin oil, and stir to combine.

Note: Greens can be cooked in advance but are at their best freshly made.

Caterina's Salad

I have no idea why this Florentine salad is called Caterina. Could it possibly be named for Caterina de' Medici who brought her own cooks and pastry chefs from Florence when she married the future King Henry of France? Caterina was a serious eater and drinker and almost died of indigestion from eating too many artichoke bottoms and chicken giblets. The salad named for Caterina is one of the few dressed with more than extra virgin olive oil and vinegar, featuring pecorino cheese, anchovies, and pine nuts, possibly a salute to her gluttonous appetite.

> ½ pound wild or tender salad greens
>
> ½ cup diced fresh pecorino cheese
>
> 3–4 anchovy fillets, chopped
>
> 2 tablespoons capers, soaked in water and rinsed of salt
>
> 2 tablespoons pine nuts
>
> 1 tablespoon red wine vinegar
>
> 3–4 tablespoons extra virgin olive oil
>
> Fine sea salt
>
> Freshly ground black pepper

1 Toss the greens in a sinkful of warm water to clean. Rinse the greens until all dirt is removed; lift out of the water and into a colander or salad spinner. Pat greens with paper towels or spin to remove excess water.

2 In a large salad bowl toss the greens with the remaining ingredients to combine.

MUSHROOMS

Funghi

*I*talians are mycophagists, mushroom-mad epicures, crazy about eating all kinds of *funghi,* both cultivated and wild. This is a world beyond the canned and cultivated white button mushrooms that were once the only options for American mushroom lovers before cremini, portobello, shiitake, oyster, and most recently porcini and other wild mushrooms began to appear on restaurant menus and in gourmet markets. In the fall Italians get excited about eating dozens of varieties of mushrooms, hunted in the countryside, purchased in shops or from roadside vendors. Some restaurants in major mushroom-producing areas become seasonal destinations, with menus that embrace mushrooms in every course, featuring raw mushroom salads, stewed mushrooms on crostini, or paired with polenta, meat, or fowl, flavoring risotto, sauced with or stuffed into pasta, grilled, roasted, or deep-fried. And now American mycophagists can join Italians in their culinary celebration dedicated to the mushroom. American sources are being tapped commercially and there's a decent supply of fresh and dried wild mushrooms available.

Most mushrooms are saprophytic plants, without chlorophyll, incapable of photosynthesis, deriving nutrition from living organisms or decaying organic matter. Microscopic fungi turn sugar to alcohol in wine making, milk into yogurt, cause bread to rise, produce penicillin. Bigger, more evolved fungi live in a symbiotic relationship with tree roots, extracting sugar and starch from the roots in exchange for minerals. Mushrooms, called carpophores by mycologists, are the fruit of the underground mycelium, a network of tiny branching filaments produced when spores germinate. When the weather is right, moist and cool, a fruit body, i.e., mushroom, develops from this web.

Fungi are classified in two major groups. Ascomycetes like morels and truffles develop spores internally that are ejected at maturity. Basidiomycetes have a central stem and rounded cap and are divided into two distinct categories. Agarics like the common cultivated mushroom, chanterelle, or oyster mushroom have radiating gills on the underside. Boletes like porcini have a spongy underside. Both kinds of Basidiomycete mushrooms reproduce when spores are discharged from the gill or pore surface, germinating to form new mycelia from which new fruits spring. Gatherers frequently make spore prints to determine a mushroom's variety, leaving mushrooms on a piece of paper, then examining the spores that drop from the gills or pores. As all mushroom hunters are aware, great care is taken to leave the mycelium intact when harvesting mushrooms so that it continues to grow and produce new mushrooms.

Mushrooms have some protein although their reputation as "vegetal meat" is unfounded since mushroom proteins aren't assimilated by human digestion. Mushrooms are around 80 percent water and therefore low in calories. They contain no fat, no cholesterol, small amounts of vitamins A, B, C, and D, and minerals calcium, phosphorous, potassium, sodium, and magnesium. Wild mushrooms generally have more nutritive value than cultivated varieties. Their unique cellular construction makes mushrooms difficult to digest in large quantities. Glutamic acid is present in large amounts, the same stuff found in monosodium glutamate, giving mushrooms a built-in flavor boost that may be responsible for the headaches and dizziness that trouble some mushroom eaters.

In the fall Italians armed with baskets and small knives stalk woods and fields searching for mushrooms, found in the mountains and foothills of almost all regions. Hunting grounds are a closely guarded secret. Traditional lore about poisonous mushrooms is often false (popular folk wisdom claims that garlic turns black when cooked with poisonous mushrooms) and whole families have been wiped out at home-cooked mushroom banquets. Every village, town, or city in Italy has an official authority (or an office full of them) who inspects mushrooms to see if they're edible but many Italians foolishly think they know better. In Trento, a northern city known for its mushrooms, the traffic policeman is the mushroom expert. Retail outlets always display health department authorization.

In Italy, wild mushrooms abound in the fall, a compensation for the end of summer, and can also be found in the spring. Mushrooms are sold fresh, dried, partially cooked and preserved under oil or vinegar, and most recently, frozen. Some are eaten raw, most cooked. Cultivated mushrooms, mostly champignons, called white button mushrooms in the United States, and brown cremini are available all year round. Italian-sounding portobello mushrooms are a new creation of American commercial mushroom growers and are actually oversized cremini, now also grown in Italy.

The freshest mushrooms should be firm and dry, without any signs of shriveling. Agarics have tightly closed gills, paler than those of older, flabbier mushrooms. The underside of boletus mushrooms will be soft and pale-colored, but will turn darker and spongy within days. Mushrooms beyond their prime should be avoided. The spongy underside of porcini can be removed if it appears too mushy. Bigger doesn't mean better and many mushroom mavens feel that small-sized specimens have more flavor.

Ideally, mushrooms should be cleaned with a mushroom brush, to whisk away dirt and grit from the stem and upper cap, and a knife to pare away the stem base and scrape off excess dirt. Never store mushrooms in a sealed plastic bag, which will make them sweat and turn soggy. Instead, wrap mushrooms in paper towels, then store in a paper bag in the refrigerator or at a cool room temperature to maintain some degree of freshness for a day or two. Baskets are preferred to bags by mushroom gatherers because air can circulate freely. Especially dirty mushrooms can be washed but should be carefully dried with paper towels.

Porcini, *Boletus edulis*, the Italians' favorite mushroom and mine too, are wild and earthy-tasting. They are eaten fresh, frozen with good success, or dried, to be used during the rest of the year in stews and risotto. Because fresh porcini are expensive and good ones aren't easy to find, when I do splurge I use stems and caps in different ways. I make soups, sauces, and risotto with lots of stems and a cap or two for show, saving large caps to grill or roast whole. When wild mushrooms aren't available I like to intensify the flavor of cultivated mushrooms with the addition of a few reconstituted dried porcini and their juices. If I'm lucky enough to have super-fresh mushrooms, I like to eat them raw, sliced paper-thin using the thinnest blade of a food processor like a mandoline, taking utmost care. But only the freshest mushrooms should be used.

Dry porcini are used in Italy to flavor sauce, risotto, and braised dishes, contributing a concentrated flavor impossible to achieve with fresh. But the finest porcini are always eaten fresh and only second- (or even third-) rate porcini, often imported from Eastern European countries, are dried and packaged in Italy. The best dried porcini are sold in clear plastic packets, a mixture of creamy-colored stem slices and caps edged with brown. Dried mushrooms that are dark, shriveled bits or crumbs should be avoided. To reconstitute dried mushrooms, soak in hot water for 30 minutes or more, remove from the water, squeeze to get rid of excess water, examine for dirt or sand, rinse, and dry with paper towels. The soaking water, which will be intensely mushroomy in flavor, can be utilized but must be carefully strained to eliminate any trace of grit. Poor-quality dried mushrooms will probably be dirty and their water will therefore taste musty and unpleasant.

In Tuscany, mushrooms are almost always paired with *nepitella,* a wild mint that grows throughout much of Italy. It's probably *Nepeta nepetella* of the genus *Calamintha,* according to botanical expert Professor Tesi from the University of Florence. Gardeners can get seeds from Sleepy Hollow Herb Farm, Jack Black Road, Lancaster, Kentucky 40444, Telephone: 606–269–7601, or B & T World Seeds, Whitnell House, Fiddington, Bridgwater, Somerset, TA5 1JE, UK. Everyone else can substitute a mixture of oregano and mint as directed in all the Tuscan mushroom recipes.

Fresh mushrooms are available at upscale markets and can be ordered from the following distributors that sell retail and wholesale and ship UPS or FedEx: Aux Delices des Bois, 4 Leonard Street, New York, New York 10013, Telephone: 212–334–1230, and Gourmet Mushrooms, P.O. Box 391, Sebastopol, California 95472, Telephone: 707–823–1743. Both sell fresh wild and cultivated mushrooms. Hans Johansson's Mushrooms & More, P.O. Box 532, Goldens Bridge, New York 10526, Telephone: 914–232–2107, sells fresh, frozen, and dried wild and cultivated mushrooms.

Cultivated or wild mushrooms can be used in the following recipes but always look for the freshest possible specimens.

History

A fourth-century compilation of Roman Apicius's recipes, *De Re Coquinaria*, includes instructions for mushrooms, prosciutto, liver, home-style desserts, bulbs, truffles, sow's vulva flavored with herbs, and *garum* (fermented anchovy essence) in Book VII, dedicated to "Food for Kings." Apicius recommends boiling mushrooms, serving them dressed with cooked grape must, vinegar, oil, and pepper or with herbs and ever-present *garum*, surely an acquired taste.

The anonymous Venetian's fourteenth-century *Book for Cook*, written in dialect, was the first to specify quantities and cooking times in recipes. The "tart of good and most perfect mushrooms" is a blend of mushrooms cooked in lard, cheese, and eggs, baked in a pastry shell, ". . . ponderous with spice, lots of mushrooms, few eggs, well-cooked."

Maestro Martino, chef to the Patriarch of Aquilea, wrote the bestseller *The Book of Culinary Art* in 1450. He inspired Bartolomeo Sacchi to write *Honest Pleasure and Health* in Latin using the pen name Platina. It was first published in 1474, an intellectual digression on food, hygiene, and alimentary ethics and all Maestro Martino's recipes, written in an era when plagiary was considered a compliment, not the object of a lawsuit. Platina warns readers about poisonous mushrooms and recommends cooking boiled and salted mushrooms in oil, served with garlicky *agliata* (see page 165) or green sauce (see page 220). Grilled mushrooms are served with pepper and cinnamon.

New-wave Protestant thinker Giacomo Castelvetro, exiled for his unorthodox religious views, wrote *A Brief Account of the Fruit, Herbs & Vegetables of Italy* in 1614. It's a heroic attempt to introduce the joys of fresh produce to the English, who took quite a few centuries to get the message. He wrote eloquently about growing and cooking vegetables and the benefits derived from eating them. "Although mushrooms are as abundant here in England as they are in Italy . . . few people seem to know much about them" states Castelvetro. He recommends cooking field mushrooms with "a little water, plenty of oil or butter, garlic, salt and pepper and a decent amount of sweet herbs. Serve them sprinkled with bitter orange juice or a little *agresto* or vinegar. Whoever eats them like this and doesn't lick their fingers does not, in my opinion, know much about true gluttony."

Mushroom Recipes

"TRUFFLED" MUSHROOMS

Funghi Trifolati

———

CESARE'S MUSHROOM *CROSTINI*

*Herbed mushroom paste on deep-fried
or grilled polenta squares*

———

RAW MUSHROOM AND TALEGGIO *CROSTINI*

*Open-faced melted cheese and mushroom
sandwich*

———

RAW MUSHROOM SALAD

*Paper-thin wild mushroom slices dressed
with oil, lemon, and Parmigiano curls*

———

**RISOTTO WITH WILD
OR CULTIVATED MUSHROOMS**

**PASTA WITH MUSHROOM
AND CHICKEN LIVER SAUCE**

———

FABIO'S MUSHROOM SOUP

Creamless smooth mushroom soup

———

**FABIO'S MUSHROOM CAPS
BAKED WITH GARLIC**

*Wild porcini mushroom caps are baked in
foil packets in a water bath*

———

GRILLED BIG MUSHROOM CAPS

Pan-roasted garlic-studded mushroom caps

"Truffled" Mushrooms
Funghi Trifolati

For 4–6 Servings   **Appetizer, Side Dish, Condiment**

*T*ruffled mushrooms, *funghi trifolati,* is just a fancy name for mushrooms cooked with olive oil, garlic, and parsley. It's the most basic of mushroom recipes, at its best when prepared with fresh porcini or other wild mushrooms, with flavors just hinted at when cultivated varieties are substituted. A few soaked porcini and their strained soaking liquid can be added to button or cremini mushrooms to make them more interesting. Truffled mushrooms can be served as an appetizer, side dish, or as a topping for grilled meat or poultry.

½ ounce dried porcini mushrooms (optional)

1 cup hot water

1½ pounds mushrooms

4 tablespoons extra virgin olive oil

2–3 garlic cloves, chopped

1 tablespoon chopped parsley

Sea salt

Freshly ground black pepper

1 Soak the dried mushrooms in 1 cup of hot water for 30 minutes. Strain and save the soaking water and rinse the reconstituted mushrooms under running water to eliminate any remaining soil. Chop the reconstituted porcini mushrooms.

2 Clean the fresh mushrooms and separate the caps from the stems. Cut them into thin slices.

3 Heat 2 tablespoons olive oil in a large nonstick skillet over moderate heat and cook the garlic until it barely begins to color.

4 Add half the sliced mushroom caps and stems and cook until they release their juices. Remove them from the pan.

5 Heat the remaining olive oil in the pan and sauté the remaining fresh mushrooms until they release their juices. Return the reserved mushrooms to the pan and add the chopped reconstituted porcini, the parsley, and ½ cup of the strained soaking water. Season with salt and pepper and cook over high heat for a few minutes to reduce the liquid, stirring often or shaking the pan. Serve hot or at room temperature but don't refrigerate.

Cesare's Mushroom *Crostini*

*C*esare Casella used to cook at his family's trattoria, Vipore, set amid olive trees in the hills outside the city of Lucca. His cooking was pure Tuscan, relying on local ingredients, delicately flavored olive oil, and herbs from his extensive herb garden outside the kitchen. Cesare would bring a crate of fresh, just-picked wild mushrooms with damp earth clinging to their stems to the table instead of a menu during mushroom season and funghi fans would thrill to an entire meal based on mushrooms. These *crostini* were always the beginning of Cesare's mushroom marathon, usually followed by a salad of sliced raw porcini or ovoli salad, fresh pasta with porcini sauce, grilled and deep-fried mushrooms. Many courses were flavored with *nepitella* wild mint. My husband Massimo always concluded these meals with a nap under the fig tree in the garden while Cesare and I sat in the late afternoon sun and gossiped. Vipore closed last year and Cesare now cooks at Coco Pazzo and Il Toscanaccio in New York. I'm sure that he gets wonderful wild mushrooms in the spring and fall, even if there isn't a fig tree to nap under. Cesare makes his mushroom *crostini* with deep-fried polenta squares but I find it too much trouble and pan-roast the polenta squares in a lightly oiled nonstick skillet. As usual I've used a blend of oregano and mint to replace unavailable *nepitella*. Lazy cooks who don't want to make polenta can substitute toasted bread.

3¼ cups water plus 1 cup hot water

¾ cup cornmeal

1 teaspoon coarse salt plus sea salt

½ pound fresh wild mushroom stems and small caps or
    ½ pound cultivated mushrooms and ½ ounce dried
    porcini mushrooms

2 tablespoons extra virgin olive oil plus more
    for frying or sautéing polenta

1 garlic clove, chopped

¼ teaspoon chopped fresh oregano

¼ teaspoon chopped fresh mint

1 teaspoon chopped parsley

Freshly ground black pepper

1 Prepare the polenta well in advance because it must cool. Bring 3¼ cups of water to a rolling boil in a 2-quart saucepan or in the top of a double boiler directly over the burner. Sprinkle the cornmeal into the water, stirring with a whisk to prevent lumping, and add 1 teaspoon coarse salt. Place the saucepan in a larger pot of boiling water or in the bottom of a double boiler and cook over low heat for 1 hour or until the polenta is cooked and glossy. Mix the polenta well with a whisk and pour into a small loaf pan 8 x 4 x 2½ inches.

2 Clean the mushrooms and separate the caps from the stems.

3 Soak the dried mushrooms in 1 cup of hot water for 30 minutes. Rinse the reconstituted mushrooms under running water to eliminate any remaining soil. Strain the soaking water and save. Mince the reconstituted porcini mushrooms.

4 Mince the fresh mushroom stems and caps.

5 Heat 2 tablespoons extra virgin olive oil in a large nonstick skillet over moderate heat and cook the garlic until it barely begins to color.

6 Add the minced mushroom caps and stems and cook until they release their juices. Add the minced reconstituted porcini mushrooms, the oregano, mint, parsley, and ½ cup of the strained mushroom soaking water. Season with salt and pepper and cook over high heat for 5 minutes to reduce the liquid, stirring often or shaking the pan. Reserve the minced mushroom paste.

7 Slice the polenta ½ inch thick and cut into squares.

8 Lightly oil a large nonstick skillet and place over high heat. Cook the polenta squares on both sides to brown and crisp. (Or deep-fry the squares the way Cesare does.) Top each polenta square with a teaspoon of the mushroom paste.

Raw Mushroom and Taleggio *Crostini*

*A*n entire Taleggio of the highest quality, a runny creamy yet lusty cheese from Lombardy brought by a friend who came to lunch, and a bunch of porcini mushroom stems to use up motivated this appetizer, not exactly traditional but wonderful nevertheless. Even my mushroomed-out family, tired of tasting dishes from this chapter, approved. Stracchino, Brie, or lightly flavored creamy cheeses can be substituted for Taleggio.

> 4 slices of country-style bread, ¾ inch thick
>
> 6 ounces Taleggio, rind removed
>
> 1 cup fresh porcini stems or cultivated mushroom caps, cleaned
>
> 3 tablespoons extra virgin olive oil
>
> Fine sea salt
>
> Freshly ground black pepper

1 Preheat the broiler. Lightly toast, grill, or broil the bread until barely colored on both sides.

2 Cover each slice of bread with one quarter of the Taleggio and place the slices on a baking sheet.

3 Place 6 inches from the broiler and cook until the cheese just starts to melt. Transfer the bread to a serving platter

4 Slice the mushrooms as thin as possible with a mandoline slicer, hand-held food processor blade, or precision knife skills.

5 Cover the melted cheese with the sliced mushrooms, drizzle with the extra virgin olive oil, and season with salt and pepper.

Raw Mushroom Salad

*T*he first time I ever had this dish it was made with *ovoli*, *Amanita caesarea*, Caesar's mushroom, supposedly a favorite of the Roman emperor. Small specimens look like eggs, with the volva, a cream-colored egg-shaped membrane, enclosing the orange mushroom that eventually bursts when the mushroom emerges. It's probably the most expensive mushroom in Italy, highly prized, hard to find in markets. Mushroom lovers can substitute porcini or even cultivated mushrooms if they're really fresh for unobtainable *ovoli* even if it's not what Caesar had in mind. Use a slicer or mandoline to create even slices. Or use the 1-mm blade of a food processor like a mandoline, running mushroom caps across the blade *with great care*. If the stems are firm enough, they can be sliced with a vegetable peeler but I prefer to save them for Fabio's Mushroom Soup (see page 206). I use a vegetable peeler to make Parmigiano curls, scraping across the cheese as if peeling a carrot. Anyone fortunate enough to have a super-fresh white truffle can slice it over the completed salad and dream of Piedmont.

½ pound *fresh* mushroom caps

1 tablespoon fresh lemon juice

2–4 tablespoons extra virgin olive oil

Salt

Freshly ground black pepper

One 4-ounce piece of Parmigiano-Reggiano, to make
 abundant cheese curls

1 Clean the mushrooms caps. Slice the mushroom caps as thin as possible, using a slicer, mandoline, or a 1-mm food processor blade like a mandoline. Mushrooms that aren't fresh won't slice well.

2 Put the sliced mushrooms on a serving platter and toss them with the lemon juice so they don't darken. Drizzle with extra virgin olive oil, season with the salt and pepper, and mix well.

3 Using a vegetable peeler, shave curls of Parmigiano-Reggiano over the mushroom salad to cover. Serve immediately.

MUSHROOMS

Risotto with Wild
or Cultivated Mushrooms

*M*ushroom caps are sliced and sautéed, stems are minced and cooked with the rice to flavor the risotto, and the caps are added before serving so they don't disintegrate. When making risotto with dried porcini the reconstituted mushrooms are cooked with rice for the entire cooking time. Good mushroom broth will guarantee the most intensely flavored risotto and can be made with some stems and broken mushrooms or with a few soaked and cleaned dried porcini and their soaking liqueur. As usual the best rice choices for risotto are Vialone Nano, Carnaroli, or Baldo—Uncle Ben's is unacceptable. Rice variety, quality, and age will determine how much mushroom broth will be absorbed during cooking and total cooking time. Tasting is the only way to know when the rice is done. See page 8 for more risotto information. Butter fans can substitute their favorite lipid for most of the olive oil. But full-flavored Tuscan extra virgin olive oil is a perfect match for woodsy mushrooms. Lazy cooks with wild mushrooms can use highly salted water instead of broth since their intense flavors will take over a risotto.

½ pound wild mushrooms—porcini stems and a few caps
    or ½ pound cultivated mushrooms plus 1 ounce dried
    porcini mushrooms

8 cups mushroom broth (made with 8 cups water, 1 celery
    stalk, 1 carrot, 1 garlic clove, 1 small onion, porcini
    stems and broken caps or a few dried porcini and
    strained mushroom soaking water) or 6 cups of water
    and vegetables or 8 cups boiling water, lightly salted

6 tablespoons extra virgin olive oil or 4 tablespoons extra
    virgin olive oil and 2 tablespoons butter

Coarse sea salt

Freshly ground black pepper

1 garlic clove, minced

¼ cup minced onion or shallot

1 cup Vialone Nano, Carnaroli, or Baldo rice

½ cup dry white wine

¼ cup grated Parmigiano-Reggiano plus additional for
    topping risotto

1 Clean the mushrooms and separate the caps from the stems. Save a few stems and broken caps to flavor the broth.

2 If you are using dried mushrooms soak them in 2 cups of hot water for 30 minutes. Rinse the reconstituted mushrooms under running water to eliminate any remaining soil. Strain the soaking water and save.

3 Make the mushroom broth with 8 cups of water, celery, carrot, garlic, onion, and a few mushroom stems and broken caps. If you are using dried porcini use 6 cups of water and a few soaked and cleaned dried porcini with their strained soaking liquid. Simmer for 20 minutes. Lightly salt.

4 Slice the mushroom caps. Heat 2 tablespoons extra virgin olive oil in a large nonstick skillet and cook the sliced mushrooms over high heat, shaking the pan, to brown. Season with salt and pepper, remove the skillet from the heat, and reserve.

5 Put the garlic and onion in a heavy-bottomed 4-quart pot, pour 2 tablespoons of extra virgin olive oil over the onion, stir to coat, and place over low heat. Cook for 10 minutes, until onions are tender but not browned.

6 Add the rice, stir to coat with the oil, and cook for a few minutes to lightly toast but not brown the rice.

7 Mince the mushroom stems and add to the rice, stirring well to combine. Add the white wine to the rice, stir to mix well, and raise the heat to maximum to evaporate the wine. Add the boiling mushroom broth or lighty salted boiling water or mush-room stock, 1 cup at a time, stirring the bottom of the pot with a *long* wooden spoon or fork, over highest heat, boiling madly. Risotto attains the temperature of molten lava! Add more water or broth when the risotto is still surrounded by liquid, slightly soupy and not dried out. After around 10 minutes of cooking begin to add water or broth ½ cup at a time, and continue adding liquid, ½ cup at a time, until rice is cooked another 5–8 minutes.

8 Taste the rice after 15 minutes. It should be firm but not raw inside under tooth since it will still continue cooking for a few more minutes. The liquid should be a lit-tle soupy because the Parmigiano, oil (or butter), and the final whipping will tighten up the sauce.

9 When rice is *al dente* and still surrounded by liquid, which should be opaque, add the mushroom slices, Parmigiano-Reggiano, additional freshly ground pepper, and the remaining extra virgin oil (or 2 tablespoons butter) and stir energetically with a long-handled wooden spoon or fork over high heat for 2 minutes to whip the ingredients together. Remove from the heat, ladle into individual bowls, and let the risotto rest for a minute before serving. Top with additional grated Parmigiano-Reggiano.

Pasta with Mushroom
and Chicken Liver Sauce

*I*talians feel strongly about Sunday lunch, an important meal to be consumed
with family members at home or in a country restaurant. When I lived in Rome
we frequently dined on Sunday at a trattoria in a cave in the village of Sacrofano,
outside the historic center and urban sprawl of Rome. The meal was always the
same—no menu and then waiters didn't bother asking what anyone wanted but
simply plunked down home-bottled wine and platters of cured meat, bowls of
olives, and toasted garlic bread drizzled with olive oil shortly after diners were
seated. Squared-off strands of pasta, *tonnarelli*, were always served with a minced
mushroom and chicken liver sauce, topped with a sprinkle of grated Pecorino
Romano cheese. The meal progressed with a selection of grilled meats and fire-
place-baked potatoes and always concluded with a bottle of dark sweet wine and a
whole plate-sized *ciambella*, a simple but heavy ring cake to be sliced off and dipped
into the wine. I never had any success reproducing the cake but Sacrofano pasta
became part of my repertoire. Vegetarians can leave out the chicken livers.

> ¼ cup extra virgin olive oil
>
> 4 ounces fresh chicken livers
>
> 2 garlic cloves
>
> ½ pound mushrooms
>
> ¼ cup (optional) plus 5–6 quarts water
>
> 2–3 tablespoons sea salt
>
> 14–16 ounces spaghetti
>
> Freshly ground black pepper
>
> ½ cup grated Pecorino Romano

1   Heat 2 tablespoons extra virgin olive oil in a large nonstick skillet and sauté chicken
livers and garlic over moderate heat until the chicken livers are browned. Remove the
chicken livers with a slotted spoon and mince in a food processor.

2   Mince the mushrooms or pulse to fine-chop in 2 or 3 batches in a food processor.
Don't crowd the mushrooms.

3   Add the remaining 2 tablespoons extra virgin olive oil to the skillet and raise the heat
to high. Add the minced mushrooms and cook until they release their juices. Add the

minced chicken livers and cook over low heat for 10 minutes, adding ¼ cup or more of water if the mixture is too dry. The mixture shouldn't be soup. Season with salt and pepper.

4 Bring 5–6 quarts of water to a rolling boil. Add 2–3 tablespoons of salt and the spaghetti.

5 Cook the spaghetti until it still offers considerable resistance to the tooth, about three quarters of the recommended cooking time. Drain, reserving 2 cups of pasta water.

6 Add the spaghetti and 1 cup of pasta water to the sauce in the skillet and cook for 3–5 minutes over high heat until the pasta is done and the sauce is well mixed with the spaghetti. Add more pasta water if the sauce becomes too dry, ¼ cup at a time, to complete the cooking. Pasta should be barely surrounded by sauce. Top with grated Pecorino Romano.

Fabio's Mushroom Soup

For 4–6 Servings   First Course

I grew up on Campbell's cream of mushroom and never realized the full potential of mushroom soup until I swooned over the intensely mushroomy creamless porcini soup at Cibrèo, my favorite restaurant in Florence. Chef-owner Fabio Picchi always has meat broth on hand but I find that the wonderful, woodsy flavor of mushrooms doesn't really need a meaty background. I use mostly stems and unattractive caps of porcini. Cremini mushrooms can be combined with soaked dried porcini to somewhat simulate the flavor of the real thing. The Tuscan herb of choice for wild mushrooms is *nepitella*, wild mint, unavailable outside the Mediterranean as far as I know. Substitute a mixture of oregano and mint to produce a similar flavor.

> ½ pound porcini mushrooms, cut into chunks or
>   ½ cremini mushrooms and 1 ounce dried porcini
>   mushrooms, soaked and cleaned in 2 cups hot water
>
> 1 small onion, chopped
>
> ½ celery stalk, chopped
>
> 1 small carrot, chopped
>
> 2 garlic cloves, chopped
>
> 4 tablespoons extra virgin olive oil
>
> 4 cups water or light homemade meat broth
>
> 1 medium all-purpose potato, peeled and cubed
>   (about 1 cup)
>
> ½ teaspoon fresh oregano, chopped
>
> ¼ teaspoon fresh mint, chopped
>
> Sea salt
>
> Freshly ground black pepper

1   Clean the mushrooms and separate caps from stems. If using dried mushrooms, soak them in 2 cups of hot water for 30 minutes. Rinse the reconstituted mushrooms under running water to eliminate any remaining soil. Strain the soaking water and save.

2   Put the onion, celery, carrot, and garlic in a heavy-bottomed 3-quart pot. Drizzle 2 tablespoons of extra virgin olive oil over the vegetables and stir to coat them with the oil.

3   Place the pot over moderate heat. Cook, stirring frequently, until the vegetables are lightly browned.

4   Add the mushrooms, potatoes, herbs, and boiling water to barely cover. Use mushroom soaking liquid if you have it. Simmer, uncovered, for 15 minutes. Season with salt and pepper.

5   Puree the soup in the food processor or with an immersion hand mixer until creamy and smooth.

6   Serve soup with a drizzle of the remaining extra virgin olive oil as a garnish.

Fabio's Mushroom Caps Baked with Garlic

For 4–6 Servings   **Main Dish**

Why does Fabio Picchi have so many wonderful mushroom recipes? It's probably because beyond the back door of his restaurant Cibrèo stands the Sant'Ambrogio market and Cecco, a porcini mushroom vendor who sells his best stuff to Fabio. And Fabio cooks the best, freshest porcini mushroom caps in aluminum foil packets, a method called *cartoccio*. He saves the stems and smaller mushrooms for the soup on page 206. This is my favorite way to cook large, well-formed mushroom caps, the essence of simplicity and almost no work, more delicate than grilled caps. Garlic slivers are inserted into the upper surface of the mushroom cap, drizzled with extra virgin olive oil, salt, and pepper, enveloped in aluminum foil, and baked in a water bath in a hot oven. Fresh oregano and mint are used instead of unavailable *nepitella to* produce a similar flavor. Fabio serves these mushrooms in their foil packets, which are opened at the table to release an intoxicating aroma of wild mushrooms.

1 pound fresh large mushroom caps, preferably porcini
    although large cultivated cremini or portobello
    mushrooms will do

3–4 garlic cloves, sliced into slivers

2–3 tablespoons extra virgin olive oil

½ teaspoon fresh oregano, chopped

¼ teaspoon fresh mint, chopped

Fine sea salt

Freshly ground black pepper

(continued)

1 Preheat the oven to 475 degrees.

2 Clean the mushroom caps.

3 Make 4 or 5 small incisions in the upper side of each cap with a paring knife. Insert a sliver of garlic in each incision.

4 Place the mushroom caps, gill side down, onto 4–6 pieces of aluminum foil, each around 12 inches in length.

5 Drizzle with extra virgin olive oil. Sprinkle the mushroom caps with the oregano, mint, sea salt, and pepper. Fold the foil over the mushrooms, crimping the edges to seal tightly.

6 Place the foil packets in a roasting pan and pour boiling water in the pan to a depth of 1 inch.

7 Bake the mushroom packets for 15 minutes. Serve the mushrooms in their foil packets and open at the table.

Grilled Big Mushroom Caps

For 4–6 Servings   Main Course

Simply grilled porcini mushrooms studded with slivers of garlic are found throughout mushroom-loving Italy in the spring and the fall, usually served as a main course since the flavors are big and meaty. Porcini mushrooms are a delicacy involving a hunt in the woods, a big expense at the market, and they're treated with respect and the greatest of simplicity. The biggest and best caps are grilled or pan-roasted by cooks without grills. A cast-iron pan with ridges makes attractive grill marks but a nonstick skillet works fine.

> 1 pound large mushroom caps
>
> 3–4 garlic cloves, cut into slivers
>
> 2 tablespoons extra virgin olive oil
>
> Fine sea salt
>
> Freshly ground black pepper

1 Clean the mushroom caps.

2 Make 4 or 5 small incisions in the upper side of each cap with a paring knife. Insert a sliver of garlic in each incision.

3 Lightly oil a large nonstick skillet and place over moderate heat.

4 Place the mushroom caps in one layer, gill sides facing up, in the skillet and cook over high heat for 4–5 minutes to brown. Turn the caps over and cook for 3–4 minutes to brown the other side. Sprinkle with salt and pepper and drizzle with remaining extra virgin olive oil and serve. Or grill over hot coals, gill sides facing up, turn and cook the other side for a few minutes until browned on both sides.

ONIONS, LEEKS, AND SPRING ONIONS

Cipolle, Porri, e Cipolline

*I*t's almost impossible to cook Italian without the onion, *cipolla*. It plays an important supporting role in most kitchens but occasionally moves to center stage with exciting results. Yellow or red onions, cured after harvesting to dry skins, are found all year in Italian regional markets. Leeks are found in the winter, replaced in the spring with white or pink-tinged just-formed onion bulbs smaller than golf balls on still-green stems, a seasonal treat.

The onion, *Allium cepa*, is a herbaceous biennial plant of the lily family that flowers in the summer, forming an attractive puffy ball that smells like onion. Leaves are cylindrical and hollow, bulbs are formed underground by scales surrounding a short stem. Some onion varieties are harvested immature, smaller than ripe onions, tender-skinned, delicately flavored, although spring onions have their own cultivars. The scent of onions makes cooks weep but onion vapors are water soluble and lessened by cool temperatures. Refrigerate or soak in cool water to cut down on tears. My editor advises me that onion vapors seek a moist warm place and if you stick out your tongue when chopping onions the tear-provoking vapors won't reach the eyes. Michael Jordan would approve.

The onion has been a Mediterranean staple from prehistory, but its origins are central Asian. It was an Egyptian object of worship, esteemed by Greeks and Romans in spite of a low-life reputation and pungent scent. Onions are depicted in the Etruscan tomb frescoes of Ceveteri, outside Rome. According to a folktale related by German etymologist Victor Hehn, when Greeks landed in Sicily they encountered the local Sikel tribe, to whom they promised peace as long as their heads were on their shoulders, as long as the land was under their feet. Unbeknownst to the Sikels, the wily Greeks had placed sand in their shoes and "heads" of onion on their shoulders under their shirts. Removing sand (land) and onions (heads), the Greeks proceeded to invade and conquer the unsuspecting Sikels. Blame it on the onion.

Although most Italian medieval and Renaissance botanical and culinary texts mention onions as an ingredient, its importance increased in the eighteenth and nineteenth centuries because the use of spices declined and cooks required something to augment the flavor of the dishes.

Ancient medical advice from Hippocrates and Pliny recommends onion for poor vision, baldness, insomnia, toothache, insect bites, worms, and as a cure

ONIONS, LEEKS, AND SPRING ONIONS

for hemorrhoids, applied locally. Late medieval doctors felt that raw onions for breakfast were effective against the plague. Modern medicine has found that onion, eaten raw, is an anticoagulant, lowers blood pressure and cholesterol, raises HDLs. Raw onion slows the digestion by raising the acidity of gastric juices and is considered an intestinal disinfectant. It's low in calories, mostly water, with moderate amounts of potassium, vitamin C, and folic acid. Friar Foreteller (*Frate Indovino*), a mythical Italian Franciscan monk, ascribes diuretic, digestive, emollient, expectorant, laxative, calming, and hemostatic properties to the onion and recommends rubbing a sliced onion on insect bites to relieve pain.

Italian regional onion cultivars include Milan Copper, Parma Golden, Bassano or Genoa Red, Milan Copper Red, Flat Red Italian, Tropea Red, Florentine Red, Barletta, and May and June spring onions. Scallions are an American import, rarely grown in Italy.

Onions are the backbone of the basic Italian *soffritto*, slowly sautéed in extra virgin olive oil with garlic, celery, and carrot, with or without cured pork, which begins many sauced dishes. Italians bake, stuff, fry, and braise onions, serve them as appetizers, on pasta, as a main dish or condiment. Spring onions are pickled or given a sweet-and-sour treatment. Florentines love red onions, and claim that their traditional, onion-based soup, *carabaccia,* was taken to France by Caterina de' Medici and renamed onion soup. The modern version of the soup has spring vegetables like fava beans and peas in addition to onions, toasted bread, and cheese. Torquato Innocenti, my favorite farmer from the Santo Spirito market, and his son sell Florentine Red onions and leeks and, as usual, have inspirational advice and recipes.

Onions should be firm with smooth, dry skins. Sprouted onions have started to deteriorate and will be soft or rotten inside. Leeks should have fresh-looking green tops and need to be carefully washed since they often have dirt between blanched root-end leaves. Store onions in a cool, dark place.

Some Italian cultivars are sold by American seed companies. White spring Barletta onion seed is available from Shepherd's Garden Seeds, 6116 Highway 9, Felton, California 95018, Telephone: 408–335–6910, Red and Yellow Milan and Red Florence seed from The Cook's Garden, P.O. Box 535, Londonderry, Vermont 05148, Telephone: 802–824–3400.

History

The Roman Apicius wrote an entire book on sauce in the first century, later incorporated in a fourth-century compilation of his recipes, *The Culinary King*. His white sauce for boiled meat combines onion, herbs, pine nuts, spice, wine, and oil, thickened with wet bread, and flavored with *garum* (fermented anchovy sauce). Many of Apicius's vegetable soups and meat preparations utilize onion and a recipe for cooked, drained, and minced lettuce is sauced with raw onion, herbs, wine, and *garum*. Best of all is the marinade for sardines, of pepper, oregano, mint, onions, oil, and vinegar, mercifully without *garum*.

The late fourteenth-century anonymous Venetian *Book for Cook* is the first cookbook to mention quantities and cooking times. The recipes have a distinct Venetian slant, with lots of spice and sweet-and-sour flavors of Eastern trade routes. The recipe for *cisame*, a sweet-and-sour sauce for fish, made of onions, vinegar, almonds, raisins, and strong spice and honey sounds like the Venetian *saor* treatment. See page 265 for the unsweetened, unspiced version that dresses eggplant.

In cultivated Renaissance-style, Bronzino (1503–72), famed Florentine Mannerist and Medici court painter, wrote rustic, somewhat silly poetry dedicated to the frying pan, freshly curdled cheese, and the onion. He rhymes enthusiastically about onions, "recommended with all animals domestic or wild" and excessively claims that "Every sweetness is left behind, when cooked in the oven to make a salad, a salad of chopped onion with purslane and cucumbers, better than all other pleasure of this life..."

Domenico Romoli, known as Panunto, "The Oily Slice," as grilled olive-oiled bread is called in Florence, wrote *The Singular Doctrine* in 1560. He claims that onions "stimulate the appetite for coitus, produce headaches and increase sperm production" when eaten raw with vinegar, but are hard to digest. These dangers, according to Romoli, disappear with cooking.

Costanzo Felici's 1569 *Of Salad and Plants Used by Man as Food*, a lengthy letter to illustrious doctor and naturalist Ulisse Aldrovandi, takes onion seriously. "In all seasons of the year, fresh or aged, perfect and with leaves, cooked and raw, in salads, paired with bread, as a condiment, in soups and tarts and many other kinds of food useful for human fare, the onion is first..." Felici claims that onion incites taste, cuts through phlegm in the body, and removes great harm from many foods.

Vincenzo Tanara's *The Citizen's Economy in Villa* (1657), a bestselling (16 printings!) book of agrarian advice, pays a lot of attention to onions. He describes health benefits and dozens of methods for cooking onions. The best and easiest is cooked under embers, dressed with oil, vinegar, salt, pepper, and *agresto*, lightly acidic cooked vinegar.

Of Pythagorean Food (1781) by Vincenzo Corrado eliminates hunks of meat and enlarges the vegetable chapter of his previously published bestseller, *The Gallant Cook* (1773), looking for another hit by capitalizing on the rage among nobles for classical philosophy. Corrado doesn't take Pythagoras's orthodox vegetarian regime too seriously and recipes contain meat, poultry, prosciutto, fish, broths, dairy products, and eggs. Onion is ". . . very greatly used in all kitchens, for without weepy onions chefs can't cook." True to his word, Corrado distinguishes his readers with 13 recipes, including the ambiguously all-purpose "In various manners, hollowed, cooked with woodcocks, sweetbreads and similar, fat or lean." Onions are parboiled, floured, dipped in egg, bread crumbs, and grated cheese and deep-fried, then used to garnish vegetable purees. Pythagoras wouldn't have approved.

Onion, Leek, and Spring Onion Recipes

WHOLE ROASTED ONIONS
Baked in the skin, dressed with balsamic vinegar

———

CESARE'S NO-TEARS STUFFED ONIONS
Twice-baked onions, stuffed with cheese and maybe a little truffle paste

———

ENZO'S HERRING AND ONION SALAD
Insalata di Aringa
Boned smoked herring marinated with red onions, carrots, celery, and bay leaves

———

TORQUATO'S RED ONION STEAKS
Thick slices of red onions are dipped in egg and pan-fried

———

AUNT ENZA'S GREEN SAUCE
Parsley flavored with onion, anchovy, hard-boiled egg, and capers, glued together with extra virgin olive oil

———

LIVIA'S GENOA MACARONI FOR ARISTOCRATS AND POOR FOLKS
Maccheroni alla Genovese
Pasta sauced with braised onions, with or without meat

PICKLED ONION-CAPER CONDIMENT FOR FAVA BEAN PUREE
Lightly marinated sliced red onions and capers

———

"HIT A LITTLE" BOILED BEEF AND ONIONS
Leftover boiled beef with tomato, onions, and red wine

———

TORQUATO'S ROAST LEEKS

———

TORQUATO'S LEEK AND BEAN SOUP

———

TORQUATO'S LEEK AND SAUSAGE *FARINATA*
Creamy cornmeal soup flavored with leeks and sausage

———

PENNE SAUCED WITH LEEKS AND LEMON
Leeks, lemon zest, and extra virgin olive oil sauce pasta

———

AIMO AND NADIA'S SPRING ONION SPAGHETTI
Spaghetti con Cipolotti
Pasta with a sweet scallion and barely tomato sauce

Whole Roasted Onions

*O*nions are roasted whole, unpeeled, in the oven, in front of a kitchen hearth or buried in embers in a one-ingredient, one-step recipe. It's the onion version of the baked potato, a traditional treatment mentioned in dozens of culinary texts but somehow totally ignored by restaurants. It must be one of the world's easiest recipes, with no peeling or preparation—onions are simply popped in the oven, cooked along with almost anything else that has to bake for at least 45 minutes. Thus prepared, onions are ready to be squeezed from their skins and dressed with extra virgin olive oil, salt, and pepper. Balsamic vinegar is often paired with onions, a classic and wonderful combination. Those lucky enough to have aged (and expensive but a little goes a long way) traditional balsamic vinegar can skip the recipe step to reduce the vinegar but everyone else should make a reduction of the commercial balsamic vinegar found on most supermarket shelves, concentrating flavors and producing a syrupy balsamic that more closely resembles the real stuff.

4 large red or yellow onions, unpeeled

¼ cup plus 1 teaspoon commercial balsamic vinegar or 2 teaspoons traditional balsamic vinegar (optional)

2 tablespoons extra virgin olive oil

Fine sea salt

Freshly ground black pepper

1 Preheat the oven to 400 degrees. Line an ovenproof pan with foil.

2 Bake the onions in the prepared pan for 45 minutes or until tender when pierced with a toothpick. Cool onions until easily handled.

3 While the onions are baking, cook ¼ cup commercial balsamic vinegar in a small saucepan for 5–6 minutes over high heat, reducing the vinegar by half to make a light syrup. Add 1 teaspoon commercial balsamic vinegar, stir, and cool.

4 When the onions are cool enough to handle, pull the root ends from each onion. Holding the onion in one hand, gently squeeze so that the cooked onion pops out of the skin in 1 piece from the root end. Cut each onion in half and then into wedges.

5 Dress the onion wedges with traditional balsamic vinegar or the reduced balsamic mixture, extra virgin olive oil, salt, and pepper. Serve warm or at room temperature.

Cesare's No-Tears Stuffed Onions

*B*aked yellow onions are sold in produce shops throughout Piedmont, a wonderful shortcut for making stuffed onions and a sign of the esteem in which they're held. Traditional stuffings are usually based on meat, but Cesare Giaccone, chef and owner of the Ristorante da Cesare in Albaretto della Torre, has lightened up the preparation with a Parmigiano cheese sauce flavored with white truffle crumbs. Cesare's cooking is local, tied to ingredients from the surrounding countryside, utilized with great style, and he uses white truffles with abandon during their brief, glorious season in the early winter. Home cooks outside truffle country can add a little truffle paste but this dish works well without any truffles too. Onion skins serve as an attractive shell for a cheese and onion filling, easier than most stuffed onion recipes because the onions aren't scooped out raw.

> 6 medium-sized yellow onions, unpeeled
>
> ¾ cup milk
>
> 1 tablespoon butter
>
> 4 teaspoons flour
>
> ¾ cup grated Parmigiano
>
> Coarse sea salt, plus 1 cup sea salt for baking stuffed
>   onions
>
> Freshly ground black pepper
>
> 1–2 tablespoons truffle paste (optional)

1 Preheat the oven to 400 degrees. Line an ovenproof pan with foil.

2 Bake the onions in the prepared pan for 45 minutes or until tender when pierced with a toothpick. Cool onions until you can handle them easily.

3 While the onions cool make a béchamel sauce. Heat the milk. Melt the butter in a small saucepan, add the flour, and cook over low heat for 2–3 minutes, stirring with a small whisk. Add the hot milk to the flour and butter mixture and stir with the whisk to thoroughly amalgamate. Cook over low heat until the sauce is as dense as sour cream. Add the Parmigiano, sea salt, pepper, and truffle paste (optional). Cool the sauce.

4   Pull the root ends from each onion. Holding the onion in one hand, gently squeeze so that the cooked onion pops out of the skin in 1 piece from the root end. Cut the onion at the stem end and re-form the skin, creating a cup.

5   Squeeze any excess liquid from 3 onion centers (save the remaining onion centers for another use). Puree them in the food processor or food mill and add to the béchamel.

6   Pipe the onion béchamel mixture into the onion-skin cups with a pastry bag or plastic bag with a ½-inch corner cut off.

7   Sprinkle a ¼-inch layer of coarse salt so that onions don't tip over into 6 individual ramekins and place the filled onions on top of the salt.

8   Bake the onions for 15–20 minutes or until browned. Serve hot.

ONIONS, LEEKS, AND SPRING ONIONS

Enzo's Herring and Onion Salad
Insalata di Aringa

*M*y husband Massimo's father Enzo was a vegetable lover. He stalked wild greens with strange names and bitter flavors that we ate minimally dressed with extra virgin olive oil and salt, without the distraction of vinegar. He would often arrive with unexpected bounty, gifts from friends in the country or irresistible items from the San Lorenzo market near where he worked. I grew up loving herring in cream sauce but it was love at first bite when I tasted my Enzo's marinated herring, a salad with the fresh crunch of carrots and celery, lightly pickled red onions, and extra virgin olive oil paired with the fishy smoky flavors of herring.

Herring is skinned, boned, and marinated in milk for 12 hours. Those lucky enough to find quality boned herring will have an easy time with this recipe. It should be prepared a day in advance since marinating is required.

> 2 whole smoked herring or 8 herring fillets
>
> 1½ cups milk
>
> 1 large red onion, coarsely chopped
>
> 2 tablespoons red wine vinegar
>
> 2 celery stalks, diced
>
> 2 carrots, diced
>
> 2 bay leaves
>
> 1 tablespoon black peppercorns, lightly cracked
>
> ¾ cup extra virgin olive oil

1 Roast the herring briefly over an open flame or hot electric burner to loosen the skin. Remove the skin and bone the herring. Or buy herring fillets.

2 Place the herring fillets in a glass bowl, cover with milk, cover the bowl with plastic wrap, and refrigerate for 12 hours or overnight.

3 Drain the herring fillets, rinse with cold water, and pat dry with paper towels.

4 Marinate the chopped onion with the vinegar for at least 15 minutes and drain.

5 Cut the herring fillets into ½-inch chunks and combine with the onions and the remaining ingredients. Marinate for at least 2 hours unrefrigerated. This salad will keep for a few days in the refrigerator if covered with olive oil. Remove bay leaves before serving.

Torquato's Red Onion Steaks

*T*orquato always has a case of red onions, a Florentine favorite, and some terrific nutritional and culinary advice about them. "They're good for the blood, diuretic, and are tasty fried, better than steak," says Torquato, who recommends lightly flouring thick onion slices, dipping them in beaten egg, and frying the "steaks" in extra virgin olive oil.

> **2–3 large red onions**
> **½ cup extra virgin olive oil**
> **1 egg, lightly beaten on a saucer**
> **Fine sea salt**
> **Freshly ground pepper**
> **Flour for dredging**

1　Cut the onions into ½-inch-thick slices.

2　Heat ¼ cup extra virgin olive oil in a large skillet until hot.

3　Beat the egg with the fine sea salt and pepper.

4　Dredge 5–6 onion slices in the flour, dip them in the beaten egg, and fry them in the extra virgin olive oil until brown, around 5 minutes. Turn the slices over, brown on the other side. Remove from the pan with a slotted spoon, drain on a paper towel, and keep warm. Add the remaining oil to the skillet and prepare the remaining onion slices in the same manner. Sprinkle with salt before serving. Serve immediately.

ONIONS, LEEKS, AND SPRING ONIONS

RED, WHITE & GREENS

Aunt Enza's Green Sauce

Makes About 1½ Cups Green Sauce   Condiment

*M*y husband Massimo's aunt Enza's cooking is Florentine with an occasional novelty picked up from the recipe section of a Franciscan calendar that hangs in her kitchen. My whole family loves her green sauce, *salsa verde*, which varies from the Italian classic of parsley, onion, anchovies, capers, and plenty of extra virgin olive oil. Aunt Enza's *salsa verde* has a chopped hard-boiled egg to give it body and it's more like paste than sauce. She serves it as a condiment for boiled meats but I use it with grilled fish or spread on small pieces of toasted country bread. All ingredients are finely minced, which Aunt Enza does by hand although a food processor does a great job. Her green sauce is glued together with first-rate extra virgin olive oil, the only kind that Aunt Enza has in her kitchen.

Torquato, my favorite farmer and recipe consultant at the nearby Santo Spirito market, suggests using arugula combined with parsley for a variation on a classic.

½ slice of stale bread

2 tablespoons salted capers

2 cups water

¾ cup Italian parsley or ½ cup parsley and ¼ cup arugula
    leaves, whole, packed in a measuring cup

½ medium red onion

2–3 anchovy fillets

½–¾ cup extra virgin olive oil

½ teaspoon red wine vinegar

1 hard-boiled egg

Fine sea salt (optional)

Freshly ground black pepper

1 Soak the bread in water, squeeze the water out, and measure 2 tablespoons of squeezed, soaked bread.

2 Soak the capers in 2 cups of water for at least 30 minutes to remove excess salt. Drain the capers and pat dry to remove excess moisture.

3 Process the capers, parsley (and/or arugula), onion, anchovy fillets, and damp bread until finely minced. Add the extra virgin olive oil and wine vinegar and combine well. Add the hard-boiled egg, quartered, and pulse to chop. Taste and season with salt, if necessary, and pepper. This sauce will keep for a few days in the refrigerator.

Livia's Genoa Macaroni for Aristocrats and Poor Folks
Maccheroni alla Genovese

For 4–6 Servings   **First Course (and Main Dish)**

*T*he narrow winding road to the restaurant Don Alfonso is flanked by hills of olive trees, lemon groves, small vegetable gardens with bamboo-staked tomatoes, bushy artichoke plants, rows of spiky onion and garlic plants, all important ingredients in local cooking. Livia and her husband, Alfonso Iaccarino, own the restaurant Don Alfonso in the tiny village of Sant'Agata sui Due Golfi, which overlooks the bays of Naples and Salerno. Don Alfonso serves fancy food like lobster and foie gras and covers food with silver domes, uncovered in unison, the kind of behavior that pleases most gastronomic guidebooks. But they haven't forgotten about traditional dishes that Livia describes with greater enthusiasm as she is always excited by her native cuisine. I fell in love with Don Alfonso's *maccheroni alla genovese*, Genoa-style short pasta, and was hooked by Livia's story of two distinctly different versions. Aristocrats ate beef braised for hours with onions, turning the onions into a creamy sauce; impoverished cooks made the same dish without the meat. Both social classes used the sauce to dress short pasta like rigatoni. Jeanne Carola Francesconi, in *La Cucina Napoletana*, claims it was served by Genovese cooks who established trattorie in Naples in the seventeenth century. The meatless version, clearly my favorite, is served at Don Alfonso but they've mercifully replaced the traditional lard with extra virgin olive oil, a move I applaud. Most Neapolitans say this dish is difficult to digest and recommend eating it for lunch.

3 pounds beef rump or bottom round roast (optional)

¼ cup extra virgin olive oil or lard

4 large red onions, chopped

1 celery stalk, chopped

1 small carrot, chopped

1 tablespoon chopped parsley

1 cup white wine

Coarse sea salt plus 2–3 tablespoons salt

Freshly ground black pepper

5–6 quarts water

14–16 ounces rigatoni

¼–½ cup grated Parmigiano

(continued)

1 Brown the meat, if you are using it, in a large heavy-bottomed pot with the extra virgin olive oil. Remove the meat from the pot with a slotted spoon and reserve.

2 Put the onion, celery, carrot, and parsley in the pot, drizzle with the extra virgin olive oil for the meatless version, stir to coat the vegetables with oil, and cook over low heat, stirring occasionally, for 15 minutes or until the vegetables are tender.

3 Add the optional meat and wine, season with salt and pepper, and cook, tightly covered, for 2–3 hours or until the meat is tender and/or the onions have turned into a cream. Remove the meat and keep warm. Measure the onion sauce and return 2 cups of sauce to the pot. Reserve the remaining sauce.

4 Bring a pot of 5–6 quarts of water to a rolling boil. Add 2–3 tablespoons of salt and the pasta.

5 Cook the pasta until it still offers considerable resistance to the tooth, about three quarters of the recommended cooking time. Drain, reserving 2 cups of pasta water.

6 Add the pasta and ½ cup pasta water to the sauce in the pot and cook for about 5 minutes over high heat until pasta is done and sauce is well mixed with the pasta. Add more pasta water if sauce becomes too dry, ¼ cup at a time, to complete cooking.

7 Top with grated cheese. Aristocrats and meat lovers should serve the braised beef with some of the onion sauce as a main dish.

Note: The meatless version of this dish is simply a braised onion sauce flavored with celery, carrots, parsley and wine, cooked about 2-3 hours until they turn into a cream.

Pickled Onion-Caper Condiment
for Fava Bean Puree

For 4–6 Servings   Condiment

*I*n the area of Martina Franca in Apulia, fava bean puree becomes a whole meal when served with a series of side dishes like sun-dried tomatoes, pickled eggplant, peppers and artichoke hearts, boiled chicory, and this pickled onion and caper condiment that I fell in love with. It may seem like a minor element on the plate but the crunchy acid onion, creamy fava puree, and bitter greens are a fantastic combination. Use this pickled onion condiment with boiled potatoes, grilled meats, or fish.

> 1 large red onion, thinly sliced
>
> 2 tablespoons capers, preferably salt-packed,
>   soaked and rinsed
>
> Vinegar
>
> Fine sea salt
>
> Freshly ground black pepper

1 Combine all the ingredients and marinate for at least 15 minutes or up to 6 hours. Drain the vinegar and serve.

ONIONS, LEEKS, AND SPRING ONIONS

"Hit a Little" Boiled Beef and Onions

For 4–6 Servings   **Main Course**

*P*icchiapo, translated literally means "hit a little," is a traditional Roman home-style dish that I learned in the kitchen of Ristorante Silvano Paris in Trastevere over 25 years ago. It was made with beef boiled for stock and never appeared on the menu, too humble for a restaurant, but perfect for the staff lunch, where I picked up some of my favorite recipes. When I moved to Florence I found the same dish with a totally different name, *francesina*. Both versions solve the problem of what to do with leftover beef, and will probably please diners who usually don't like boiled meat. Even my son Max likes it.

> 1 pound boiled beef (leftovers are fine)
> 3 large red onions, sliced
> 3 tablespoons extra virgin olive oil
> ½–1 cup beef broth
> ½ cup tomato pulp, fresh or canned
> ½ cup red wine
> Coarse sea salt
> Freshly ground black pepper

1 Cut the boiled beef into bite-sized pieces.

2 Place the onions in a large nonstick skillet. Drizzle with the extra virgin olive oil and stir to coat the vegetables with the oil. Cook over moderate heat for 10 minutes or until the onions have wilted.

3 Add the beef, ¼ cup broth, tomato pulp, red wine, salt, and pepper and simmer, stirring occasionally, over low heat for 15–20 minutes. If the sauce dries out, add more broth, ¼ cup at a time. Serve hot.

Torquato's Roast Leeks

"*T*hey're the asparagus of the winter" was Torquato's sales pitch one morning for a pile of fantastic-looking leeks, one of his best winter vegetables. As usual Torquato Innocenti and his son, Valerio, my favorite farmers at the outdoor Santo Spirito market, were full of wonderful recipes for their bounty. "Roast them like asparagus, in a pan, with oil" was the extent of Torquato's recipe, too easy to ignore. "Save the green tips for soup or a *frittata*." Mediterranean cooking expert Paula Wolfert suggested blanching the leeks first, then pan-roasting them, which shortens cooking time and yields more tender leeks.

> 1½ pounds trimmed leeks
>
> 4 quarts water
>
> Fine sea salt
>
> 2 tablespoons extra virgin olive oil
>
> 1 tablespoon minced Italian parsley
>
> Freshly ground black pepper

1 Cut large leeks in half lengthwise. Split smaller leeks three quarters of length, leaving 2 inches of the bulb end intact. Rinse the leeks carefully to eliminate all dirt.

2 Bring 4 quarts of water to a rolling boil, add salt and leeks, and blanch for 4–5 minutes or until just tender. Remove the leeks with a slotted spoon and refresh in cold water. Squeeze the leeks, then blot with paper towels to remove excess water.

3 Put the leeks in a large nonstick skillet, drizzle with extra virgin olive oil, and shake the pan to coat the leeks with the oil.

4 Cook over high heat, turning the leeks until lightly browned. Season with salt and pepper, sprinkle with parsley, and serve hot or at room temperature.

Torquato's Leek and Bean Soup

*T*his is the soup that uses up the green tips of the leeks that Torquato is always telling me to save. It has an even better flavor than leek and potato soup and is easy to make, especially if you've got some cooked beans on hand. Good-quality canned beans can be substituted by cooks in a hurry.

> 1 pound leeks
>
> 4 cups bean broth from homemade beans (not canned),
>   homemade stock, or lightly salted water
>   (or any combination)
>
> 1 teaspoon fresh sage, minced
>
> 3 tablespoons extra virgin olive oil plus more for garnish
>
> 2 cups cooked white beans
>
> Coarse sea salt
>
> Freshly ground black pepper

1   Trim the roots from the end of the leeks and peel off the tough outer leaves. Cut off the green tops. Slice leeks in half lengthwise and carefully rinse in warm water to eliminate all dirt between the leaves.

2   Simmer the leek greens and trimmings in 4 cups liquid (bean broth, homemade stock, or lightly salted water) for 20 minutes. Remove leek trimmings with a slotted spoon and discard.

3   Thinly slice the white part of the leeks.

4   Put the leeks and the sage in a heavy-bottomed 3-quart pot, drizzle with the extra virgin olive oil, and stir to coat.

5   Cook the leeks over moderate heat for 10 minutes, stirring occasionally.

6   Add the beans, 3 cups of leek broth, salt, and pepper and simmer for 15 minutes.

7   Puree one third of the soup in a food processor until smooth and add back to the rest of the soup.

8   Serve with a drizzle of extra virgin olive oil and freshly ground pepper.

Torquato's Leek and Sausage *Farinata*

For 4–6 Servings   **First Course**

"Have you ever had *farinata*, a polenta soup, with leeks and sausage?" asked Torquato. Polenta fans will enjoy the recipe that he related, a wonderful marketing technique that sent me straight to my kitchen. I bought the leeks, stopped off at the butcher shop for fresh sausage, and reproduced Torquato's recipe for dinner with positive results.

> 2 leeks, about 2 cups chopped
>
> 6 cups water
>
> 1–2 teaspoons salt
>
> 1 cup cornmeal
>
> 1 pound sausage, casing removed
>
> 3 tablespoons extra virgin olive oil plus more for garnish
>
> Freshly ground black pepper
>
> ½ cup grated Parmigiano-Reggiano

1 Trim the roots from the end of the leeks and peel off the tough outer leaves. Cut off the green tops and save for soup (see page 226). Slice the leeks in half and carefully rinse in warm water to eliminate all dirt between the leaves. Cut the leeks into ½-inch slices.

2 Bring 6 cups of water to a rolling boil in a 3-quart pot. Add 1–2 teaspoons salt and sprinkle the cornmeal into the water, stirring with a whisk to prevent lumping. Place the pot in another, larger pot of boiling water (or the bottom of a double boiler over boiling water) and cook over low heat for 45 minutes or until creamy.

3 While the polenta is cooking, sauté the sausage over high heat in a large nonstick skillet, mashing with a wooden spoon to crumble the sausage. Remove the sausage with a slotted spoon and add to the polenta. Traditionalists will utilize the fat rendered by the sausage but I throw it out.

4 Place the leeks in the skillet, drizzle with extra virgin olive oil (or use sausage fat), and cook over low heat for 10 minutes or until soft.

5 Add the leeks to the polenta and continue cooking until the *farinata* is done, 45 minutes in all.

6 Ladle the *farinata* into soup bowls and top each bowl with a sprinkle of grated cheese, a drizzle of extra virgin olive oil, and a few twists of freshly ground pepper.

Penne Sauced with Leeks and Lemon

For 4–6 Servings   **First Course**

*C*ountess Lisa Contini is one of the greatest home-cooks in Tuscany. She cooks lunch for her family and guests, always a crowd at Tenuta di Capezzana, the Contini family's estate that produces fine wine and extra virgin olive oil in the hills west of Florence. She served me pasta flavored with lemon peel and herbs a few years ago, such a winning combination that I added it to my asparagus sauce. If leeks are the asparagus of the winter, as Torquato claims, it makes perfect sense to use them for this sauce. Leeks are boiled, then pureed with lemon peel and parsley, whipped with extra virgin olive oil, finished with thinly sliced shreds of leek for a nontraditional but tasty sauce for short pasta.

> **4–6 trimmed medium leeks**
>
> **1 tablespoon lemon juice**
>
> **5–6 quarts plus 1–2 cups water**
>
> **2–3 tablespoons salt**
>
> **1 teaspoon minced lemon zest**
>
> **1 tablespoon chopped Italian parsley**
>
> **¼ cup quality extra virgin olive oil**
>
> **Sea salt**
>
> **Freshly ground black pepper**
>
> **14–16 ounces penne or other short pasta**
>
> **½ cup grated Parmigiano**

1   Remove the roots and any tough bruised outer leek leaves. Split each leek in half lengthwise and rinse carefully to eliminate any dirt between the leaves. Slice a small piece of leek into the thinnest possible half-rings to make ¼ cup and toss with the lemon juice. Set aside.

2   Bring 5–6 quarts of water to a rolling boil, add 2–3 tablespoons salt, and cook the split leeks for 6–8 minutes until soft, totally tender. Remove the leeks from the pot with a slotted spoon, refresh in cold water, drain, and squeeze lightly to remove excess water. Reserve the leek cooking water.

3   Puree the leeks in a food processor with lemon zest, parsley, extra virgin olive oil, ½ cup leek cooking water, salt, and pepper; transfer the sauce to a 3-quart pot.

4   Add 1–2 cups water to the leek cooking water and return it to a rolling boil. Add the pasta and cook until it still offers considerable resistance to the tooth, around three quarters of the recommended cooking time. Drain, reserving 2 cups of pasta water. Add the pasta, ½ cup pasta water, and the marinated leek rings, drained, to the leek puree in the pot and cook over highest heat for 3–5 minutes until the pasta is almost cooked and the sauce coats the pasta. Add more pasta water, ¼ cup at a time, if sauce gets too dry. Sauce should surround pasta but be slightly liquid since cheese will thicken it.

5   Add grated Parmigiano-Reggiano, heat for an additional minute to melt the cheese, and serve immediately.

Aimo and Nadia's Spring Onion Spaghetti
Spaghetti con Cipolotti

For 4–6 Servings   **First Course**

*T*he restaurant Aimo and Nadia is inconveniently located, a distant cab ride
through the ugly suburbs of Milan. It was once an unattractive Tuscan trattoria that served some of the best food in Italy, simple but elegant, relying on first-
rate seasonal ingredients. But Aimo and Nadia upgraded to full-fledged restaurant
status over 10 years ago, with silver service plates, crocheted doilies, cloches lifted
in unison, all the things I dislike about fancy dining. But in spite of the formal
decor and ambiance, Nadia's food under the cloches is still the same, irresistible.
The menu always has new and interesting dishes but Aimo knows that I simply
have to have a taste of spaghetti sauced with spring onions. I had to beg for the
recipe but it was worth it.

Aimo uses spring onions, which look like scallions with bulb bottoms. They're
sliced very fine but I've never found anything that resembled even a tiny piece of
onion and felt the sauce had the smooth texture of a puree. I tried whipping the
cooked spring onions with the additional extra virgin olive oil and the resulting
sauce was creamy. Both versions have their merits.

6 tablespoons extra virgin olive oil

2 fresh bay leaves

1 sprig fresh thyme, minced

1 sprig fresh oregano, minced

3 garlic cloves, minced

1 pound scallions or spring onions, white part only, sliced
    as thin as possible

½ teaspoon chopped fresh hot red pepper

½ cup fresh ripe tomato pulp (peeled, seeded, and
    chopped tomatoes with juice)

1 cup vegetable broth, made with scallion greens, 1 bay
    leaf, and any vegetable trimmings on hand

5–6 quarts water

2–3 tablespoons salt

14 ounces spaghetti

6 basil leaves, cut into thin strips

1 Heat 3 tablespoons extra virgin olive oil in a large nonstick skillet over low heat and add the bay leaves, thyme, and oregano. Cook for a minute or two.

2 Add the garlic, scallions, and hot pepper and cook for 10 minutes or until the scallions are soft.

3 Add the tomatoes and ½ cup vegetable broth and simmer for 5 minutes. Add more broth if the sauce appears too dry. (Puree the sauce if desired and return it to the skillet.)

4 While the sauce is cooking bring 5–6 quarts of water to a rolling boil. Add 2–3 tablespoons salt and the spaghetti.

5 Cook the spaghetti until it still offers considerable resistance to the tooth, around three quarters of the recommended cooking time. Drain, reserving 2 cups of pasta water.

6 Add the spaghetti and 1 cup pasta water to the sauce in the skillet and cook for 3–5 minutes over high heat until the pasta is done and the sauce is well mixed with the spaghetti. Add more pasta water, ¼ cup at a time, if the sauce becomes too dry, to complete the cooking.

7 Divide the pasta into 4–6 portions and top each with a few basil strips and some of the remaining extra virgin olive oil.

PEPPERS: SWEET AND HOT

Peperoni e Peperoncini

*B*ack in the dark age of vegetables before the 1980s, peppers were green, eaten raw or subjected to a rice and meat stuffing. I grew up thinking green referred to color but when I moved to Italy I encountered a world of sweet summer peppers, bright red or yellow, perishable, sold in huge piles in my neighborhood market. They were distinctively flavored, sensuously textured, light-years beyond the undeveloped tastes of early-harvested immature green peppers. And I found hyper-red, horn-shaped hot peppers sold fresh in the late summer and fall, threaded into strands to be dried and used during the rest of the year.

Peppers are another New World import from the dangerous but exciting nightshade or Solanaceae family, of the genus *Capsicum*. On January 2, 1493, Columbus wrote in his diary of all sizes, shapes, and colors of ". . . their pepper, of a quality better than pepper and no one eats without it, finding it beneficial to health. In Hispaniola we could load 50 caravels a year . . ." Unfortunately for Columbus the plant was well suited to the Mediterranean climate, eliminating the need for New World pepper trade. They were grown as a domestic alternative to expensive, imported pepper and, as a cheap local surrogate, got no attention in cookbooks or from court chefs. Doctors, however, viewed them as powerful medicine.

Peppers are mostly water and therefore low in calories. They have lots of vitamins A and C and folic acid and are high in fiber. According to folk medicine, hot peppers improve digestion and, applied externally, alleviate muscular pain. They're analgesic, antibiotic, anticoagulant, antioxidant. Capsaicin, an essential oil contained in peppers, causes the burning sensation and stimulates the brain to secrete endorphin, which blocks pain and induces euphoria. Hot pepper may be a dieter's best friend because it speeds up metabolism and calories are burned faster. Friar Foreteller, *Frate Indovino*, a mythical Italian Franciscan monk whose yearly calendar is filled with folk wisdom, name days, religious holidays, recipes, home cures, and gardening tips attributes diuretic, antirheumatic, and analgesic powers to peppers. He's got home remedies with hot peppers in different forms: infusions for diarrhea, cough, arthritis, and sea sickness, tincture for muscular pain and swelling, pomade for chilblain, rheumatism, and neuralgia. Hot pepper is ". . . above all a remedy for hemorrhoids, used internally or externally, in various preparations."

Black pepper dominates historic Italian cookbooks, which chronicle the cuisine of the rich, who had no need to substitute the New World import for more expensive and therefore more prestigious imports. So peppers don't get any good press until the late 1700s.

Sweet peppers are grown in most of Italy. Cultivars include the Asti square, Cuneo "meaty," bull's horn, long Marconi, Calabria green. Out-of-the-way villages grow local varieties available regionally but not nationally. Italians roast and peel peppers, then dress them with extra virgin olive oil or stew them with garlic, onion, and tomato. Whole peppers are pickled under grape pomace in northern Piedmont, served with *bagna cauda* (see page 166). Sicilians bake peppers with a bread crumb, pine nut, currant stuffing. Neapolitans stuff peppers with pasta. In the southern region of Basilicata, peppers are dried in the sun, like tomatoes, and used during the winter months, fried in oil until crisp or reconstituted in water, then cooked with scrambled eggs. Sweet green pickling peppers are known as *friarelli* in the Naples area, green cigarettes elsewhere.

Hot red pepper is called *peperoncino* regardless of cultivars. Italy's spiciest pepper is said to be the *diavolillo*, "little devil," small, bright red, and *hot,* a favorite in southern Italy, worn against the evil eye and used to liven up many simple foods.

Gardeners can choose Italian cultivars from Shepherd's Garden Seeds, 6116 Highway 9, Felton, California 95018, Telephone: 408–335–6910, which sells seed for red and yellow Corno di Toro bull's horn sweet peppers; Seeds of Change, P.O. Box 15700, Santa Fe, New Mexico 87506, Telephone: 800–957–3337, has red and yellow Corno di Toro and cherry peppers for stuffing; The Cook's Garden, P.O. Box 535, Londonderry, Vermont 05148, Telephone: 802–824–3400, has Corno di Toro and Marconi sweet pepper seeds; Pinetree Garden Seeds, Box 300, New Gloucester, Maine 04260, Telephone: 207–926–3400, sells seeds for the Corno di Toro; and Nichols Garden Nursery, 1190 North Pacific Highway, Albany, Oregon 97321–4598, Telephone: 503–928–9280, has *peperoncino* and cherry peppers for stuffing.

History

*T*uscan doctor M. Pietro Andrea Mattioli translated classical Greek physician Dioscoride's *Discussions on Material Medicine* in 1557 from Latin to common Italian, adding modern sixteenth-century commentary that includes Italy's first mention of the pepper. Mattioli writes of "Indian pepper . . . long fruits like little horns, green first, red when ripe, that appear to be made of coral . . . each small taste valorously roasts the tongue and palate . . . "

Vincenzo Corrado's 1781 *Of Pythagorean Food* proposes a dietary regime for nobles and literary-minded readers of delicate digestion that includes meat and fish broth, dairy products, and eggs, all out of the question on Pythagoras's fifth-century B.C. animal-rights regime, the original Mediterranean diet. Corrado is the first cookbook author to pay attention to peppers, which he calls *peparoli*. He writes in his introduction that they're ". . . vulgar rustic food but lots of people like them . . . green, fried and sprinkled with salt or cooked over coals, dressed with salt and oil."

Pepper Recipes

STUFFED PEPPER STRIPS INSPIRED
BY ANNA BOLOGNA

—

TUNA AND FIREPLACE
OR STOVE-TOP-GRILLED PEPPERS
Tonno e Peperoni

—

SWEET AND SOUR GREEN PEPPERS
AND RED ONIONS
*Antipasto salad of green peppers
and red onions*

—

FABIO'S YELLOW PEPPER SOUP
Zuppa di Peperoni Gialli

MASSIMO'S STEWED PEPPERS
AND POTATOES *PEPERONATA*
Tuscan version of a Roman classic

—

PEPPER EXTRACT
Concentrato di Peperoni
*Pepper puree slow-baked to
simulate sun-drying of a traditional
Neapolitan condiment*

—

CHICKEN WITH PEPPERS, PIEDMONT-STYLE
*Chicken substitutes for rabbit in a traditional
pepper, red wine, and spice stew*

—

VINCENZO'S SUMMER VEGETABLE *CIAMBOTTA*

Stuffed Pepper Strips
Inspired by Anna Bologna

*A*nna Bologna is a fantastic home-cook and I've been lucky enough to eat in both her dining room and kitchen at Braida, the Bologna family winery. Her husband, Giacomo, a legendary wine maker from the village of Rocchetta Tanara, changed the way the wine world viewed Barbera, once considered nothing more than rustic quaffing wine for local consumption. Giacomo, through careful selection and wood aging, produced a special Barbera of elegance and style along with his everyday easy drinking version known as La Monella as well as sparkling Moscato d'Asti, the most entertaining of dessert wines. His stand at the yearly wine fair in Verona was always crowded with clients and friends who would stop by for a chat and a taste of his wines. And since Italians don't drink without eating a little something, Anna would serve her sensational caper and anchovy-stuffed cherry peppers. I came up with a recipe for those who want to capture the flavor of Anna and Roberto's peppers with ripe bell peppers. Cooks who want to duplicate the real thing will have to grow or get red cherry peppers, poach them whole, and carefully drain. Purists will want to use anchovies packed in salt, rinsed with vinegar, and carefully dried, but canned will do for most. Roberto and Anna both insisted on Sicilian salt-packed capers, rinsed, then dried for a few hours or overnight. Drink the Bologna family's Barbera La Monella or Bricco del Uccellone, eat the peppers, and dream of Piedmont. Serve with country-style bread.

2 large red bell peppers (or 25 cherry peppers)

¾ cup water (optional)

¾ cup red wine, Barbera or Dolcetto

¾ cup red wine vinegar

1 teaspoon coarse sea salt

1 fresh hot pepper or dried chili pepper to taste

24 or more anchovy fillets

2 tablespoons salt-packed capers, unrinsed

½–¾ cup extra virgin olive oil

1   Slice the top and bottom off the bell peppers. Cut the pepper cylinder to form a long rectangle. Cut the peppers into ¾ inch x 3 inch-strips. (Or pull the stems off the cherry peppers, remove the seeds, and core with a melon-baller.)

2   Combine ¾ cup water, the red wine, vinegar, salt, and hot pepper in a small saucepan and bring to a boil. (If using cherry peppers, eliminate the water.)

3   Cook the pepper strips in the boiling liquid for 6–8 minutes or until tender; remove with a slotted spoon and cool. (Cook the cherry peppers for 30 seconds, remove, and cool upside down on paper towels.)

4   Put an anchovy fillet on each pepper strip. Push the end of a toothpick through the anchovy fillet ½ inch from the end of the pepper strip. Put a caper on the toothpick, gently fold the pepper strip, and push the toothpick through the other end. (Or wrap an anchovy around a caper and stuff it inside each cherry pepper.)

5   Marinate the toothpicked pepper strips or stuffed cherry peppers with extra virgin olive oil to cover peppers in a glass container for at least 2 hours. (Cover the stuffed cherry peppers with extra virgin olive oil in a jar. Store in the refrigerator.) Oil left over after serving peppers can be used to dress full-flavored salads. Peppers submerged in oil will last almost indefinitely.

Tuna and Fireplace
or Stovetop-Grilled Peppers
Tonno e Peperoni

For 4–6 Servings   **Appetizer**

I'm lucky—I've got a cooking fireplace in my kitchen. It was one of the features that convinced my husband, Massimo, and me to buy our apartment in the center of Florence. Wood is delivered, up a huge flight of stairs, by short, muscular, red-faced (who wouldn't be) Ernesto, who specializes in combustible deliveries— wood, charcoal, or gas tanks. When I've got a fire going I often roast a few peppers, placed close to the flame on a piece of aluminum foil, turned when they get black and blistered. I also like to cook peppers on my *tostapane*, a stove-top grid that sits directly over a gas burner. Wrap a wire grid or cake cooling rack with a double thickness of aluminum foil and place directly over a gas flame to fill in for the *tostapane*. Peppers can also be grilled over hot coals or on a cast-iron, ridged grill pan, which produces authentic-looking grill marks.   *(continued)*

Grilled peppers are usually marinated with garlic and anchovies but I love the addition of capers and chunks of canned tuna, a classic appetizer from Piedmont. First-rate tuna is a must—the most prized Italian tuna is *ventresca*, belly, usually packed in 1 piece, more like meat than fish. Domestic tuna packed in spring water is unacceptable although leftover grilled tuna marinated with a little extra virgin olive oil can be substituted for canned tuna. Italian tuna is unavailable in the United States.

For a more elegant presentation, cut roasted peppers into 2-inch-wide strips, puree the remaining ingredients, spread a layer of puree on the pepper strips, and roll the pepper strip around the filling.

> 4 red and/or yellow peppers
>
> 2 tablespoons salt-packed capers, soaked and rinsed
>
> 1 garlic clove, minced
>
> 2–3 anchovy fillets, minced
>
> 3–4 tablespoons extra virgin olive oil
>
> 2 tablespoons chopped basil
>
> Fine sea salt
>
> Freshly ground black pepper
>
> 8–10 ounces canned tuna, packed in olive oil, drained (or
>   fresh tuna, poached or grilled)

1 Roast the peppers set on a piece of aluminum foil in front of a fireplace. Or grill over hot coals. Or wrap a wire grid or cake-cooling rack with a double thickness of aluminum foil and place directly over a gas flame. Or use a cast-iron ridged grill pan over high heat. Turn the peppers with tongs when the skin is blackened until the entire pepper is charred.

2 Place the peppers in a plastic bag and cool them until they're easily handled.

3 Peel off the charred skin, discard the seeds, and core. Drain the peppers in a colander but don't rinse with water.

4 Cut the peppers into strips and dress with the capers, garlic, anchovies, extra virgin olive oil, basil, salt, and pepper.

5 Marinate for at least 1 hour or up to 1 day. Sprinkle the peppers with chunks of tuna and serve.

Sweet and Sour Green Peppers
and Red Onions

*E*nzo, who used to be the headwaiter at Cibrèo, contributed quite a few south-ern dishes to my favorite Florentine restaurant. The best is this irresistible appetizer, one of 4 or 5 room-temperature salads that appear on Cibrèo's summer-time menu, perfect for when it's too hot to think about cooking or eating. Green pickling peppers around 3 inches long are used in this dish. Green peppers, cut into strips, can be substituted but should be peeled since they have tougher skins.

> ¾ pound green pickling peppers or green peppers
>
> 3 tablespoons extra virgin olive oil
>
> ½ cup water
>
> 1 teaspoon coarse sea salt
>
> 1 tablespoon sugar
>
> 3 tablespoons red wine vinegar
>
> 1 medium red onion, sliced thin

1 Remove the stems from the pickling peppers. Or peel the green bell peppers with a swivel-bladed vegetable peeler, core, and cut the peppers into strips.

2 Place the stemmed pickling peppers or green pepper strips in a large nonstick skillet, pour 1 tablespoon extra virgin olive oil over the peppers, and stir to lightly coat. Cook over moderately high heat for 5 minutes to lightly brown, stirring often.

3 Add ½ cup water, the salt, sugar, and vinegar, bring to a boil, and transfer the con-tents of the skillet to a serving dish. Mix the onion with the warm peppers, drizzle with remaining extra virgin olive oil, stir to evenly distribute the onions, and cool. Serve at room temperature.

PEPPERS: SWEET AND HOT

RED, WHITE
& GREENS

Fabio's Yellow Pepper Soup
Zuppa di Peperoni Gialli

Fabio Picchi, owner-chef of the restaurant Cibrèo in Florence, cooks like a Tuscan granny. He's never served pasta in his restaurant—not really Tuscan and there was no room on the stove in the tiny kitchen that served both his restaurant and less expensive trattoria. He's enlarged the kitchen but hasn't added pasta to his menu, which features seasonal soups as a first course. But even when yellow peppers aren't in season locally he makes his signature soup, a yellow pepper and potato puree garnished with a sprinkle of Parmigiano and a C-shaped drizzle of extra virgin olive oil. Fabio always has stock on hand but I make his soup with water and don't miss the flavor of meat.

> 1 medium onion, chopped
>
> 1 celery stalk, chopped
>
> 1 carrot, chopped
>
> 2 garlic cloves, chopped
>
> 2 tablespoons extra virgin olive oil plus more for garnish
>
> 1½ pounds yellow peppers, seeded and cut into chunks
>
> ¾ pound potatoes, peeled and cut into chunks
>
> 3 cups boiling water or light stock
>
> 1 tablespoon sea salt
>
> 1 small hot red pepper or 1 pinch chili pepper flakes
>
> 2 tablespoons grated Parmigiano-Reggiano

1 Place the onion, celery, carrot, and garlic in a 4-quart heavy-bottomed pot. Drizzle with extra virgin olive oil, stir to coat, and cook over low heat for 10 minutes or until vegetables are soft.

2 Add the peppers, potatoes, 3 cups of boiling water or stock, salt, and hot pepper. Simmer for 15–20 minutes or until the potatoes are tender. Puree the soup in the food processor or with an immersion mixer until smooth and transfer back to the pot to keep warm.

3 Ladle the soup into bowls and top each with a sprinkle of grated Parmigiano and a C-shaped drizzle of extra virgin olive oil.

Massimo's Stewed Peppers
and Potatoes *Peperonata*

I learned to make *peperonata*, peppers stewed with onions and tomato at the restaurant Silvano Paris over 25 years ago when I first came to Italy. I peeled garlic, cleaned the guts from cases of fresh anchovies, rolled cannelloni, paid attention in the kitchen, and took careful notes. I'd return home to try out my new Roman recipes on Massimo, my super-Tuscan husband. "Where are the potatoes?" he asked when I made the classic Roman version of *peperonata*. "In Tuscany we put chunks of potato in our *peperonata*—much better," he insisted. And he was right.

> 1 large red onion, chopped
>
> 2 garlic cloves, chopped
>
> 3 tablespoons extra virgin olive oil
>
> 4 red and/or yellow bell peppers, seeded and
>   cut into strips
>
> ½ cup tomato pulp
>
> 2 medium potatoes, peeled and cut into ¾-inch cubes
>
> Coarse sea salt
>
> Freshly ground black pepper
>
> ¼ cup boiling water (optional)

1 Put the onion and garlic in a 4-quart heavy-bottomed pot and drizzle with extra virgin olive oil. Stir to coat the vegetables with the oil and place the pot over low heat. Cook the onions for 10 minutes or until soft.

2 Add all remaining ingredients except the water and simmer for 20 minutes or until the potatoes are cooked. The peppers should expel enough liquid to cook the potatoes but if the mixture appears too dry add ¼ cup boiling water. Serve warm or at room temperature.

Pepper Extract
Concentrato di Peperoni

*W*hile tracking down the story of tomato paste in Naples I found a reference for concentrated pepper paste, supposedly an older tradition. According to Jeanne Carola Francesconi's *La Cucina Napoletana*, pepper paste was used in sauces and Neapolitan cooking before the eighteenth-century diffusion of the tomato. The same technique—cooking, passing through a fine sieve, then sun-drying—for making tomato paste was applied to the ripe red or yellow pepper. Although none of my friends in the Naples area had ever heard of pepper paste I decided to try it and the results were wonderful. Pepper paste can be spread on toasted garlic bread (see page 163), thinned down with olive oil to sauce pasta, or used as a condiment with grilled or poached fish or chicken. Cooks who want to revive this lost Neapolitan tradition will want to cook their paste longer, to an almost claylike consistency, then jar the paste topped with a layer of extra virgin olive oil although I prefer the softer paste produced by this recipe. Fans of spicy food will enjoy the addition of hot pepper.

> 3 pounds ripe red and/or yellow peppers,
>   seeded and cut into large pieces
> 1 cup boiling water
> 1 hot pepper (optional)
> ½ teaspoon sea salt
> Extra virgin olive oil

1   Cook the peppers in a 4-quart pot with 1 cup boiling water and optional hot pepper. Cover the pot and cook over low heat for 15–20 minutes or until the peppers are tender when pierced with a knife.

2   Preheat the oven to 150 degrees.

3   Drain the peppers, cool, and press them through the fine disk of a food mill to remove the skin and make a smooth sauce. Add the salt to the pepper sauce.

4   Pour the pepper sauce into a 10 x 14-inch nonstick baking pan. Bake for 5–6 hours until concentrated and the thickness of tomato paste. Cool the pepper paste and transfer to a glass bowl or jar. Cover with a layer of extra virgin olive oil and store in the refrigerator in a jar with a tight-fitting lid.

Chicken with Peppers, Piedmont-Style

For 4–6 Servings   **Main Dish**

*P*iedmont is a northern region that takes peppers seriously. They're roasted, marinated, and pickled under grape pomace, the leftovers of the wine making process. I love the stew made with rabbit, peppers, red wine, and spice but I've substituted chicken for rabbit since it's easier to find and few diners are squeamish about eating chicken. I've skinned the chicken to make it leaner, just like rabbit. Peppers will be easier to digest if peeled with a swivel-bladed vegetable peeler and will melt into the sauce.

> 1 large onion, minced
>
> 2 celery stalks, minced
>
> 2 carrots, minced
>
> 2 ounces salt pork, *pancetta*, or sausage, chopped
>
> 2 garlic cloves, minced
>
> 1 tablespoon minced fresh rosemary
>
> 3 tablespoons extra virgin olive oil
>
> 4 red or yellow peppers, seeded and cut into strips
>
> 1 chicken, about 3–4 pounds, skin and fat removed,
>   cut into 8–10 serving pieces
>
> Sea salt
>
> Freshly ground black pepper
>
> 3–4 whole cloves or 1 pinch powdered clove
>
> 1 pinch cinnamon
>
> 2 medium tomatoes or ½ cup canned tomato pulp,
>   coarsely chopped
>
> 1½ cups red wine (Barbera)
>
> 2 tablespoons red wine vinegar
>
> 1 pinch nutmeg

1   Put the chopped onions, celery, carrots, salt pork, garlic, and rosemary in a large 4-quart pot. Pour 2 tablespoons extra virgin olive oil over the vegetables and stir to coat with the oil. Place over low heat and cook until the vegetables are lightly browned, 10–15 minutes.

(continued)

2   Prepare the peppers. Those who have trouble digesting peppers should peel them. Everyone else can slice the tops and bottoms off the peppers to form a cylinder, remove the seeds and the white membrane, and cut the peppers into strips.

3   Season the chicken pieces with salt and pepper and drizzle with 1 tablespoon extra virgin olive oil. Mix to coat the chicken pieces lightly with the oil.

4   Cook the chicken pieces in a wide nonstick skillet over medium heat, around 3–5 minutes, until lightly browned. Turn the pieces to brown evenly.

5   Transfer the chicken pieces with a slotted spoon to the large pot with the cooked vegetables.

6   Add the cloves, cinnamon, pepper strips, tomatoes, and 1 cup red wine to the chicken pieces. Season with salt and pepper and stir to mix. Raise the heat and bring to a boil; lower the heat and simmer, uncovered, for 30–40 minutes, stirring occasionally, adding more wine, up to ½ cup, if necessary.

7   When the chicken is done, remove with a slotted spoon to a serving platter. Add the vinegar and nutmeg to the peppers and cook for 5 minutes over medium-high heat. Pour over the chicken and serve.

Vincenzo's Summer Vegetable *Ciambotta*

For 6–8 Servings   **Main or Side Dish**

My friends Vincenzo Masucci and Florentine Nilo Checchi introduced me to inexpensive Roman osteria dining 25 years ago, cheaper, they insisted, than installing a kitchen. Vincenzo and Nilo ate out every day, had coffee sent up from a nearby bar, and lived in a penthouse duplex with an elevator, marble and mirror bathroom the size of a suite, sauna, terraces overlooking the Campidoglio in the heart of Rome but no kitchen. Rome continues to evolve as it has for centuries, all our old osteria hangouts have closed or turned into cheap Chinese restaurants. Vincenzo and Nilo put in a well-equipped kitchen flanked by Moroccan temple doors. Nilo offers Tuscan suggestions and taunts but Vincenzo cooks what he pleases, often drawing from dishes his mother, who came from a mountain village outside Paestum, made when he was a kid. "We used to eat *ciambotta* twice a week in the summer," he told me when he made this mixed vegetable stew of ripe bell peppers, eggplant, tomato, and potato, "and my mother always told us it was Padre Pio's favorite dish." It was probably her favorite since it's so easy to make.

Vincenzo calls it *ciambotta*, *The Food of Rome and Lazio* by Oretta Zanini de Vita has an almost identical recipe for *cianfotta*, and Luigi Carnacina's *La Buona Vera Cucina* transforms the regional dialect name into correct Italian, *gianfottere*, "John Fuck." Carnacina limits himself to the recipe with no explanation about the profane title. It's a dish that must have been born of necessity and its name may have been the response of an annoyed cook in a hurry with limited summertime basics on hand when asked what was for lunch by John.

2 onions, chopped

2 garlic cloves, chopped

1 tablespoon chopped fresh Italian parsley

4 tablespoons extra virgin olive oil

1 medium eggplant, cut into ¾-inch cubes

2 ripe bell peppers, sliced into strips

2 medium boiling potatoes, peeled and cut
  into ¾-inch cubes

2 tomatoes, juiced, seeded, and coarsely chopped

2 tablespoons capers, rinsed

Sea salt

Freshly ground black pepper

1 tablespoon chopped fresh basil

1 Put the onions, garlic, and parsley in a large heavy-bottomed pot and drizzle with the extra virgin olive oil. Stir to coat the vegetables with the oil and place over moderate heat. Cook for a few minutes until the onions are soft but not colored.

2 Add the eggplant cubes, pepper strips, potatoes cubes, chopped tomatoes and their juice, capers, salt, and pepper and cook over low heat, tightly covered, stirring occasionally, for 40 minutes or until the potatoes are tender and all the vegetables have melted into a sauce. Uncover and evaporate excess liquid if necessary.

3 Add the basil and cool. Serve at room temperature.

POTATO

Patata

*I*talians haven't always been crazy about the potato, a strange New World import of Central and South American origin, a member of the dangerous, often poisonous Solanaceae family along with tomatoes and tobacco. It's easy to understand the resistance to this homely underground vegetable. Although its flowers are attractive, potato leaves and fruit are both poisonous—only the hidden fleshy growth known as a tuber is edible. Lumpy, dull, brown-skinned potatoes aren't as attractive as flashier members of the family like red peppers or purple eggplant. Mr. Potato Head is nobody's idea of Prince Charming. But potatoes are easy to grow, even at high altitudes, keep well over the winter, and are cheap and filling. Eventually, the entire Italian peninsula and its islands were won over by the ugly tuber.

Spanish explorers brought the potato to Europe in 1536 and 1538. A few specimens were sent to Pope Pius V sometime between 1566–72 and were grown as ornamental plants for their attractive flowers. Barefoot Carmelite monk Nicolo' Doria brought potatoes from Spain to Italy and planted them in a convent garden in Genoa in 1585 but not just for their flowers. He wrote that potatoes could be ". . . eaten in slices, in the manner of truffles or mushrooms, fried and floured . . ." But in spite of Doria's enthusiasm potatoes didn't catch on until late in the eighteenth century.

Neither fruit nor root, the potato is an enlarged end of a subterranean stem. It stores energy in the form of starch, supporting "eyes" from which new stems are created. Potatoes are divided into two distinct types—yellow-fleshed, all-purpose with medium starch and firmer high or medium starch white-fleshed. New potatoes are immature, thin-skinned potatoes of any color. Recipes prepared with different potato types vary widely.

Potatoes are relatively low in calories, high in potassium and vitamin C, with protease inhibitors which protect the body from viruses, and serotonin, a neurotransmitter with calming effects. Green or sprouted potatoes contain toxic alkaloids concentrated near the skin and should be avoided. Friar Foreteller—whose calendar hangs in many Italian kitchens, complete with lunar phases, daily inspirations, saints' days and holidays to be celebrated, folk philosophy, gardening and wine-making advice, recipes, and home cures—recommends using sliced raw potatoes on burns, chapped skin, chilblains, and contusions. The friar advises those suffering from gastric ulcers, gallstones, hemorrhoids, and diabetes to take a syrup of raw potato and carrot juice combined with honey and lemon.

Italians fry, roast, braise, and boil potatoes, cooked or dressed with extra virgin olive oil. Boiled potatoes are a favorite of those suffering from digestive ills, condemned to eat the diet known as "white," *bianco*. Boiled starchy potatoes are molded into *gnocchi* that may range from feather-light to lead, depending on the skill of the cook. Outside Florence, in the town of Mugello, ravioli are stuffed with a mixture of mashed potato enriched with meat sauce, too complicated to think about making. My favorite dishes are the simple ones that highlight the earthy, starchy flavor of the potato, distracting with only a few simple additional ingredients. Potatoes are the perfect match for first-rate, fruity extra virgin olive oil, less sweet and greasy than butter.

Local cultivars are disappearing rapidly, replaced by American and Dutch varieties with higher yields. Torquato Innocenti, my favorite farmer at the Santo Spirito market in Florence, buys his seed potatoes at an agricultural consortium that supplies local farmers. He's full of advice for his tasty kennebec potatoes, including the recommendation to never go anywhere by car without a potato. "Slice a potato in half and rub the cut side on the windshield," recommends Torquato, "and water will slide right off the glass." Automotive travelers take note.

History

I couldn't find any historic potato recipes in spite of all the evidence of growing potatoes from the late sixteenth century on. But *Dr. Amal Speaks . . . on Food and Medicinal Plants*, written in 1950, says that potatoes were considered the most plebeian of foods, thought to cause leprosy, which may explain the absence of potato recipes.

Potato Recipes

CLAUDIA'S POTATO FRITTERS

Subrich di Patate

Silver-dollar-sized fritters flavored with herbs and cheese

———

ROMAN EGGLESS POTATO *FRITTATA*

———

TUSCAN BAKED POTATOES

Dressed with extra virgin, better than butter

———

NANO'S BOILED POTATOES AND BALSAMIC VINEGAR

———

AUNT ENZA'S ROAST POTATOES

CESARE'S TUSCAN FRIES

———

TORQUATO'S STEWED POTATOES

Patate in Umido

———

FABIO'S NOT REALLY RUSSIAN POTATO SALAD

———

SICILIAN POTATO SALAD

———

CESARE'S FISH BAKED ON POTATOES

Claudia's Potato Fritters
Subrich di Patate

*C*laudia Verro, chef-owner with her husband, Tonino, of the restaurant La Contea in the village of Neive, makes the kind of home-style cuisine often ignored by restaurants. The intoxicating magic of white truffles entices gastronomes to visit Piedmont in the autumn, distracting most palates from the truffleless dishes of the other three seasons. Claudia's *subrich* (say su-BRICK) potato fritters are a perfect example of this culinary oversight. *Subrich* are a wonderful appetizer, served with a glass of sparkling wine. Truffleless cooks can console themselves with Claudia's recipe.

> 1 pound russet or yellow-fleshed potatoes
> 2 egg yolks
> 2 tablespoons grated Parmigiano
> Fine sea salt
> A few gratings of nutmeg
> 2 tablespoons minced fresh herbs—parsley, rosemary, thyme, sage
> 2 fresh bay leaves, minced
> 1 garlic clove, minced
> Freshly ground black pepper
> Extra virgin olive oil for frying

1 Carefully scrub the potatoes. Place them in cold, salted water to cover. Bring to a boil and cook for 35–35 minutes or until tender when pierced with a toothpick. Drain the potatoes and set aside until cool.

2 Peel the potatoes and put them through the fine disk of a food mill or grate with the fine blade of a food processor.

3 Combine the potatoes with the egg yolks, Parmigiano, nutmeg, minced herbs, and garlic and season with salt and pepper. Shape the potato mixture into balls the size of a walnut and flatten each ball into a disk.

4 Heat 2 tablespoons extra virgin olive oil in a large nonstick skillet over moderate heat. Cook the *subrich* for a few minutes on each side until lightly browned. Remove to drain on paper towels. Add more oil when necessary and cook the remaining *subrich*. Serve immediately or keep warm in the oven.

Roman Eggless Potato *Frittata*

For 4–6 Servings   **Appetizer**

*A*fter I spent months in the kitchen of Roman restaurant owner Silvano Paris, he sent me to a friend's restaurant in Trastevere for another point of view. The food was different, more Italian, less regional, with dishes like *insalata russa* made with fresh potatoes and carrots, frozen peas, and homemade mayonnaise, rice salad with pickled vegetables and hot dog bits, and crème caramel. I wasn't enthusiastic about most of the cooking but I loved the rustic mixed appetizer cart with a potato *frittata* centerpiece, a golden brown disk on a large plate surrounded by platters of sweet-and-sour pearl onions, grilled eggplant, marinated peppers, zucchini, and fresh anchovies bathed in extra virgin olive oil. The potato *frittata* was my favorite *antipasto* on the cart, a hash brown potato pancake with onions and garlic.

> 2 pounds russet potatoes
> Sea salt
> ¼ cup extra virgin olive oil
> 2 medium yellow onions, sliced
> 2 garlic cloves, sliced
> Freshly ground black pepper

1 Carefully scrub the potatoes. Place the potatoes in cold, salted water to cover. Bring to a boil and cook for 35–35 minutes or until tender when pierced with a knife. Drain the potatoes and set aside until cool.

2 Heat the extra virgin olive oil in a large nonstick skillet and cook the onions and garlic over low heat for 10 minutes or until soft.

3 Peel and slice the potatoes while the onions are cooking. Add the potatoes to the onions and mash with a wooden or plastic fork to reduce the potatoes to a pulp and combine well with the onions. Or grate the potatoes on the medium blade of a food processor for a less rustic look and combine well with the onions. Season with salt and pepper.

4 Gently press the potatoes and onions with a spatula or pancake turner to form an even pancake. Cook the *frittata* over low heat for 10–15 minutes or until the bottom of the *frittata* forms a firm crust.

5 Place a plate over the *frittata* and invert the skillet. Slide the *frittata* back into the skillet and cook the other side for 10 minutes. Slide the *frittata* onto a round platter and serve hot or at room temperature.

Tuscan Baked Potatoes

*M*y super-Tuscan husband Massimo has always enjoyed trying new foods, but with a few limits. When I decided to introduce him to baked potatoes I went to the market and purchased 2 of the largest potatoes I could find, shaped just like American baking potatoes. I soured my own cream since sour cream isn't available in Italy, found chives at a fancy produce stand, and improvised a stove-top potato baker with a wire-grid toaster and an upended pot large enough to cover 2 huge-by-Italian-standards potatoes. Massimo called them "footballs," very American, very big. I forked open the crisp-skinned baked potatoes and spooned some of the sour cream chive mixture into my potato, added salt and pepper. Massimo was skeptical, had a taste of my potato, then went to work on his own, pouring some wonderful extra virgin olive oil into his "football." I stubbornly relished the familiar taste of my potato and couldn't believe that he'd skip my wonderful homemade sour cream and chives until I tasted his potato. Once again my stubborn Tuscan was right.

> 1 large russet potato, around ½ pound
> 2 tablespoons best-quality extra virgin olive oil
> Fine sea salt
> Freshly ground black pepper

1 Preheat the oven (or toaster oven) to 425 degrees.

2 Scrub the potato to remove every trace of dirt. Dry carefully with a paper towel. Sprinkle the potato with a few drops of extra virgin olive oil and rub the skin to barely coat with oil.

3 Bake the potato for 1 hour or until tender when pierced with a toothpick.

4 Pierce the potato skin with a fork to open the potato and dress with extra virgin olive oil, salt, and pepper.

Nano's Boiled Potatoes
and Balsamic Vinegar

*I*s this the only recipe from Emilia-Romagna with no fat grams? I learned about it with difficulty from Nano Morandi, owner of Hosteria Giusti in Modena, one of my favorite restaurants. It's next to (and supplied by) Nano's 390-year-old *salumeria,* which sells cured meat and cheese, the finest local products including prosciutto, salami, Parmigiano, and aged balsamic vinegars. In the tiny four-table Hosteria, all pasta is hand-rolled and a heavy dusting of just-grated first-rate Parmigiano tops many dishes. Cholesterol rules. But probably the best vegetable dish is boiled potatoes with Nano's oldest balsamic vinegar. His own private cask of balsamic vinegar is over 20 years old, and bears little resemblance to the stuff you find at your local supermarket. Most balsamic vinegar is an industrial effort to capitalize on the name and mystique of this unique product. Traditional balsamic vinegar is precious, expensive, over $100 a bottle, used by the drop. It's made in attics, aged in 5 different kinds of wood, condensed and refermented over years. Boiled potatoes are considered the perfect foil for the complex lingering flavors of aged balsamic vinegar. Those not lucky enough to have Modena's traditional balsamic vinegar hanging out in the cupboard can substitute the following vinegar reduction for the real stuff. But those who can indulge should.

> 2 pounds yellow-fleshed potatoes
>
> Sea salt
>
> 2 teaspoons aged Aceto Balsamico Tradizionale di
>   Modena or ¼ cup plus 1 teaspoon industrial balsamic
>   vinegar
>
> Freshly ground black pepper

1 Carefully scrub the potatoes. Place the potatoes in a pot with water to cover. Bring to a boil, add salt to taste, and simmer until tender, 20–30 minutes, depending on potato size. Drain potatoes and peel when just cool enough to handle.

2 If you are using it, cook ¼ cup industrial balsamic vinegar in a small saucepan for 5–6 minutes over high heat, reducing vinegar by half to make a light syrup. Add 1 teaspoon industrial balsamic vinegar, stir, and cool.

3 Slice the warm potatoes. Drizzle with real or reduced balsamic vinegar, salt, and pepper.

POTATO

Aunt Enza's Roast Potatoes

*M*y husband Massimo's aunt Enza is a wonderful cook. Her food is traditional Tuscan with a few new dishes that she's picked up from the culinary tips on her Franciscan calendar-almanac. She uses first-rate extra virgin olive oil for everything, even deep-frying. Aunt Enza crowds the table with classic Tuscan vegetable dishes and then apologizes that there's nothing to eat. Should she rinse off a few leaves of lettuce? All festive meals at Enza's conclude with her tiramisù, garnished with *AUGURI*, BEST WISHES, written with chocolate bits on top. But her very best specialty is roast potatoes, crispy, flavored with rosemary, sprinkled with sea salt, drenched with extra virgin olive oil. Aunt Enza recommends removing excess starch from the potatoes by soaking them for five minutes in cold water and then drying the potatoes with a linen towel (paper towels are fine) to prevent them from sticking to the pan. I use a nonstick pan for best results and no stirring during baking although I soak and dry the potatoes too.

> 2½ pounds yellow-fleshed potatoes
> ¼ cup extra virgin olive oil
> 2 teaspoons fine sea salt
> Freshly ground black pepper
> 2 tablespoons fresh rosemary

1 Preheat the oven to 400 degrees.

2 Peel the potatoes, cut into quarters lengthwise, and then cut into ½-inch chunks. Place the potatoes in a bowl of cold water for 5 minutes to remove excess starch.

3 Drain the potatoes and pat dry with paper towels. Place the potatoes in one layer in a large nonstick roasting pan. Drizzle with extra virgin olive oil and sprinkle with salt, pepper, and rosemary.

4 Bake the potatoes for 1 hour or until well browned, stirring after 30 minutes of cooking to evenly brown. Some types of potatoes may need an extra 15 minutes. Serve immediately.

POTATO

Cesare's Tuscan Fries

Super-Tuscan cook Cesare Casella prepared these rustic-looking fried potatoes at his restaurant, recently closed, in the hills outside Lucca. Tuscan fries are potato sticks a little larger than fast-food fries, deep-fried in extra virgin olive oil with whole sprigs of fresh rosemary, sage, and thyme, whole garlic cloves, and *peperoncino* hot peppers. Warning: this dish is expensive to make in Italy and even more of a luxury elsewhere, hence the $11 charge for an order at Coco Pazzo and Il Toscanaccio in New York, where Cesare is currently making these potatoes. The difference in flavor between full-bodied, fruity olive oil and neutral, tasteless vegetable oil produced with solvents is worth the expense for those who love deep-fried vegetables. Oil can be strained and reused two or three times to lower the cost of frying. Tuscan traditionalists deep-fry in a black iron (but not cast-iron) pan with sloping edges but any deep-fryer will do.

> 1½ pounds all-purpose yellow-fleshed potatoes,
>   peeled and cut into sticks
> 2 sprigs rosemary
> 3–4 sprigs sage
> 2 sprigs thyme
> 4 cups extra virgin olive oil
> 4 garlic cloves
> 2 hot peppers
> Fine sea salt

1 Soak the potatoes in warm water for at least 5 minutes. Drain and pat dry with paper towels.

2 Rinse and dry the herbs.

3 Heat the oil to 340 degrees in a deep-fryer or black iron pan. Gently add the potato sticks to the hot oil, being careful not to crowd the fryer. Fry the potatoes until lightly colored. Add the herbs, garlic cloves, and hot peppers and cook a few minutes more until potatoes are browned.

4 Remove the potatoes and herbs from the fryer or pan and drain them on paper towels. Sprinkle with salt and serve immediately.

POTATO

Torquato's Stewed Potatoes
Patate in Umido

I love Torquato's recipe for stewed potatoes, *patate in umido*, easily made with ingredients on hand in most pantries. Potatoes are braised with water, onions or leeks, garlic, and herbs and lightly spiced with red pepper. Fabio Picchi, chef-owner of Cibrèo in Florence does the same dish but uses meat stock, always on hand in his restaurant but never in my kitchen.

1–2 garlic cloves, finely minced

1 small hot red pepper or chili pepper flakes to taste

2 tablespoons chopped parsley

2 teaspoons chopped fresh herbs—rosemary, sage, marjoram

3–4 tablespoons extra virgin olive oil

2 pounds russet or yellow-fleshed potatoes, peeled and cut into ¾-inch cubes

½ cup tomato pulp, fresh or canned

2 cups boiling water or light homemade stock

Coarse sea salt

1   Put the garlic, hot pepper, and herbs in a large nonstick skillet, drizzle with extra virgin olive oil, and stir to coat. Cook, stirring often, over moderate heat until the garlic begins to color.

2   Add the potatoes, tomato pulp, 2 cups water or stock, and the salt and simmer for 20–30 minutes or until the potatoes are tender and the sauce is creamy. Serve warm.

Fabio's Not Really Russian Potato Salad

For 4–6 Servings   **Side Dish**

I've never understood the Italian affection for the appetizer known as "Russian" salad, made with diced potatoes and carrots, frozen peas, and tons of mayonnaise. I always thought that Fabio Picchi's vegetable *composta* or compote, a salad of diced beets, new potatoes, carrots, and green beans, dressed simply with extra virgin olive oil, stained dark purply-red, looked more Russian than the pale mayonnaise-swirled so-called "Russian" salad. Beets can be baked in the oven or boiled.

> 2 quarts water
>
> Fine sea salt
>
> 1 cup cubed carrots (cut into ½-inch cubes)
>
> 1 cup cut-up green beans (cut into ½-inch lengths)
>
> 1 cup cooked, peeled, and diced beets (previously boiled
>   until tender or baked in the oven)
>
> 1½ cups yellow-fleshed potatoes, peeled and cut into
>   ½-inch cubes
>
> ¼ cup extra virgin olive oil
>
> 1 teaspoon chopped Italian parsley
>
> Freshly ground black pepper

1   Bring 2 quarts of water to a rolling boil. Add the salt and the carrots and cook until tender. Remove the carrots with a slotted spoon and drain.

2   Cook the green beans in the boiling water for 3–6 minutes or until tender, remove with a slotted spoon, refresh in cold water and drain.

3   Cover the potatoes with water in a small pot, add salt, and cook for 15–20 minutes or until the potatoes are tender. Remove with a slotted spoon and drain.

4   Combine all the ingredients and mix well. Marinate for at least 1 hour before serving.

POTATO

Sicilian Potato Salad

Sicily has some of the most wonderful vegetables in the world, sold in bustling outdoor markets but not often found on restaurant menus, considered too common to take seriously. But Sicilians eat a lot of vegetables at home and I've been lucky to be able to sit at quite a few Sicilian kitchen tables. I fell in love with this potato salad spiked with Sicilian salted capers at a country lunch with Marchesa Anna Tasca Lanza, author of *The Heart of Sicily* (Clarkson Potter, 1993) and owner of the Regaleali Cooking School. After a morning of swimming, an easy-to-deal-with summery lunch was quickly assembled: freshly baked golden semolina bread dipped in extra virgin olive oil and sprinkled with oregano; grilled coils of sausage; potato salad; sliced ripe tomatoes; *pecorino* cheese and peeled prickly pears and figs for dessert. The mayonnaise-less potato salad has been a favorite ever since. Dried wild mountain oregano is used by Sicilians to flavor this dish but American cooks should look for quality fresh dried herbs and avoid anything that's been hanging around in a spice rack for years.

> 2 pounds yellow-fleshed or red-skinned boiling potatoes
> Fine sea salt
> 2–3 tablespoons salt-packed capers
> 2 cups water
> 1 large red onion, thinly sliced
> 2 teaspoons quality dried oregano
> ¼ cup extra virgin olive oil
> 2 teaspoons vinegar
> Freshly ground black pepper

1 Carefully scrub the potatoes and place them in cold salted water to cover. Bring to a boil and cook for 35–35 minutes or until tender when pierced with a knife. Drain the potatoes and set aside to cool.

2 While the potatoes are cooking, rinse the capers and soak them in 2 cups of water for 15 minutes, and drain.

3 Peel the potatoes and cut them into ½-inch slices. Combine the potatoes with the capers and all the remaining ingredients. Marinate the potato salad for at least 30 minutes or up to a day.

Cesare's Fish Baked on Potatoes

*C*esare Benelli, owner-chef with his wife Diane of the Ristorante Al Covo is one of the great cooks of Venice. He's taken me marketing for fish and to vegetable gardens in the Venetian lagoon, stalking the best local produce for his restaurant. He's obsessed with raw ingredients, *materia prima*, and uses heirloom cornmeal for polenta, the finest Carnaroli rice for risotto, pasta made by Latini. Cesare bakes whole baby monkfish on a layer of thinly sliced potatoes to keep the fish from sticking to the pan and to slightly thicken the sauce of fish juices and white wine. He doesn't serve the potatoes, which don't look good, he claims. But I do. Cesare uses baby monkfish tails, 8 inches long, but any firm-fleshed white fish will do.

> 4 baby monkfish tails or fish fillets, about 5–6 ounces each
>
> 1 large potato, russet or yellow-fleshed
>
> 2 shallots, minced
>
> 3 tablespoons extra virgin olive oil
>
> ½ cup dry white wine
>
> ½ cup fish stock or water
>
> Fine sea salt
>
> Freshly ground white pepper
>
> 1 tablespoon minced parsley

1   Preheat the oven to 425 degrees. Lightly oil a flameproof pan large enough to hold the fish in one layer.

2   Peel the potato and cut it into thin slices. Put the potato slices in one layer on the prepared pan.

3   Put the fish fillets on the potatoes, sprinkle the shallots over the fish, drizzle with the extra virgin olive oil, white wine, ¼ cup fish stock or water, salt, and pepper.

4   Bake the fish for 15 minutes. Remove the baking pan from the oven and transfer the fish to a serving dish. Add the remaining ¼ cup fish stock to the baking pan and cook over high heat, gently stirring to deglaze the pan and lightly reduce the sauce.

5   Transfer the contents of the pan into a strainer and strain the sauce over the fish without pressing the potatoes. Sprinkle the sauced fish with parsley and serve. Rustics like me can serve the potatoes even if Cesare doesn't.

RED RADICCHIO

Radicchio Rosso

*I*t's easy to spot in salads at trendy restaurants, hipper than arugula, purplish-red shreds or cupped white-veined leaves of yet another easily mispronounced Italian designer lettuce. But once you've learned to say rah-DEE-key-oh you're ready to start cooking because red radicchio is at its best grilled, braised, roasted, or stir-fried, in risotto or saucing pasta, and it's low in calories and easy to cook. Bitter, but not nasty, is an element of its grown-ups-only flavor.

Red radicchio is a member of the chicory family *Cichorium intybus*, which grows wild throughout the Mediterranean and beyond, ever prized by foraging Italians. Cultivation probably tamed some of the plant's inherent bitterness. But, according to Veneto culinary historian Giuseppe Maffioli, modern red radicchio was developed south of Treviso in the late 1860s by Belgian garden consultant Francesco Van Den Borre, who was hired to "do" the garden of Villa Palazzi in the then-fashionable English style. He was most likely familiar with the Belgian blanching-sprouting technique used on endive. He messed around with the local lettuce. Son Aldo followed in his father's footsteps and by the end of the 1800s cultivation methods of red radicchio were being promoted by a local agricultural association.

In northern Italy, in the Veneto region, the towns of Chioggia, Verona, Castelfranco, and Treviso have each developed distinct varieties of red radicchio. Chioggia is a tight, purple-red ball aswirl with bulging, pumped-up white veins. Verona is small, loose-leafed, soft, ovoid. Castelfranco looks more like a yellowish-green and wine-freckled ball of tender lettuce unfolding gently like a rose, and is frequently subjected to a simple blanching. But Veneto's entry in the Gastronomic Hall of Fame is Treviso's red radicchio, bittersweet, expensive, seasonal, exposed to a complicated forcing-blanching-sprouting technique that results in elongated, sun-starved, spider-mum-like spears of purple red with an impressive pearly white central rib, held together by a pointed, peeled root.

If there were a vegetable rights movement, Treviso growers would surely be accused of harassment. Selected seeds are planted in early summer, green-red leafed heads are harvested in the fall with root system intact, packed tightly in long furrows in a plastic tunnel, removed as needed for the next stage. Plants are

RED RADICCHIO

transferred to low cement pools covered with plastic where life goes on, roots absorb warm spring water (once this process was done in the stalls, and the roots were immersed in cow manure), and the plants begin to sprout. Looking worse for wear, with unattractive rotting outer leaves and a long hairy taproot, plants are moved indoors to a warm, moist environment, draining onto sawdust for a few days, forcing the development of the sprout even more. When this stage is complete plants are trimmed of rotten outer leaves (lots) to expose the heart, which has sprouted in the center tender etiolated white and red leaves. The hairy taproot is cleaned up, carved to one third the length of the red radicchio head, and the trimmed, shaved Treviso is given a rinse, crated, and ready for market, traditionally traumatized vegetables. Clearly this is not a practical procedure, and forced Treviso radicchio sells for twice as much as easier-to-grow more coercible varieties. It's not a simple business to jump into since first-rate seeds of easy-to-mutate red radicchio, produced with enclosed pollination of selected specimens by growers, are never sold. And the market is mined with hybrids.

Red radicchio is low in calories, high in potassium, vitamins A and C, and folic acid, and contains anthocyanins, said to reduce risk of cardiovascular disease. Like most bitter vegetables, it's supposed to be good for the blood. A promotional pamphlet claims that radicchio has sedative, diuretic, and purifying powers and that those who eat it will live 100 years.

Most forced Treviso red radicchio is sold regionally, although fancy green-grocers throughout Italy will often carry it. Outside northern Italy it's easier to find Chioggia, Verona, or unforced Treviso, and the same selection is either grown or imported into the United States. Two men from Veneto, Lucio Gomiero and Carlo Boscalo, and Fresh Western Marketing, a grower-shipper, successfully raise quality red radicchio with family heirloom seeds in California. They are experimenting with the forcing procedure. Call 408–758–1390 and ask for Noel for more information. Radicchio isn't easy to grow but Shepherd's Garden Seeds, 6116 Highway 9, Felton, California 95018, Telephone: 408–335–6910, Pinetree Garden Seeds, Box 300, New Gloucester, Maine 04260, Telephone: 207–926–3400, The Cook's Garden, P.O. Box 535, Londonderry, Vermont 05148, Telephone: 802–824–3400, sell seeds. Start your own selective breeding program.

If red radicchio isn't available, the following recipes can be all be prepared with Belgian endive, which is subjected to a similar forcing regimen. A combination of Belgian endive and red radicchio is probably the best approximation of the bittersweet crispy sprout sensation of Treviso.

Fans of red radicchio should consider a pilgrimage to Veneto during the cold winter months. Area restaurants are rarely without this much-prized vegetable but the true radicchio lover will head for Ristorante Le Tre Panoce in Conegliano, owned by chef Armando Zanotto, author of *Il Radicchio in Cucina*, a cookbook with 617 recipes ranging from appetizers to dessert using Treviso and Castelfranco varieties. Armando will prepare an extensive all-radicchio menu concluding with radicchio grappa for those who just can't get enough of a good thing. Guess the shape of the restaurant's business card.

So what's the best easiest way to cook red radicchio? The basic minimalist recipe roasts it with a few drops of extra virgin olive oil and a sprinkle of salt and pepper, in the oven, on a grill, or in a nonstick pan or griddle, not until crunchy or wilted or still red but really cooked, tender. The dry heat of a hot oven or grill will brown and crisp outer leaves, while a nonstick pan will brown and soften them—both methods slightly caramelize the outer leaves. The radicchio heart will be soft, well done, almost creamy with lengthy cooking, with a more bitter than sweet flavor balance—no fuss, no cholesterol, low calorie, low fat. Where has this vegetable been hiding?

History

*C*astor Durante's *Treasure of Health*, published in 1586, is a medical manual that details the health benefits and culinary applications of vegetables. He mentions wild chicory called radicchio, which aids inflammations of the stomach and maintains a healthy liver although it contains little nutriment. Durante recommends eating radicchio boiled in water and dressed with oil, vinegar, and raisins, raw in salad, cooked in meat broth.

Giovanni Rizzi, a poet from Treviso, rhymed in Italian about radicchio in 1876.

> *If you look at it, it's a smile* (sorriso)
> *If you eat it, it's paradise* (paradiso)
> *. . . radicchio from Treviso*

The first edition of the Treviso Radicchio Fair, held under the sixteenth-century Arcade of the Palace of the Three Hundred in the center of Treviso, December 19, 1889, had 56 exhibitioners and awards for early, late, and variegated radicchio. Francesco Van Den Borre, the creator of the first forced radicchio, was on the jury. The fair, suspended during World Wars I and II, has become an important yearly event for growers although Castelfranco, Dosson, Rio San Martino, Mogliano Veneto, and Zero Branco all host festivities dedicated to red radicchio. Fans planning a December visit to Treviso can call the local tourist board (Telephone: 0422–547–632) to find out the dates of the fair.

Radicchio (or Endive) Recipes

RADICCHIO "IN SOUR"
Radicchio in Saor

———

CESARE'S RED RADICCHIO
OR BELGIAN ENDIVE *PASTICCIO*

———

RAW RADICCHIO SALAD WITH SALT PORK

———

CESARE'S TRENETTE WITH RADICCHIO
AND SHRIMP

RISOTTO WITH RADICCHIO
OR BELGIAN ENDIVE

———

GRILLED OR PAN-ROASTED RADICCHIO

———

GRILLED RADICCHIO
OR BELGIAN ENDIVE CHRYSANTHEMUMS

Radicchio "in Sour"
Radicchio in Saor

*I*n the Veneto, fresh sardines, eggplant, and radicchio are all given the *saor* treatment, marinated with cooked onions, vinegar, pine nuts, and raisins. The combination of bitter, sour, and sweet is a winner and this dish improves after marinating for a day or two. Leftover grilled or baked radicchio can be used, eliminating half the work of this dish.

> 4 radicchio heads, quartered, or Belgian endive
>   split in half
> 4 tablespoons extra virgin olive oil
> Fine sea salt
> Freshly ground black pepper
> 2 onions, thinly sliced
> 3 tablespoons red wine vinegar
> 2 tablespoons raisins, soaked in ¼ cup hot water
> 2 tablespoons pine nuts

1 Drizzle the radicchio quarters or the split endive with 2 tablespoons extra virgin olive oil, salt, and pepper in a large nonstick skillet or griddle.

2 Cook the radicchio or endive over moderate heat for 10 minutes per side on all sides until tender and lightly browned. Remove the radicchio from the skillet.

3 Put the onions in the skillet, drizzle with 2 tablespoons extra virgin olive oil, season with salt and pepper, and stir to coat the onions with the oil. Cook over moderate heat, stirring often, until the onions are soft but not brown.

4 Add the vinegar, raisins, and pine nuts and cook over high heat for a minute or two, evaporating most of the liquid.

5 Layer the onion mixture with the cooked radicchio or Belgian endive beginning and ending with onions and marinate for a few hours or overnight. Serve at room temperature.

Cesare's Red Radicchio
or Belgian Endive *Pasticcio*

I never make lasagna because my husband Massimo hates it. It's not Tuscan and
it's heavy, two serious drawbacks. But I can sneak in a vegetable *pasticcio* (say
pah-STEE-cho) that I learned from Cesare Benelli, chef-owner of the Ristorante Al
Covo in Venice. Cesare cooks with freshest fish and vegetables from the Venetian
lagoon and feels that the delicate flavors of local bounty would be overpowered by
butter or cream. He uses half milk and half vegetable or chicken stock in his sauce,
lighter than béchamel but still creamy. I love the results. Sweet nutty Parmigiano-
Reggiano contrasts with the adults-only flavors of radicchio. It's a perfect party dish
that can be assembled and baked at the last minute. Almost any cooked vegetable
but especially mushrooms, asparagus, wild greens, or artichokes can be substituted
for the radicchio for other seasonal *pasticci*.

> 6 radicchio heads or 8 Belgian endive, cut into strips
> 6 tablespoons extra virgin olive oil
> 1–2 garlic cloves, minced
> Sea salt
> Freshly ground black pepper
> 1 pound wide lasagna pasta, preferably fresh
> 4 tablespoons flour
> 1½ cups hot milk
> 1½ cups vegetable or chicken stock
> 1 cup grated Parmigiano-Reggiano

1 Preheat the oven to 400 degrees. Lightly oil a 9 x 12-inch baking dish.

2 Put the radicchio or Belgian endive strips in a large nonstick skillet. Drizzle with 3
tablespoons extra virgin olive oil, stir to coat, and sauté over moderate heat for 5
minutes or until wilted and lightly browned. Add the garlic, season with salt and pepper, and transfer the radicchio to a bowl.

3 Bring a large pot of water to a boil, salt the water, and add the lasagna. Cook the
lasagna partially for only half the recommended time. Fresh pasta will be done in a
minute or two, dry boxed pasta will take longer. Bear in mind that pasta, fresh or
dry, will complete its cooking in the oven. Drain pasta and place strips on a cloth
towel to dry.

4   Heat the remaining extra virgin olive oil in a medium saucepan. Add the flour, stirring with a small whisk, and cook over low heat without browning. Add the hot milk and stock, whisking constantly to produce a smooth sauce. Add salt and pepper to taste.

5   Spread a few spoonfuls of the sauce on the bottom of the prepared baking dish, cover completely with a layer of pasta, and top with one quarter of the cooked radicchio and one quarter of the sauce. Sprinkle with one quarter of the Parmigiano. Repeat the process, layering the lasagna, radicchio, béchamel, and Parmigiano, ending with the Parmigiano.

6   Bake for 15–20 minutes or until golden brown. Cool for 10 minutes before serving, necessary so that the pasta and sauce settle and can be easily sliced.

Raw Radicchio Salad with Salt Pork

For 4–6 Servings   **Side Dish**

*A*rmando Zanotto's *Il Radicchio in Cucina* has hundreds of recipes for radicchio, most of them not the best of ideas. He combines radicchio with just about anything, from ketchup to caviar but does include a few traditional recipes, including this wonderful dressing for raw radicchio. Lard or salt-cured *pancetta* is used in Veneto although salt pork or quality bacon can be substituted.

> 3 red radicchio heads or 4 Belgian endive, cut into strips
> 2 tablespoons extra virgin olive oil
> Fine sea salt
> Freshly ground black pepper
> 2 ounces salt pork or bacon, diced
> 1 teaspoon red wine vinegar

1   Dress the radicchio with the extra virgin olive oil, salt, and pepper in a salad bowl.

2   Cook the salt pork or bacon in a small skillet until lightly browned. Add the vinegar and pour over the radicchio. Mix well to combine; serve immediately.

Cesare's Trenette
with Radicchio and Shrimp

*H*ere's another wonderful red radicchio recipe from Cesare Benelli, chef-owner with his wife, Diane Rankin, of the Ristorante Al Covo in Venice. Cesare buys wonderful Treviso radicchio and super-sweet tiny *scampi*, baby langoustines at the Rialto market, both unavailable to most non-Venetian cooks. Cesare lived in Texas for a few years and says that Belgian endive and shrimp can substitute for Treviso radicchio and *scampi*. Purists should consider a trip to Venice in the winter to taste the real thing.

> 5–6 quarts water
>
> 2–3 tablespoons sea salt
>
> 14–16 ounces linguine or trenette
>
> 3 red radicchio heads or 4 Belgian endive, cut into strips
>
> ½ pound shelled shrimp
>
> 2 garlic cloves, minced
>
> 3–4 tablespoons extra virgin olive oil
>
> 1 cup shrimp or fish stock
>
> Freshly ground black pepper
>
> 2 tablespoons chopped parsley

1   Bring 5–6 quarts of water to a rolling boil. Add 2–3 tablespoons salt and the pasta.

2   While the pasta is cooking, put the radicchio or Belgian endive, shrimp, and garlic in a large nonstick skillet. Drizzle with extra virgin olive oil, stir to coat the vegetables and shrimp with the oil, and cook for 2–3 minutes over moderate heat to wilt the radicchio. Season with salt and pepper.

3   Cook the pasta until it still offers considerable resistance to the tooth, about three quarters of the recommended cooking time. Drain, reserving 1 cup of pasta water.

4   Add the pasta to the skillet with the radicchio and shrimp. Add the shrimp or fish stock and cook over highest heat, stirring, to complete pasta cooking, which should take 3–4 minutes. Add some of the reserved pasta water if the sauce is too dry. Sprinkle with the parsley and serve.

Risotto with Radicchio or Belgian Endive

For 3–4 Servings **First Course**

*T*his is a classic Veneto risotto, rice bonded to a vegetable with an unusual technique. Rice and its clinging starch link up with butter or oil to thicken a sauce which is created by melting a chopped vegetable in broth. Fairly frequent stirring is a must, but the steam is good for your skin. At the last moment butter and Parmigiano cheese are whipped in, a final frenzy of enrichment that adds an emulsified creamy quality to risotto. The consistency should be of just-cooked oatmeal, thickened just enough to slowly slide across a tipped plate. A spoon won't stand up in it. First-rate rice will result in the best risotto. Vialone Nano, Carnaroli, or Baldo are all correct. Although all recipes call for broth, most home cooks don't have homemade stock on hand. Most Italians use the *dado* or bouillon cube, loaded with MSG and mystery. If you have light veal, chicken, or vegetable broth, use it, but I never do so. I use water and add a larger quantity of the vegetable flavoring than most recipes and a few drops of brandy to finish for greater flavor. Butter and Parmigiano are always whipped into the risotto before serving. I use less butter (or none at all) and add a spoonful of extra virgin olive oil for richness. Risotto, like pasta, doesn't wait for guests and should be made to order, never in advance.

½ onion, chopped

4–5 tablespoons extra virgin olive oil (or 3 tablespoons
   extra virgin olive oil and 2 tablespoons butter)

1 large radicchio head or 2 Belgian endive,
   cut into thin strips

1 cup Italian rice for risotto

¼ cup dry white wine (optional)

8–10 cups lightly salted boiling water or lightly salted
   vegetable broth (made with 1 onion, 1 garlic clove,
   1 carrot, 1 celery stalk, radicchio trim, and a few
   parsley stems, cooked for 15 minutes)

1 tablespoon brandy

½ cup grated Parmigiano-Reggiano (and more cheese
   if desired)

Freshly ground black pepper

(continued)

1 Put the chopped onion in a heavy-bottomed 4-quart pot or saucepan and pour 2 tablespoons extra virgin olive oil over them. Stir the vegetables to coat with the oil. Cook over moderate heat for 10 minutes, stirring frequently, until the onions barely begin to brown.

2 Add the radicchio and cook for a minute or two to wilt and evaporate any liquid that forms.

3 Add the rice, stir to coat with the oil, and cook for a few minutes to lightly toast. Add an extra tablespoon of oil if there doesn't seem to be enough to toast the rice.

4 Add the white wine, if desired, and evaporate over high heat.

5 Add the boiling water or the vegetable broth, 1 cup at a time, stirring the bottom of the pot with a *long* wooden spoon or fork, over high heat, boiling madly. Risotto attains the temperature of molten lava and it's wise to keep one's distance while stirring. Add more salted boiling water or broth when risotto is still surrounded by liquid, not dried out. After 10 minutes of cooking add boiling liquid ½ cup at a time. Begin to taste the rice after another 5 minutes of cooking; it should be firm under tooth, *al dente*, and slightly soupy since it will still cook for a few minutes. The Parmigiano cheese and final whipping will tighten up the sauce.

6 Add the brandy, cheese, pepper, and the remaining 2 tablespoons extra virgin olive oil (or 2 tablespoons butter) and stir energetically with a long-handled wooden spoon or fork over high heat to whip the ingredients together.

7 Remove from the heat, ladle into individual bowls, and let the risotto rest for a minute before serving. Top with additional Parmigiano, if desired.

Grilled or Pan-Roasted Radicchio

*T*his is the simplest way to cook radicchio; two ingredients plus salt and pepper, half an hour, and a pan. The dish is served throughout Veneto during the winter months. Although it's at its very best prepared with Treviso-style radicchio, other kinds of radicchio or even Belgian endive will yield positive results.

> 3 radicchio heads or 4 Belgian endive
> 3 tablespoons extra virgin olive oil
> Fine sea salt
> Freshly ground black pepper

1 Cut the radicchio heads in quarters (or the Belgian endive in half lengthwise), cutting through the heart to keep sections from falling apart. Wash and dry carefully.

2 Drizzle the radicchio or endive with the extra virgin olive oil, salt, and pepper. Grill over low heat (charcoal, wood, or gas) for 10 minutes per side on all three sides (two split sides and the rounded edge) until the outer leaves are blackened and the heart is tender when pierced with a knife. Or cook in a nonstick pan or griddle over low heat for 10 minutes per side on all three sides. Stove-top cooks move the pan to a back burner and cook radicchio for up to 45 minutes—overcooking is often preferred. Serve immediately.

RED RADICCHIO

Grilled Radicchio or Belgian Endive Chrysanthemums

*T*his is a fancy version of grilled radicchio or Belgian endive, inspired by reading Armando Zanotto's obsessive *Il Radicchio in Cucina*. Recipe #540 in his book is for radicchio "*alla giudea*," fried Jewish-style, a cooking method applied to artichokes in the Roman Jewish tradition. Armando simply opens the leaves of the radicchio and fries the whole heads in a few inches of oil until brown and crisp, a great idea for lovers of deep-frying. It inspired me to try the Roman brick-pressed cooking method for artichokes (see page 29) on heads of radicchio or Belgian endive, twice-cooked, pressed with a weight until flat and crispy with a tender heart. Since Armando often calls radicchio "red flowers" in his recipes I decided it looked like a pressed chrysanthemum.

> 3–4 medium-sized radicchio heads or 6 Belgian endive
> 3 tablespoons extra virgin olive oil
> Fine sea salt
> Freshly ground black pepper

1 Discard any blemished outer leaves of the radicchio or Belgian endive. Cut the tips and top third off long heads of Treviso or the Belgian endive and reserve for salad or risotto. Round heads of radicchio can be left whole. Make incisions lengthwise without cutting though the base of the Belgian endive or long Treviso. Slice the round radicchio into 8 wedges without cutting all the way through the base. Carefully rinse and drain the radicchio or Belgian endive.

2 Heat 2 tablespoons extra virgin olive oil in a large nonstick skillet. Sprinkle the radicchio or Belgian endive with salt and pepper and cook over low heat, turning occasionally to brown evenly, for around 25–35 minutes or until tender when pierced with a toothpick. Cook the round radicchio standing up on the base end for 10 minutes. Remove the radicchio or endive from the pan and drain on paper towels.

3 Heat the remaining extra virgin olive oil in the skillet. Carefully open the leaves of the radicchio or Belgian endive and place the opened heads, base end up, in the skillet. One large head of radicchio may take up the entire skillet. Cover the radicchio or Belgian endive with a heavy plate. Put a weight (traditionalists should use a brick) on the plate and cook the radicchio over moderate heat for 5 minutes or until well browned. Remove to a serving platter and serve.

TOMATO

Pomodoro

*I*t's almost impossible to think of Italian cooking without the tomato—fresh, canned, sauce, or sun-dried. It's the perfect condiment for pasta, the best thing that ever happened to a pizza, the red of the Italian flag, colors red, white, and green. Surely the world would be a little sadder without tomato sauce or sliced ripe tomatoes dressed with extra virgin, salt, and pepper, or even a minimalist tomato straight from the vine, warm from the sun.

The tomato, *Lycopersicon lycopersicum,* is a member of the Solanacea or nightshade family along with potato, tobacco, and eggplant, exotic New World wonders. Grown as a short-lived perennial in its native, western South American habitat, most of the world treats the tomato as an annual. Plants are usually started indoors, transplanted outside when all danger of frost is over and the first flower buds begin to open. Tomatoes need from 20–30 days after flowering to achieve full size and another 3–4 weeks to complete maturation. Green chlorophyll deteriorates as yellow carotenoids and red lycopene form during the tomato's metamorphosis from green to red. Acid components are transformed; starch is converted to sugar; pH lowers; fruit flesh becomes progressively softer; skin thinner and more fragile with advanced ripening. All these processes are activated by the gas ethylene, naturally produced by the tomato or artificially supplied by commercial growers for uniform harvest or off-plant ripening. New tomato varieties have been created to suit a wider range of growing conditions, maximize size, yield, and the ability to ship without bruising. Some modern hybrids are early ripening, of great interest to those who don't live in a Mediterranean climate with at least 12 hours of daily summer sun. Many new cultivars are self-pollinating, eliminating the need for insect fertilization. Great effort is invested to improve the tomato because it's big business. American industrial production is worth over $1 billion annually. Italy ranks second. Commercial growers are interested in bigger fruit, uniform ripening, and longer shelf life. Biogenetic engineers employed by agroindustrialists are making plenty of promises for the tomato but flavor and health aren't high on their list of priorities.

Ripe tomatoes have lots of vitamin A, good vitamin C, and potassium. Green tomatoes have higher vitamin C and half the vitamin A. Ripe seasonal tomatoes have higher nutritive values (not to mention more flavor) than greenhouse or hydroponic fruits. The tomato contains up to 94 percent water and is therefore low in calories. According to Friar Foreteller (*Frate Indovino*)—a mythical Italian Franciscan monk whose yearly calendar is filled with a wonderful mixture of folklore, religion, health, and gardening tips—tomatoes aid digestion, cure constipation, eliminate kidney stones and urinary inflammations, and purify the blood. The friar's wisdom includes vague instructions for a hemorrhoid remedy of tomato and pork fat.

Italians embraced the tomato quickly after Genovese navigator Cristoforo Colombo brought seeds back to the Old World from his second voyage of discovery, although most of Europe didn't bother eating this bizarre New World import. Strange-scented leaves, unusual appearance, and membership in the often-dangerous nightshade family deterred most diners. The tomato traveled from Spain to Italy, where adventurous gastronomes soon realized that it was more than just an ornamental shrub. In an era without instant global communication it took the tomato only 50 years to appear in Italian botanical texts that describe the New World import and refer to its culinary applications. Recipes in cookbooks that include the tomato don't appear until the late 1600s.

Seeds for exotic discoveries like tomatoes were probably channeled through the usual recipients of knowledge—the Church with its medicinal monastery gardens, wealthy aristo-agronomists, and botanical gardens. The tomato may have found its way from the New World to Tuscany through the gardens of Cosimo de' Medici, who loved the countryside, was fascinated by botany, and experimented with new fruits and vegetables. Ruling Spanish aristocracy may have welcomed the tomato to Naples shortly after its discovery. Sicily also had strong contacts with Spain through which the tomato may have been introduced into noble gardens.

Each area of Italy has its own favorite tomatoes—varieties that rarely leave the zone of production since the very best tomato is eaten just picked. They're usually named for their shape or locality—pear, plum, ox heart, pendant, lightbulb, or San Marzano (outside Naples), Pachino (southern Sicily), Roma, or Vesuvio. In my local vegetable market the preferred tomato is the *riccio fiorentino,* the Florentine curl, deeply ridged pumpkin-shaped as described in the sixteenth century by Filici (see page 279). If Cinderella had been Florentine, her carriage would probably have been made of this attractive fruit. At the beginning of the season its stem end is colored deep green, fading into a midsection of pale green highlighted by a blush of orange, a mere hint of the brilliant rich red of the fully ripened *riccio*. It has a thin skin, and firm meaty flesh. Sliced in half, its scalloped ridges look like petals of a flower, lined with a coral-colored pith to which the seeds are attached. They are easily removed with a squeeze, just like juicing a lemon or orange. The ripe *riccio* tastes sweet from the heat and light of summer, heightened by a touch of acidity that gives this tomato a clean, mouth-filling flavor. It's an all-purpose tomato and can be used raw or cooked, unripe, hard, and green, pink-tinged, barely on the road to maturity, or ripened to maximum intensity. Parma and Genoa also claim the *riccio* as their own. Low yield and vulnerability to disease have deterred commercial growers who opt for American hybrids; knowledgeable farmers and home gardeners continue to grow the *riccio* for its fine flavor.

The San Marzano cultivar is Italy's most famous sauce tomato. It's named after the area where *fiaschella,* "little flask," tomatoes were grown in the volcanic soil outside Naples. There, it was responsible for the development of a canning industry in the 1800s. Cans were called *buatte,* transforming the French *boîte* into Neapolitan dialect. It's a perfect baking and sauce tomato, holds up to heat, thick with pulp, easy to skin.

The canning industry's newest format for the tomato is pulp, a seeded and skinned dice of raw tomato pieces packed in juice, perfect for lazy cooks who like a chunky sauce. Laws that regulate plum and paste producers don't regulate the pulp canners and quality varies greatly. Mutti is probably my favorite brand in Italy although it's hard to find. Pomi' is available in the United States, although it's packed in concentrated juice. My favorite brand in the United States is Muir Hill organic tomato pulp. Anyone lucky enough to find a jar of tomato puree by L'Orto di Lucania will be in for a treat since it's the finest jarred tomato product I've ever tasted.

First-rate canned tomatoes, whole, pulp, or sauce, homemade, domestic, or imported from Italy, guarantee the best results in all nonseasonal preparations.

Little tomatoes with the "ini" diminutive (*pomodorini* in Italian with a variety of dialect names) are sold in clusters like grapes, still on the vine, looking like a bunch instead of a basket of cherry tomatoes, tasting sweet, intensely tomatoish. The entire plant is harvested at the end of the season, tied, and hung in courtyards, surely the easiest method of preserving tomatoes. They may wrinkle a bit but are considered the perfect cooking tomato in much of southern Italy and are used whole. The Principe di Belmonte is a popular variety.

A typically southern approach to preserving results in the sun-dried tomato (*pomodori secchi*). Tomatoes are split in half, lightly salted, and set out on wire trays in the morning for a serious session of Mediterranean sun, brought indoors in the evening. After a few days of this treatment they're preserved under extra virgin olive oil plain, or with oregano, garlic, and grated pecorino cheese. Tomato variety is of utmost importance, as anyone who has ever endlessly chewed a tough, leathery, meatless sun-dried tomato will attest. A first-rate sun-dried tomato should taste concentrated, pulp reduced to an essence held together by a thin (not leathery) skin, preserved (and therefore flavored) with quality olive oil. In Italy sun-dried tomatoes are served as an appetizer, often part of an "under oil" (*sott'olio*) course of preserved olives, mushrooms, and eggplant. Or two sun-dried tomatoes are sandwiched with a filling of bread crumbs, garlic, and herbs and pan-fried.

Tomatoes are also preserved in the form of paste, a process that evaporates almost all water content, yielding essence of tomato. Paste is classified as single, double, or triple concentrate, customarily sold in tubes, although I've never come across triple concentrate. In Sicily, paste is known as *estratto*, made by drying tomato sauce in the hot Sicilian sun on long boards, slanted to facilitate drainage. Other regions dry tomatoes in the sun for a few days, pass them through a sieve, mix the pulp with salt, and dry, covered with gauze to keep insects away, for a few more days. Concentrated tomato paste is then stored in a jar, covered with a layer of olive oil. Ten pounds of fresh tomatoes yield approximately 1 pound of concentrated paste. It's used freshly made as a snack spread on bread like preserves with a drizzle of extra virgin olive oil, or during the tomatoless winter as an enrichment to sauce.

But it is as sauce that tomatoes really claim their place in the Gastronomic Hall of Fame, fresh or preserved, raw or cooked, green or ripe, a

TOMATO

full-flavored balance of sweet and sour. Tomato sauce tops pasta daily on most of Italy's tables year round, made with fresh tomatoes in season and preserved products for the rest of the year. Northern cooks may begin their sauce with butter while central and southern Italians opt for extra virgin. Tomato sauce is flavored with sautéed garlic, onion, celery, carrot, salted pork products, spicy *peperoncino* hot peppers, or all of the above. Italian flat-leafed parsley, basil, and oregano are the herbs of choice.

Tomatoes for sauce should be seeded, an almost effortless step, by slicing tomatoes in half and squeezing, like citrus fruit, into a strainer over a bowl to catch any of the precious juice, which can be added back to the tomatoes. Skin tomatoes before seeding if the peel is thick or you're offended by bits of skin and prefer a silkier, more elegant sauce. Drop tomatoes into boiling water for 10 seconds, remove with a slotted spoon, and slip off the skin. Or peel tomatoes with a vegetable peeler or sharp paring knife.

Never refrigerate tomatoes! Or buy refrigerated tomatoes. Cool temperature destroys texture and flavor, resulting in insipid, pulpy fruit.

Shepherd's Garden Seeds and Seeds of Change (see page 135 for addresses and phone numbers) have the Costoluto Genovese, another name for the *riccio fiorentino*, my favorite tomato, well worth growing for home gardeners. Most seed catalogs have the plum tomato cultivars San Marzano and Roma, ideal for sauce, canning, or sun-drying, and the Principe Borghese, the Italian *pomodorino* used for sauce or harvested in bunches still on the plant, appended in a dry sunny courtyard to preserve.

Vine-ripened local tomatoes will yield the best results in the following recipes, although mediocre specimens can be livened up with the addition of a little vinegar and sugar. When tomatoes aren't in season quality canned tomatoes, either whole plum or chopped pulp, should be used. Although out-of-season tomatoes may look good it's only an illusion—they're close to flavorless, and should be avoided.

History

The first mention of the tomato in Italy occurs in Tuscan doctor M. Pietro Andrea Mattioli of Siena's 1557 translation (from Latin to Italian) of *Discussions on Material Medicine* by the Greek physician Dioscoride. Mattioli included his modern sixteenth-century commentary and placed tomatoes in his mandrake chapter, befitting a fellow member of the nightshade family. He described green tomatoes ripening to red, to be eaten fried like mushrooms or juiced as sauce.

Costanzo Felici, in a March 10, 1572, letter to his botanical pen pal Ulisse Aldrovandi, writes about the "*Pomo d'oro* or *pomo del Peru* . . . either intense yellow or vigorously red, either round or ridged in slices like a melon . . ." He unenthusiastically reports the vegetable fried and sprinkled with a mild vinegar (*agresto*), not too impressed with the ". . . new thing . . . easily more attractive than tasty."

Antonio Latini's 1692 cookbook, *The Modern Steward,* focuses on noble food and wine service along with recipes and even includes a chapter on "maccheroni, lasagna and little dumplings." Latini was a cook for cardinals, dukes, and counts, rewarded for his culinary efforts with the title of cavalier. The tomato, in its first cookbook appearance, is used in recipes for sauce, stewed, and combined with eggplant and herbs in a "Spanish" soup.

Florentine monastery cook Francesco Gaudenzio was an early tomato enthusiast. His 1705 *Panunto Toscano* recommends cooking chopped tomato with ". . . oil, pepper, salt, minced garlic and wild country mint. Gently fry, stirring often, and add, if you will, tender eggplant and summer squash . . . "

Vincenzo Corrado's 1781 *Of Pythagorean Food* proposes a dietary regime for nobles and literary-minded readers of delicate digestion that includes meat and fish broth, dairy products, and eggs, all out of the question on Pythagoras's fifth-century B.C. animal-rights vegan diet. Corrado is from Naples, a city of tomato-worshipers, and he declares them "tasty bites and universal sauce" not only flavorful but good for the digestion, especially in the summer. He describes round yellow tomatoes with skin that needs to be removed, either by rolling on hot coals or dipping in boiling water. Seeds, he warns, must be removed. Corrado recommends stuffing tomatoes with garlic, anchovy, parsley, oregano, salt, and pepper, sprinkling with bread crumbs and oil, and baking in the oven. "Turkish" tomatoes are stuffed with cooked rice and egg yolks, then floured and deep-fried. He concludes his chapter with both fat and lean sauce advice, cooking tomatoes with lard, prosciutto, onion, bay, Spanish pepper, and herbs or else with oil, garlic, basil, oregano, and parsley, passing either sauce through a sieve, typical behavior for a professional chef.

Neapolitan Ippolito Cavalcanti, Duke of Buonvicino, wrote *Theoretical-Practical Cooking* in 1837, a cookbook of both refined Frenchified recipes of the noble aristocracy and gutsy Neapolitan traditional dishes. The duke includes a recipe for a sauce of quick-cooking seeded and juiced tomatoes, sieved, cooked with lard or oil to thicken up, to use on "fish, meat, chicken, eggs or whatever you want." His "Maccheroni in all ways" recipe calls for "red sauce from braised [meat]" to dress pasta, the first reference I've found that pairs pasta with tomato sauce in which meat has cooked, documenting a street food tradition firmly entrenched in Naples by the nineteenth century.

Did the duke ever eat pizza at the world's first pizzeria, which opened in Naples in 1830? Or at King Ferdinand I's Capodimonte estate, equipped with a pizza oven at the insistence of his wife Maria Caroline? Two generations of Neapolitan *pizzaioli* (pizza cooks) claim to have made pizza for both King Ferdinand I and II. But was it topped with tomato? The Neapolitan nobles may have been among the first to plant tomatoes in their country gardens. And they may have been the first to taste tomato on a pizza, prepared in their own villa ovens by local *pizzaioli*. But without a doubt, on June 11, 1889, Raffaele Esposito prepared three kinds of pizza, including one with a topping he named to honor his Queen, Margherita, of red tomatoes, white mozzarella, and green basil, the colors of united Italy's flag. Were the Neapolitan nobility making an effort at politically correct gastronomy? Probably,

since pizza with basil, mozzarella, and tomato was mentioned in an 1847 book by Emanuele Rocco on local, lower-class customs and therefore couldn't have been invented especially for the Queen.

It seems fitting that *In Armida's Vegetable Gardens* was written by a poet from Naples, a city of vegetable lovers, known as "leaf eaters," according to a local expression. Silvio Salvatore Gargiulo's book of "Italo-Neapolitan Verses," published in 1922, includes a poem entitled "The Tomato" in Neapolitan dialect that speaks of love, desire, pasta ,and tomato sauce, concluding with a feast of a pound of sauced pasta per person.

> *A thin strand of pasta returns from exile*
> *and tomato sauce laughs happily . . .*
> *garlic, onion and even the saucepan*
> *all go into rapture.*
> *The tomato sauce cries with joy*
> *because she has been alone for so long*
> *She says: Come here, my beauty,*
> *my husband, come and comfort me*
> *And with an embrace the party began*
> *everyone attacked half a kilo apiece!*

Tomato Recipes

Raw Tomato Salad

*I*talians have devised hundreds of treatments for tomatoes but they're probably at their very best eaten raw, sliced thick or roughly chunked, dressed with fresh basil, salt, pepper, and extra virgin olive oil. Ripe red as well as green fading to pink semi-ripe tomatoes are used for salads in Italy. Refined diners may prefer their tomatoes skinned (use a vegetable peeler for best results) but most Italians don't bother. A sprinkle of vinegar will heighten flavors but a wonderful summer tomato doesn't need too much enhancement. As usual, first-rate extra virgin olive oil produces the best results. Soak up the leftover oil and exuded tomato juice straight from the platter with dense country-style bread.

> **2 pounds tomatoes**
> **3–4 tablespoons extra virgin olive oil**
> **1 teaspoon red wine vinegar (optional)**
> **Fine sea salt**
> **Freshly ground black pepper**
> **Fresh basil, chopped, ripped into pieces or cut into strips**

1   Slice the tomatoes ½ inch thick and put in one layer on a large serving dish.

2   Dress the tomatoes with extra virgin olive oil, optional vinegar, and season with salt and pepper. Top with the basil and serve.

Rustic Tomato-Rubbed Garlic Bread
Fettunta al Pomodoro

For 4–6 Servings   **Appetizer**

*A*lmost everyone has encountered *bruschetta* even if they can't pronounce it. Raw tomatoes and herbs roughly chopped atop a slab of garlic bread are found in restaurants all over the world. But there's an even easier way to make this typical Tuscan *merenda* or snack, with no peeling or chopping. First garlic, then split tomatoes are rubbed across toasted country bread, which is then doused with extra virgin olive oil in a summery version of Florentine *fettunta* (fey-TUNE-ta), easier to pronounce than *bruschetta* (bru-SKAY-ta).

> 2–3 plum tomatoes
> 6 ¾-inch slices of country bread
> 1 garlic clove, unpeeled
> 6 tablespoons extra virgin olive oil
> Fine sea salt
> Freshly ground black pepper

1 Slice the tomatoes in half like oranges and squeeze each half to remove the seeds and juice.

2 Toast the bread until barely browned.

3 Rub the unpeeled garlic over one side of the toasted bread. Rub the cut side of the tomato onto the garlicked surface of the bread. The tomato will grate itself into the rough surface of the bread.

4 Place the bread slices on a serving dish and drizzle with extra virgin olive oil, season with salt and pepper, and serve.

TOMATO

RED, WHITE
& GREENS

283

Tomato and Mozzarella Salad from Capri
Insalata Caprese

For 4–6 Servings   Appetizer, Main Course

Insalata caprese, the salad from Capri, is the perfect summertime dish for lazy cooks in a hurry. Slicing is the hardest part. Bright red tomato slices are interspersed with juicy white mozzarella and whole green basil leaves, drizzled with a little extra virgin, sea salt, and a twist of pepper. The salad was created in the 1950s, a substitute for the sumptuous cooking at the Trattoria da Vincenzo for summertime regulars out for a light lunch. They'd order a ripe, just-picked tomato and a fresh, locally made *fior di latte*, cow's milk mozzarella—no buffalo on the island of Capri. The salad has evolved on Capri to include a few leaves of *rughetta*, wild arugula, and a pinch of dried wild oregano, both island products; everywhere else in Italy the salad is limited to tomato, mozzarella, and basil. The dressing is always a drizzle of extra virgin olive oil. Vinegar would destroy the delicate flavor of fresh mozzarella and is never used. Because the Capri salad is so simple, first-rate ingredients are imperative. Mozzarella should be fresh, white, locally made or imported. Both yellow, rubbery, processed mozzarella wrapped in plastic and hothouse tomatoes are unacceptable. If fresh mozzarella isn't available locally, it can be ordered from Mozzarella Company, 2944 Elm Street, Dallas, Texas 75226, Telephone: 800–798–2954.

¼ cup loosely packed fresh basil leaves
¼ cup loosely packed arugula(optional)
2 pounds ripe tomatoes, sliced ½-inch thick
1 pound fresh mozzarella, sliced ¼-inch thick
1 pinch first-rate dried oregano (optional)
3–4 tablespoons extra virgin olive oil
Fine sea salt
Freshly ground black pepper

1 Tear basil (and optional arugula) into bite-pieced pieces. Alternate slices of tomato, mozzarella, and basil leaves on a serving platter. Scatter the arugula and oregano on top (if you choose to use them). Drizzle the salad with extra virgin olive oil, season with salt and pepper, and serve.

Torquato's Herb
and Garlic Baked Tomatoes

*T*orquato and Valerio Innocenti sell two kinds of tomatoes in the summer at their stand in Piazza Santo Spirito. "The Florentine curl—use it for salad or sauce; and plum tomatoes for sauce or baking," advises Torquato. "Chop garlic and basil, add *olio buono* (good oil), fill split tomatoes, and bake." Maria di Fazio, my voice of Apulia, stuffs her tomatoes with bread crumbs, grated pecorino cheese, garlic, and basil. Marchesa Anna Tasca Lanza, author of *The Heart of Sicily* (Clarkson Potter, 1993), bakes tomatoes with the typical Sicilian stuffing of bread crumbs, pine nuts, and currants. I love all versions of baked stuffed tomatoes but Torquato's simple recipe is my favorite.

> 15 plum tomatoes
> 4 garlic cloves
> ½ cup tightly packed basil or parsley
> ¼ cup extra virgin olive oil
> Fine sea salt
> Freshly ground black pepper

1 Preheat the oven to 400 degrees.

2 Split the tomatoes in half lengthwise and scoop out the seeds with a teaspoon.

3 Put the tomatoes, split side up, on a nonstick or lightly oiled baking sheet in one layer.

4 Mince the garlic and basil in a food processor and add extra virgin olive oil to make a fragrant herb paste. Season the paste with salt and pepper.

5 Smear about ½ teaspoon herb paste in each tomato half.

6 Bake in the preheated oven for 30–40 minutes. Cool and serve.

Fabio's Tomato Aspic

Fabio Picchi, owner and chef of the restaurant Cibrèo in Florence, cooks like a Florentine granny with a spicy palate. He takes full advantage of seasonal abundance from the Sant'Ambrogio market next to his restaurant. Fabio's recipes are wonderful but imprecise, quantities are vague, and I've got to pay strict attention so he doesn't skip an ingredient or a step. His refreshing summery tomato aspic is simple and uses traditional ingredients in a novel way, creating a spicy tomato sauce with a wiggle, barely jelled, more fun than a formal aspic. Bright red, speckled with herbs, zapped with chili and garlic, Fabio's appetizer is a far cry from the ladies-lunch image of conventional, transparent consommé aspics. Even my gelatin-hating husband and son love this dish. Double the extra virgin for more authentic Tuscan flavor.

1½ pounds plum tomatoes

1 envelope unflavored gelatin

3 tablespoons fresh minced basil or parsley
    or a combination of both

3 garlic cloves, minced

1 small hot red pepper, minced, or chili pepper flakes
    to taste

1–1½ teaspoons salt

3 tablespoons extra virgin olive oil plus additional
    for garnish

1 Split the tomatoes in half and squeeze the halves into a sieve over a small bowl to remove juice and seeds. Press the mixture in the sieve and reserve the liquid and pulp.

2 Puree the tomatoes in a food processor and pass through a food mill or strainer to remove the skins. (Or peel, seed, juice, and process tomatoes until smooth if you don't have a food mill.) Add the reserved juice to the pulp and measure 2 ¼ cups of tomato.

3 Sprinkle the gelatin over ¼ cup tomato pulp in a medium-sized bowl, stir, and soak for 3 minutes. Heat ½ cup tomato pulp until boiling, add to the softened gelatin, and stir to dissolve the gelatin. Add the rest of the tomato pulp, the basil, garlic, hot pepper, salt, and extra virgin olive oil. Divide the mixture into 6 lightly oiled ½-cup molds and chill for at least 3 hours. Unmold and top with a drizzle of extra virgin.

Lisa's "Slide" Pasta with Raw Tomato Sauce
Pasta allo Scivolo

For 4–6 Servings   **First Course**

Countess Lisa Contini from the Tenuta di Capezzana, first-rate producers of wine and extra virgin olive oil, is one of the great home-cooks of Tuscany. She serves this nontraditional cold pasta to winery guests in the torrid Tuscan summer. Raw tomato sauce slides off chilled pasta, hence Lisa's name.

> 1 pound tomatoes
> 1–2 garlic cloves
> 3 tablespoons extra virgin olive oil
> 2–3 tablespoons chopped Italian parsley, basil, or arugula
> Fine sea salt plus 2–3 tablespoons salt
> Freshly ground black pepper
> 5–6 quarts water
> 14–16 ounces spaghetti

1 Peel the tomatoes with a vegetable peeler or by blanching in hot water if desired. Cut the tomatoes in half and squeeze the juice and seeds into a strainer over a bowl. Reserve the juice and pulp.

2 Mince the garlic in a food processor. Add the tomatoes, their strained juice, 2 tablespoons olive oil, and herbs to the garlic in the processor bowl. Pulse to rough-chop for a rustic chunky sauce or partially puree for a more elegant texture. Season with salt and pepper and marinate in a nonreactive bowl while making the pasta.

3 Bring 5–6 quarts of water to a rolling boil. Add 2–3 tablespoons salt and the spaghetti and cook *al dente*, until it still offers resistance to the tooth. Drain the pasta and refresh with cold water. Toss with 1 tablespoon of extra virgin olive oil and chill for up to an hour.

4 Toss the pasta with the marinated tomato sauce just before serving, never in advance, because tomato liquid will sog up pasta. Sauce will be slippery.

5 To serve hot: Cook the spaghetti until it still offers considerable resistance to the tooth, three quarters of the recommended cooking time. Drain the pasta, reserving 1 cup of the pasta water. Cook the pasta and sauce in a skillet, mixing to combine well, for 3–4 minutes to finish cooking the pasta. Add some of the starchy pasta water if sauce becomes too dry.

TOMATO

Titina's Move It! (*Sciue' Sciue'*) Pasta

*T*itina and Costanzo Vuotto own the pensione La Pineta on Capri and Titina is one of the island's best cooks. She prepares lunch next to the pool in the summer and taught me to make *sciue' sciue'* pasta, easier to prepare than pronounce (say shoo-AYE shoo-AYE). It's regional dialect, a slang expression to accelerate movement in an area known for its languid Mediterranean pace. Local cherry tomatoes packed with flavor called *pomodorini di spugnito* are hurried into a sauce with garlic, cooked with *al dente* spaghetti, sprinkled with a fistful of fragrant basil. A *cerasiello*, red hot cherry pepper, sometimes makes *sciue' sciue'* pasta even livelier.

> 5–6 quarts water
>
> 2–3 tablespoons salt plus fine sea salt
>
> 14–16 ounces spaghetti
>
> 2 garlic cloves
>
> 1 small hot red pepper or chili pepper flakes to taste
>
> 3 tablespoons extra virgin olive oil
>
> 1 pound cherry tomatoes
>
> 3–4 tablespoons coarsely chopped fresh basil

1 Bring 5–6 quarts of water to a rolling boil. Add 2–3 tablespoons salt and the spaghetti and cook until it still offers considerable resistance to the tooth, about three quarters of the cooking time.

2 While the pasta is cooking, sauté the garlic cloves and hot pepper in the oil over moderate heat in a large nonstick skillet. When the garlic barely begins to color add the cherry tomatoes and season lightly with the sea salt. Cook over high heat until the tomatoes loose their shape.

3 Drain the spaghetti and add it to the skillet along with 1 cup of pasta cooking water. Cook over high heat, stirring frequently, to amalgamate the tomatoes and pasta and to complete cooking. Add more pasta water if the sauce gets too dry.

4 Sprinkle with chopped basil before serving.

TOMATO

Fresh-Tasting Tomato Sauce and Spaghetti

For 4–6 Servings   **First Course**

*A*lmost all tomato sauce recipes call for at least 30 minutes of cooking but I make my tomato sauce in less than 10 minutes by using a large skillet instead of the conventional saucepan. The tomatoes cook faster on the larger surface of the skillet and taste fresher than sauces subjected to 45 minutes of heat. Pasta is added to the sauce in the skillet to finish cooking both pasta and sauce together. This basic tomato sauce can easily be prepared while waiting for the pasta water to come to a boil. Ripe seasonal tomatoes, preferably plum or sauce tomatoes which have a lower water content, should be used when available but first-rate canned tomato pulp is a fine choice for the rest of the year. I rarely peel fresh tomatoes when I make sauce but those who wish to peel should.

> 1½ pounds tomatoes or 2 cups tomato pulp
>
> 1–2 garlic cloves, minced
>
> 3–4 tablespoons extra virgin olive oil
>
> Fine sea salt plus 2–3 tablespoons salt
>
> Freshly ground black pepper
>
> 5–6 quarts water
>
> 14–16 ounces spaghetti
>
> 3 tablespoons chopped fresh basil or any combination of
> fresh herbs, chopped
>
> ½ cup grated Parmigiano-Reggiano for topping pasta
> (optional)

1 Peel the tomatoes, if desired, with a vegetable peeler or by blanching the tomatoes in boiling water. Cut the tomatoes in half and squeeze the juice and seeds into a strainer over a bowl. Chop or process the tomatoes and add to the reserved juice. Or measure 2 cups of canned tomato pulp or drained plum tomatoes.

2 Put the garlic in a large nonstick skillet and drizzle with 1 tablespoon extra virgin olive oil. Place over moderate heat and cook until the garlic barely begins to color.

3 Add the tomatoes to the skillet and cook over moderately high heat for 5 minutes or until the tomatoes look cooked and most but not all the liquid has evaporated. Add fine sea salt and pepper to taste.

(continued)

4   For a smooth sauce, blend the cooked tomatoes in a food processor with the remaining extra virgin olive oil and return the sauce to the skillet. For a chunky sauce, add the remaining oil before serving.

5   Bring 5–6 quarts of water to a rolling boil. Add 2–3 tablespoons salt and the spaghetti; cook until it still offers considerable resistance to the tooth, around three quarters of the cooking time.

6   Drain the pasta, reserving 2 cups of the cooking water. Add the drained *al dente* pasta, ½ cup pasta cooking water, and the basil to the skillet with the tomato sauce. Cook over high heat, stirring to mix sauce and pasta, until the pasta is cooked. Add more pasta water if the sauce becomes too dry. Serve immediately, topped with Parmigiano if desired.

Torquato's Green Tomato Sauce

*T*orquato has lots of suggestions for green tomatoes, fantastic for those who love tart flavors. Greater acidity, more vitamin C, consistent texture, and a delicate, barely tomato flavor are good reasons to harvest tomatoes when they're just beginning to change from green to pink, but well before they turn red. Green tomato *frittata* and floured and fried green tomato slices are two of Torquato's favorites but I love his green version of a traditional Florentine *carrettiera*, or "teamsters'" pasta, spicy, garlicky, shot with parsley, although Torquato's sauce is green or pale pink instead of bright ripe red.

> 1½ pounds green or firm green to pink tomatoes
> 5–6 quarts water
> 2–3 tablespoons salt plus coarse sea salt
> 14–16 ounces spaghetti
> 2–3 garlic cloves
> 1 hot red pepper or chili pepper flakes to taste
> 3 tablespoons extra virgin olive oil
> 2 tablespoons chopped Italian parsley

1 Peel the tomatoes, if desired, with a vegetable peeler or by blanching in hot water. Cut them in half and squeeze the juice and seeds into a strainer over a bowl. Chop or process the tomatoes and add to the reserved juice.

2 Bring 5–6 quarts of water to a rolling boil. Add 2–3 tablespoons salt and the spaghetti and cook until it still offers considerable resistance to the tooth, around three quarters of the cooking time.

3 While the pasta is cooking, put the garlic and hot pepper in a large nonstick skillet and drizzle with 1 tablespoon extra virgin. Place over moderate heat until the garlic barely begins to color, add the tomatoes, and cook over moderately high heat for 5 minutes or until the tomatoes soften and most but not all the liquid has evaporated. Season with coarse sea salt.

4 Blend the tomato sauce in a food processor with the remaining olive oil, ½ cup pasta cooking water, and parsley to emulsify.

5 Put the sauce back in the skillet, add the drained pasta, and ½ cup pasta cooking water. Cook over high heat, stirring to mix sauce and pasta, until the pasta is cooked *al dente*. Add more pasta water if the sauce gets too dry.

TOMATO

Massimo's *Panzanella* Summer Vegetable and Bread Salad (and My Matzoh-nella)

For 4–6 Servings   **First Course**

*M*y husband, Massimo, taught me to make traditional Florentine *panzanella,* also called *pan molle* or *pan bagnato,* a refreshing first-course salad of tomatoes, cucumber, basil, and onion combined with soaked and squeezed stale Tuscan bread, dressed at the last minute with extra virgin olive oil and a little wine vinegar. Florentine sixteenth-century Mannerist painter Bronzino didn't include tomatoes when describing *panzanella* in a poem dedicated to the onion. He was clearly wild about this salad of oil and vinegar, dipped bread, raw onion, tender purslane, cucumber, basil, and rucola, "better than all other pleasures of this life." *Panzanella* is easy to prepare but it's impossible to make with first-rate bread. Some non-Tuscan cooks substitute toasted country bread but the resulting salad really doesn't taste like *panzanella.* I wanted to find an easy alternative to country-style bread and came up with matzoh, which takes to soaking and squeezing quite well, creating an easily made Tuscan-style salad for Passover. *Panzanella* (or Matzoh-nella) is at its best freshly made, and will turn into a soggy mess if it sits for too long.

> 5–6 slices of stale bread or 4 ounces matzoh
> 1 red onion, coarsely chopped
> 1 tablespoon red wine vinegar
> 3–4 ripe tomatoes
> 1 cucumber, peeled, seeded, and cut into chunks
> 1 bunch arugula (or purslane), cut into bite-sized pieces
> 3 tablespoons coarsely chopped basil
> 3–4 tablespoons extra virgin olive oil
> Fine sea salt
> Freshly ground black pepper

1 Preheat the oven to 250 degrees.

2 Toast the bread in the preheated oven for 20–30 minutes or until dry.

3 Soak the bread or matzoh in a bowl of water for 10 minutes (matzoh will take less time) until soft. Squeeze all the water out of the bread or matzoh and measure 2 cups. Place in a large serving bowl and refrigerate at least 30 minutes.

4 Marinate the onion with the vinegar for at least 10 minutes.

5 Peel the tomatoes with a vegetable peeler or by blanching in hot water if desired. Cut the tomatoes in half, squeeze the juice and seeds into a strainer over a bowl, and save the juice for another use (sauce or soup). Cut the tomatoes into chunks.

6 Combine the onion, tomatoes, cucumber, arugula, and basil with the damp bread or matzoh, dress with the extra virgin olive oil, season with salt and pepper, and serve.

Massimo's "*Farranella*" Emmer (or Barley) and Tomato Salad

For 4–6 Servings

*O*ne summer my husband Massimo, son Max, and I vacationed in the Lucca area about an hour from Florence. We rented an apartment on the grounds of a villa, above a greenhouse where the lemon trees from the formal gardens were stored in the winter. We discovered a local specialty, *farro*, emmer in English, an ancient grain similar to barley, traditionally used in bean soup. We bought lots of it at a grain and bean store in Lucca since it was unknown in Florence. Massimo made a salad with all the ingredients of *panzanella*, substituting boiled emmer for soaked and squeezed bread, a terrific idea that's become a summertime favorite. Use soft wheat berries, usually found in health food stores, or barley if emmer is unavailable.

> 1 cup emmer or barley
> 6 cups water
> 1 red onion, coarsely chopped
> 2 tablespoons red wine vinegar
> 3–4 ripe tomatoes
> 1 cucumber, peeled, seeded, and cut into chunks
> ½ cup arugula and/or purslane
> 2 tablespoons coarsely chopped basil
> 3–4 tablespoons extra virgin olive oil
> Fine sea salt
> Freshly ground black pepper

1 Put the emmer or barley in a 3-quart pot and add 6 cups of water. Bring to a simmer and cook for 40–50 minutes or until the emmer or barley is tender. Drain, rinse with cold water, and chill for at least 30 minutes.

(continued)

2   Marinate the onion with the vinegar while the emmer or barley is cooking.

3   Peel the tomatoes with a vegetable peeler or by blanching in hot water if desired. Cut the tomatoes in half, squeeze the juice and seeds into a strainer over a bowl, and save the juice for another use. Cut the tomatoes into chunks.

4   Combine the onion, tomatoes, cucumber, arugula, and basil with the emmer or barley, dress with extra virgin olive oil, season with salt and pepper, and serve.

Torquato's Tomato Broth and Garlic Bread Soup
Pappa all'Acquacotta

For 4–6 Servings   **First Course**

*T*orquato Innocenti grows vegetables outside the city of Florence, sells them at the Santo Spirito market, and relates vague but excellent recipes in Tuscan dialect to anyone who has time to listen, although many shoppers become impatient with his soft-sell approach to produce.

Torquato's *pappa all'acquacotta*, an easily prepared soup, has become a favorite in my home. The recipe combines elements of two traditional Tuscan soups. *Pappa al pomodoro* is a Florentine bread and tomato soup, the consistency of oatmeal; *acquacotta*, a specialty of the Maremma, land of the Tuscan cowboy, is a mushroom-tomato broth served over toasted country bread, often garnished with an egg poached by the heat of the broth. Torquato's version combines garlic, basil, and *peperoncino*, hot red peppers, in a simple tomato broth ladled over a slice of toasted bread rubbed with garlic, drizzled with an extra virgin olive oil garnish. Eggs, lightly poached in the tomato broth, placed over the toasted bread, sprinkled with freshly grated Parmigiano cheese, make this into a one-dish meal.

1 pound tomatoes

1–2 garlic cloves, minced

1 hot red pepper or chili pepper flakes to taste

1 tablespoon extra virgin olive oil plus more for garnish

3 cups water

Salt

4–6 slices of country-style bread, toasted

1 unpeeled garlic clove

2 tablespoons chopped fresh basil

4–6 eggs (optional)

¼–½ cup grated Parmigiano-Reggiano (optional)

1 Peel the tomatoes, if desired, with a vegetable peeler or by blanching the tomatoes in boiling water. Cut the tomatoes in half and squeeze the juice and seeds into a strainer over a bowl. Chop or process the tomatoes and add to the reserved juice.

2 Put the garlic and hot pepper in a 3-quart heavy-bottomed nonreactive pot. Drizzle the garlic and hot pepper with 1 tablespoon of extra virgin olive oil and stir to coat. Place the pot over moderate heat and cook until the garlic barely begins to brown.

3 Add the tomatoes and water, bring to a simmer, salt lightly, and cook for 5–10 minutes. Taste the tomato broth and correct seasoning if necessary.

4 Toast the slices of country-style bread and rub each slice with an unpeeled garlic clove, which will grate itself onto the toast's hardened surface.

5 Put a slice of garlicked toast in each soup bowl. Ladle the tomato broth over the toast, sprinkle with chopped basil, and garnish with a swirl, or "C" as the Tuscans call it, of olive oil.

6 For an easy one-dish meal or a more substantial starter, poach 1 egg per person in the tomato broth and place it on the toasted garlicked bread. Ladle the broth over the egg, sprinkle with the chopped basil, and top with the grated Parmigiano-Reggiano cheese.

TOMATO

Massimo's Eggs in Purgatory

For 4–6 Servings   Main Course

*M*y husband Massimo is my favorite Florentine home-cook. He's a master at the grill, cooks a mean plate of pasta, and can scare up a quick meal from an empty pantry when I've been too busy to shop for groceries. His cooking is simple, fast, super-Tuscan, heavy-handed with extra virgin olive oil. I love Massimo's eggs in purgatory, a one-skillet preparation of eggs poached in a bright red garlicky tomato sauce, said to resemble the flames of purgatory. The best part of eating this dish is the act known in Italian as *la scarpetta*, "the little shoe," mopping up the sauce with a small piece of bread, perfectly admissible table manners in a country that takes a good sauce seriously. Provide plenty of first-rate rustic bread.

> 1–2 garlic cloves, minced
> 2–3 tablespoons extra virgin olive oil
> 2 cups tomato pulp, fresh or canned
> Fine sea salt
> Freshly ground black pepper
> 4–8 eggs

1 Put the garlic in a large nonstick skillet and drizzle with extra virgin olive oil. Place the skillet over moderate heat and cook until the garlic barely begins to color.

2 Add the tomatoes and cook over moderate heat for 5 minutes, until the excess liquid has evaporated. Add salt and pepper.

3 Carefully break the eggs into the tomato sauce, sprinkle lightly with salt and pepper, and cook the eggs until the whites are set and the yolks are as soft as safety dictates. Slide the eggs and sauce onto a large round platter.

RED, WHITE
& GREENS

Alfonso's Fish Poached in "Crazy Water"
Pesce all'Acqua Pazza

I first learned about the *acqua pazza*, "crazy water," method of cooking fish from Alfonso and Livia Iaccarino, owners of the restaurant Don Alfonso in Sant'Agata sui Due Golfi between Positano and Sorrento. The restaurant is formal, elegantly appointed, serving creative cuisine that impresses the guidebooks along with some traditional dishes "born of poverty," as Livia puts it. I'm wild about their fish poached in a light tomato and garlic broth, made crazy with a little hot pepper. Livia explained that the dish was made by poor farmers who grew vegetables and fished to supplement small incomes. They cooked fish and vegetables in sea water flavored with garlic and a few cherry tomatoes from the cluster that hung from the rafters, enriched at the last minute with a drizzle of extra virgin olive oil. Rock fish (*scorfano*) and the basslike *pezzogna* are favored by Alfonso but red snapper, bass, bream, turbot, or any other delicately flavored white fish can be used.

> 1 garlic clove, sliced
>
> 2-3 tablespoons extra virgin olive oil
>
> ½ pound ripe cherry tomatoes, cut in half, or cubed plum tomatoes
>
> 1 fresh hot red pepper or chili pepper flakes to taste
>
> 1 cup lightly salted water
>
> 1½ pounds fish fillets
>
> Freshly ground pepper
>
> 1 tablespoon chopped Italian parsley
>
> Country-style bread, toasted

1 Put the garlic in a large nonstick skillet, drizzle with 1 tablespoon extra virgin olive oil, and cook over low heat until soft. Add the tomatoes, hot pepper, and 1 cup lightly salted water and bring to a simmer. Cook for 3–4 minutes or until the tomatoes have softened.

2 Put the fish fillets in the skillet, sprinkle with salt and pepper, and cover. Cook over low heat for 5–10 minutes or until the fish is done. Remove the fish to a platter with a slotted spoon, top with the pan juices, sprinkle with parsley, and drizzle with the remaining extra virgin olive oil. Serve with toasted country-style bread.

Fabio's Livorno-Style Fish
Pesce alla Livornese

Fabio Picchi, chef-owner of the restaurant Cibrèo in Florence, makes fish Livorno-style, cooked in a thick tomato sauce. It's one of the few great fish recipes in Tuscany, named for the city on the coast known in English as Leghorn. Fabio usually uses a member of the shark family, smooth hound (*palombo*), but red mullet and salt cod are also prepared Livorno-style. Red snapper, fresh tuna, or any firm-fleshed white fish can be substituted with success.

> 1½ pounds fish fillets
> Flour
> Fine sea salt
> Freshly ground black pepper
> 3 garlic cloves, minced
> 2 tablespoons chopped Italian parsley
> 1 fresh hot red pepper or chili pepper flakes to taste
> 2 tablespoons extra virgin olive oil
> 3 cups tomato pulp
> ½ cup fish stock or clam juice

1 Lightly coat the fish fillets with flour and season with salt and pepper.

2 Put the garlic, parsley, and hot pepper in a large skillet, drizzle with extra virgin olive oil, and cook over medium heat until the garlic barely begins to color. Add the tomatoes and fish stock and bring to a simmer.

3 Put the fish fillets in the skillet and immerse in the simmering tomato sauce so the fillets are covered. Cook over lowest heat, barely simmering, for 5–10 minutes or until the fish is cooked.

Graziella's Sun-Dried Tomatoes

For 24 Stuffed Sun-Dried Tomatoes   **Appetizer**

Graziella, who works for Marchesa Anna Tasca Lanza, author of *The Heart of Sicily* (Clarkson Potter, 1993), gave me a jar of her stuffed sun-dried tomatoes after a stay at Regaleali, the Tasca family winery estate and site of Anna's cooking school. It's really the only recipe I've ever found in southern Italy that uses sun-dried tomatoes as an ingredient, an embellishment on the commonly found sun-dried tomatoes marinated in olive oil, eaten as a snack or antipasto or condiment with bread—never used to cook with. Graziella uses split plum tomatoes dried in the Sicilian sun, sandwiched with a filling of grated pecorino sheep's milk cheese, garlic, red hot pepper, and oregano, all produced at Regaleali. She makes dozens of jars of her stuffed sun-dried tomatoes covered with extra virgin olive oil, to be used all winter long. I'm too lazy to put up a year's supply of stuffed tomatoes but don't mind making a jar's worth, which I keep in the refrigerator even though Graziella says they last forever in the pantry. Old, leathery-looking, discolored sun-dried tomatoes should be avoided.

> 3 garlic cloves, minced
>
> 1 tablespoon dried oregano
>
> ½ cup coarsely grated Pecorino Romano
>
> 1 small hot red pepper, minced, or chili pepper flakes
>   to taste
>
> 48 sun-dried tomatoes
>
> Extra virgin olive oil

1 In a small bowl, combine the garlic, oregano, grated cheese, and hot pepper.

2 Place half the sun-dried tomatoes, skin side down, on a clean surface. Sprinkle each tomato with 1 teaspoon of the cheese mixture and cover with another sun-dried tomato, skin side up to make a sandwich.

3 Pack the tomato sandwiches in a sterilized jar or small glass bowl and cover with extra virgin olive oil. Press down on the tomatoes to eliminate air between layers and add more oil if necessary. Store the tomatoes refrigerated for at least 2–3 weeks before eating.

TOMATO

WINTER SQUASH

Zucca

*W*inter squash? A whole chapter on winter squash? Italy has interesting winter squash preparations rarely seen on restaurant menus, a world beyond split acorn baked with brown sugar and butter. Torquato Innocenti, my favorite farmer at the Santo Spirito market, sells squash by the slice, offered with his usual recipes and cooking advice, a great reason for a squash chapter. And even ardent squash haters may enjoy some of the recipes. My almost antivegetarian son Max loves the soups, gnocchi, and risotto but barely tasted the other recipes, rejected for being "too vegetable."

Different kinds of squash have varying nutritional values—sugar content ranges from 4–16 percent, water from 79–95 percent, and in flavor and texture go from insipid and watery to sweet and firm, depending on cultivar, growing conditions, and ripeness. Squash can be rich in fiber, calcium, and potassium and high in beta-carotene, a precursor of vitamin A. Fully ripe and therefore deeper-colored squash have more carotene. Vitamin A aids in the growth and repair of body tissues, defends mucous membranes, which reduces infection and protects against air pollution, activates the secretion of gastric juices necessary for protein digestion, and prevents night blindness. Squash is an antioxidant and helps to prevent the formation of free radicals. All good reasons to eat squash.

As a member of the Cucurbitacae family of melons and gourds, squash plants have long vinelike shoots with tendrils and unisexual flowers. Staminate males fertilize the ovaries of pistillate females, producing a large berry called a "pepo." Male winter squash flowers can be deep-fried, baked, or braised just like zucchini flowers.

Most books claim that squash, *Cucurbita maxima* or *moschata*, is a New World discovery, and that the *lagenaria* genus of squash, originally from India, was introduced early to Italy and was well known by Roman cooks. Professor Tesi, a fruit and vegetable specialist at the University of Florence, is of a different opinion. He claims that *Cucurbita* squash is originally from Asia, and pumpkin and zucchini (*Cucurbita pepo*) are New World imports. One botanical source identifies Old World examples by their round soft stems, New World pumpkins by sharp polygonal-shaped stems. The Latin for winter squash in Apicius's recipes is *cucurbitas*. So Italians must have known about winter squash before the discovery of America. Since the imported squash resembled a familiar vegetable and tasted better it must have made its way into Italian kitchens with ease.

Lumpy-looking marine squash from coastal Chioggia, a dark green warty-skinned squashed globe with deep orange flesh, is called *zucca barucca* by Venetians. It's starchier than most winter squash and a mixture of winter squash and sweet potato can be substituted for it. Risotto, gnocchi, and soup made from this squash are frequently found on regional winter tables in Veneto and Friuli.

Many Italian recipes require peeling winter squash, easier said than done since many have hard skins that laugh at a knife. Place a piece of newspaper on the floor and drop the squash, which will probably break into manageable-to-peel pieces. Use a sharp heavy knife and keep your hands behind the blade.

Italian traditional squash varieties include Chioggia marine, Neapolitan full or long. Hybrids and non-Italian varieties like butternut and Hubbard are invading the market. American cooks have a wider selection of squash to choose from. Use any firm-textured winter squash like Hubbard, banana, or butternut, or, if squash is too tasteless, a combination of sweet potato and squash. Chioggia marine squash can be ordered from Fratelli Ingegnoli, Corso Buenos Aires 54, Milan 20124.

History

Winter squash stars in three recipes of the first-century Roman millionaire epicure Apicius, who organized banquets of delicacies like flamingo tongues and camel heels but also paid attention to vegetables. He blew his entire fortune on culinary festivities and poisoned himself when he realized that his funds were running low and he'd have to change his dining habits. Apicius's legend survives in a fourth-century compilation of his recipes, *De Re Coquinaria*. Most dishes are dressed with *garum*, a fermented anchovy sauce, probably a cover-up for rotten food. Squash puree with herbs, sweet and sour squash with garlic, herbs, dates, pine nuts, honey and vinegar, and deep-fried squash slices dressed with wine are all flavored with *garum*, surely an acquired taste.

Although bizarre Florentine writer Anton Francesco Doni wrote a book titled *The Squash* in 1551, it's not really about squash. Doni claims it's a "register of chatter, balderdash, fibs, wild daydreams and castles in the sand," although contemporary critics viewed it as "an act of protest against pretentious names currently the rage." Doni mentions three different kinds of winter squash which can be candied, boiled, and braised with eggs, roasted, stewed with spice, fried with sauce, dressed with *agresto* (a cooked vinegar).

Giacomo Castelvetro's 1614 *A Brief Account of the Fruit, Herbs & Vegetables of Italy* attempts to convince the English to eat more vegetables the way the Italians do. He concludes his autumn chapter with a discussion of "marine squash," thus named because weak swimmers can tie two dried gourds to their chests and remain afloat; kids use them the same way to learn to swim in rivers. Large squash are used to make tasty soups, cooked in good broth, thickened with bread crumbs, grated cheese, spices or pepper, and beaten eggs.

In Vincenzo Corrado's 1781 *Of Pythagorean Food*, a regime for nobles and literary-minded readers of delicate digestion that includes meat and fish broth as well as eggs and dairy products, he details three different kinds of squash—*zucchette* in the spring, summer long squash, and hard-skinned, reddish-yellow-fleshed winter squash. Recipes, as usual, sound inviting, for soups, flans, "Spanish-style" squash with chick-peas, red pepper powder, garlic, and herbs, fried fritters with ricotta, and sweet-and-sour squash with candied citron, lemon peel, and cinnamon.

Winter Squash Recipes

SIGNORA ADA'S PENNE WITH SQUASH SAUCE

*Pasta dressed with slow-cooked
braised squash*

———

**FRANCO'S PASTA WITH WINTER SQUASH
AND POTATOES**

*Diced potatoes and squash, boiled with pasta,
dressed with extra virgin olive oil, parsley,
and grated pecorino*

———

LEDA'S SQUASH GNOCCHI

———

SQUASH RISOTTO

———

FABIO'S CREAMY CREAMLESS SQUASH SOUP

Squash, potato, and hot pepper puree

SQUASH, BEAN, AND PASTA SOUP

———

TORQUATO'S MUSHROOM-STYLE SQUASH

*Quick-fried mushroom pieces with garlic
and parsley*

———

**VALERIO'S ROAST SQUASH
AND POTATOES WITH ROSEMARY**

*Chunks of squash and potatoes roasted
with rosemary*

———

**AGOSTINA'S AND THE DUKE'S
MARINATED SQUASH AND ONIONS**

*Squash dressed with a sweet-and-sour
onion mint sauce*

Signora Ada's Penne with Squash Sauce

For 4–6 Servings   First Course

Signora Ada has a stand next to Torquato at the Santo Spirito market and when he's absent she sells me vegetables and gives me cooking advice. "When I make this pasta no one can believe that the sauce is made with squash," she claimed, and my family, not major squash fans, enthusiastically agrees. The sauce is made the same way as Torquato's mushroom-style squash, cooked slowly to a mushier consistency, and used to dress short pasta. A sprinkle of Parmigiano-Reggiano is optional.

> ¾ pound winter squash, peeled and cut into ¾-inch cubes, about 2 cups
>
> 3 tablespoons extra virgin olive oil
>
> 2 garlic cloves, minced
>
> 2 tablespoons chopped Italian parsley
>
> Fine sea salt plus 2–3 tablespoons salt
>
> Freshly ground black pepper
>
> 5–6 quarts water
>
> 14–16 ounces penne or rigatoni
>
> ¼–½ cup grated Parmigiano-Reggiano (optional)

1 Put the squash in a heavy-bottomed 3-quart pot, drizzle with extra virgin olive oil, and stir to coat the squash. Cook over moderate heat until the squash is soft. Add the garlic and parsley and season with salt and pepper.

2 While the squash is cooking, bring 5–6 quarts of water to a rolling boil. Add 2–3 tablespoons salt and the pasta and cook until it still offers considerable resistance to the tooth, about three quarters of the recommended cooking time.

3 Drain the pasta, reserving 2 cups of the cooking water. Add the drained pasta and 1 cup pasta cooking water to the squash. Cook over high heat, stirring to mix sauce and pasta, until the pasta is cooked *al dente* and lightly coated with sauce. Add more pasta water if the sauce gets too dry.

4 Serve with grated cheese if desired.

RED, WHITE
& GREENS

Franco's Pasta with Winter Squash and Potatoes

For 4–6 Servings   First Course

*F*ranco Ricatti of the superlative restaurant Bacco in Apulia, in the heel of the Italian boot, mentioned this dish as an example of home-style regional recipes never found in restaurants. It's the winter version of pasta sauced with zucchini and potatoes, diced and cooked in the same pot as the pasta, drained and finished with extra virgin olive oil and grated Parmigiano. I like to spice up this simple pasta with garlic and hot red pepper and skip the cheese.

> 5–6 quarts water
>
> ¾ pound squash, peeled and cut into ¾-inch cubes, about 2 cups
>
> 1 large yellow-fleshed potato, peeled and cut into ¾-inch cubes
>
> 2–3 tablespoons salt plus coarse sea salt
>
> 14–16 ounces spaghetti
>
> 1–2 garlic cloves, chopped
>
> 1 small piece of hot red pepper or chili pepper flakes to taste
>
> 2 tablespoons chopped Italian parsley
>
> 2–3 tablespoons extra virgin olive oil
>
> ½ cup grated Parmigiano-Reggiano (optional)

1 Bring 5–6 quarts of water to a rolling boil. Add the squash, potato, and 2–3 tablespoons salt. Cook for 2 minutes, add the pasta, and cook until it offers considerable resistance to the tooth, about three quarters of the recommended cooking time.

2 While the pasta is cooking, put the garlic, hot pepper, and parsley in a large nonstick skillet and drizzle with 1 tablespoon extra virgin olive oil. Place the skillet over moderate heat and when garlic begins to sizzle remove from the heat.

3 Drain the pasta and the vegetables, reserving 2 cups of the cooking water.

4 Put the drained pasta and vegetables in the skillet with the garlic and add 1 cup pasta cooking water. Cook over highest heat, stirring, until the pasta is cooked, surrounded by a creamy sauce. Add more cooking water if the sauce dries out.

5 Serve the pasta in bowls, topped with a drizzle of olive oil and optional cheese.

Leda's Squash Gnocchi

*L*eda della Rovere cooks at her family's restaurant in Manzano, the chair capital of Italy, in the untouristed region of Friuli, between Venice and ex-Yugoslavia. Her food is earthy, based on first-rate local ingredients, and although she reads all the food magazines her cooking remains firmly rooted in her native tradition. Leda makes wonderful squash gnocchi, often leaden in the hands of lesser cooks who use more flour. She steams winter squash, then drains to eliminate excess water, but I find that baking is easier. Leda uses marine squash, I use a butternut-like squash in Florence, but a combination of butternut and sweet potato also produces fine results. Leda uses smoked ricotta, a specialty of Friuli rarely found outside the borders of the region. Although it's not dry like smoked (but not salty) ricotta, smoked provola can be used.

¾ pound uncooked winter squash, to make about 1 cup
    pureed cooked

¼ pound sweet potato, about ½ cup pureed cooked

2 eggs

Fine sea salt plus 2–3 tablespoons salt

1–1½ cups sifted flour

4–5 quarts water

2–3 tablespoons melted butter

6 fresh sage leaves, chopped

Freshly ground pepper

½ cup grated smoked provola (or other smoked cheese)

1 Preheat the oven to 400 degrees.

2 Cut the squash in half and bake it in a pan with the sweet potato for 1 hour or until tender. Cool the squash and sweet potato.

3 Peel the squash and sweet potato and put through the fine disk of a food mill or grate with the fine disk in the food processor. Measure 1½ cups of squash and sweet potato puree.

4 Combine the squash, eggs, salt, and 1 cup of flour to make a paste firm enough to shape with a spoon but softer than dough. Fold in more flour, ¼ cup at a time, if necessary.

(continued)

WINTER SQUASH

5 Bring 4–5 quarts of water to a rolling boil. Add 2–3 tablespoons salt.

6 Push half-teaspoonfuls of dough, which will be sticky, into the boiling water, 6–8 in the pot at the same time, and cook until they rise to the surface. If gnocchi don't float after 2 or 3 minutes, use a wooden spoon to gently dislodge them from the bottom of the pot. Remove the gnocchi with a slotted spoon and cool on a clean surface. Reserve the cooking water to heat up the gnocchi for serving.

7 Melt the butter over low heat in a large nonstick skillet and add the sage. Season with salt and pepper.

8 Bring the cooking water back to a boil, add the gnocchi, and cook for 3–4 minutes to heat. Drain carefully, reserving 1 cup cooking water.

9 Put the gnocchi in the skillet with the butter and sage, add ½ cup cooking water, and cook over high heat, shaking the skillet to gently mix, until gnocchi have formed a creamy sauce.

10 Put the sauced gnocchi in individual bowls, top with the cheese, and serve immediately.

Squash Risotto

"CHIOGGIA VEAL" reads the sign next to the warty, green-skinned marine winter squash in the Venice Rialto produce market, succinctly defining provenance (the nearby coastal city of Chioggia) and the tender but meaty quality of this local vegetable. At a Halloween squash risotto cook-off between Natale Rusconi, managing director of the Hotel Cipriani in Venice, and his head chef, Renato Piccolotto, I learned two different ways of making this Venetian winter specialty and although Chef Piccolotto's version was brighter, more attractive, Natale's, zapped with *peperoncino* chili pepper, was easier to execute. His risotto is served in a hollowed-out squash, an elegant and practical presentation, since the rice is flavored with the scraped-out squash. Both cooks used marine squash but Hubbard, banana, or butternut squash can be substituted. If squash is tasteless, use a mixture of squash and sweet potato.

> 1 small onion, chopped
>
> 1 tablespoon minced fresh rosemary
>
> 1 small piece of hot red pepper or 1 pinch chili pepper flakes
>
> ¼ cup extra virgin olive oil
>
> 1 cup rice for risotto, Carnaroli or Vialone Nano
>
> 1 pound winter squash, peeled and chopped, about 2 cups
>
> ¼ cup white wine (optional)
>
> 8–10 cups simmering lightly salted vegetable broth (made with 1 onion, 1 garlic clove, 1 carrot, 1 celery stalk, and a few parsley stems, cooked for 15 minutes) or simmering water
>
> Salt (optional)
>
> ½ cup grated Parmigiano-Reggiano (and additional cheese for the table, if desired)

1   Put the onion, rosemary, and hot pepper in a heavy-bottomed 4-quart pot, drizzle with 2 tablespoons extra virgin olive oil, and stir to coat the onion with the oil. Cook over low heat until the onion is soft.

2   Add the rice, stir to coat with the oil, and cook for a few minutes to lightly toast.

3   Add the squash and stir to combine with the rice. Add the wine if you are using it and raise the heat to evaporate the wine.   *(continued)*

4   Add the simmering vegetable broth (or boiling water and a little salt) 1 cup at a time, stirring frequently with a *long* wooden spoon or fork, over highest heat. Boiling risotto attains the temperature of molten lava and it's wise to keep one's distance while stirring. Add more vegetable broth when risotto is still surrounded by liquid, stirring often. After about 10 minues of cooking begin to add broth ½ cup at a time. Taste the rice after about 15 minutes of cooking. It should be firm under tooth, *al dente*, since it will still cook for a few minutes. Liquid should be a little soupy because the Parmigiano cheese, oil (or butter), and final whipping will tighten up sauce, which should be opaque, bathing individual kernels.

5   Add the grated cheese and the remaining extra virgin olive oil (or 2 tablespoons butter) and stir energetically with a long-handled wooden spoon or fork, over high heat to whip the ingredients together.

6   Remove from heat, ladle into individual bowls, and let risotto rest for a minute before serving. Top with additional Parmigiano if desired.

Fabio's Creamy Creamless Squash Soup

For 6–8 Servings   **First Course**

Fabio Picchi and Benedetta Vitale of the restaurant Cibrèo in Florence cook like Tuscan grannies, using seasonal vegetables to great advantage. Flavors are typically Florentine, creamless, enriched with extra virgin olive oil and a zap of spicy *peperoncino* hot pepper, grown by Fabio's father. Creamy, creamless soups and polenta are the usual first-course choices. "Pasta isn't really Florentine," claims Fabio, "so we don't serve it." I suspect the logistics of cooking pasta in a tiny kitchen with two restaurants to service may also figure in Fabio's anti-pasta stance.

Cibrèo's smooth golden orange soup pairs squash with a sprinkle of amaretti cookie crumbs, echoing the combination of northern Mantua's *tortelli,* fresh pasta stuffed with squash and amaretti cookies, but is far easier to prepare. Fabio, like many restaurant cooks, always has meat broth conveniently on hand and uses it as the base of this soup, but I prefer water, always available in my kitchen. Stock makers, canned broth lovers, and bouillon cube users can substitute their favorite form of broth but vegetarians and lazy cooks like me won't miss the flavor of meat.

1 celery stalk, chopped

1 medium carrot, chopped

1 medium onion, chopped

2 tablespoons extra virgin olive oil plus more for garnish

1 pound winter squash, peeled and cubed
    (Hubbard, banana, or butternut), about 3 cups

½ pound all-purpose potatoes, peeled and cubed,
    about 1½ cups

1 whole hot pepper

3½ cups boiling water or light stock

2 teaspoons coarse sea salt

1 amaretti cookie for garnish

1   Put the chopped celery, carrot, and onion in a 3-quart pot and drizzle with extra virgin olive oil. Stir to coat the vegetables with the oil and place over low heat. Cook, stirring occasionally, for 10 minutes or until the vegetables are tender but not brown.

2   Add the squash, potatoes, and hot pepper and cover with the boiling water or broth. Season with salt.

(continued)

WINTER SQUASH

3 Bring to a simmer and cook for 20 minutes or until the vegetables are tender.

4 Remove and discard the hot pepper and blend the vegetables and their broth in a food processor or with an immersion mixer until smooth. Keep the soup hot.

5 Place the amaretti cookie in a small plastic bag and crush to form fine crumbs.

6 Ladle the soup into bowls and garnish with a pinch of amaretti crumbs and a drizzle of extra virgin olive oil.

Squash, Bean, and Pasta Soup

For 6–8 Servings   **First Course**

*A*lthough the warty, green-skinned, orange-fleshed winter squash called the *zucca barucca* is found in markets all over the region of Veneto whenever I asked what to do with it everyone always replied "risotto." "Only risotto?" I asked and my reward was this recipe for a hearty winter soup of beans and squash, flavored with rosemary, and with pasta, "just like *pasta e fagioli*" I was told. It's packed with protein, easy to prepare if you've got cooked white beans on hand. Lazy cooks can opt for canned beans with lesser results but watch out for salt. Forget about the rule to never break spaghetti and snap off 2-inch lengths, or use a small, tubular pasta. But this soup also tastes terrific without the pasta.

¾ pound winter squash, peeled and cut into
    ¾-inch cubes, about 2 cups

¼ cup extra virgin olive oil

1 small onion, chopped

3 cups cooked white beans

3 cups bean cooking water, meat or vegetable broth,
    or water

Coarse sea salt

Freshly ground black pepper

1 cup boiling water

5 ounces short pasta or broken spaghetti

1   Put the squash in a heavy-bottomed 4-quart pot, sprinkle with 2 tablespoons of extra virgin oil, and toss to coat. Place over high heat to lightly brown.

2   Reduce the heat to low, add the onion, and cook, stirring occasionally, until the onion begins to brown. Add the beans, cooking water, broth, or water, and season with salt and pepper; simmer for 10–15 minutes or until the squash is tender.

3   Blend one third of the soup in a food processor and return it to the pot or use an immersion blender and blend to a chunky consistency.

4   Add 1 cup of boiling water and the pasta to the soup and cook until the pasta is done (timing will depend on the size of the pasta), stirring often to prevent sticking. Serve with a drizzle of extra virgin olive oil. Eliminate this last step for a pasta-less winter vegetable soup. Soup can be ladled into bowls and topped with a drizzle of extra virgin olive oil.

Torquato's Mushroom-Style Squash

*L*istening to Torquato Innocenti, my favorite farmer at the Santo Spirito market, talking about vegetables is better than researching in Renaissance libraries, reading botanical, herbal, and medical books, or talking to chefs. His Tuscan accent and attitude are reflected in his culinary-dietary advice, never a mention of butter or cream, not part of his palate. His recipes are always simple outlines, related while he weighs, bags, and calculates the price of his vegetables without the help of a calculator. "Cut the squash into pieces, fry in a puddle of oil, and sprinkle with garlic and parsley, both good for the blood," was Torquato's minimalist sales pitch for his tan-skinned, deep orange-fleshed squash. It sounded too good to be true—no steaming or baking, 10 minutes, one pan. Stir-frying eliminates the excess moisture and lightly caramelizes the squash's natural sugar, easier, faster, and tastier than baking.

> 1½ pounds squash, peeled and cut into 1-inch cubes,
>   about 4½ cups
>
> 3 tablespoons extra virgin olive oil
>
> Fine sea salt
>
> Freshly ground black pepper
>
> 1 garlic clove, minced
>
> 2 tablespoons chopped Italian parsley

1 Put the squash in a large nonstick skillet, drizzle with extra virgin olive oil, stir to coat the squash, and season with salt and pepper. Turn heat to medium-high and cook the squash, shaking the pan to prevent burning, for 5–10 minutes or until the squash is tender.

2 Add the garlic and parsley to the squash, stir to combine, and serve hot or at room temperature.

Valerio's Roast Squash
and Potatoes with Rosemary

*T*orquato doesn't come to market by himself anymore. He's slowing down a little and needs help shifting crates, weighing, adding, making change, wrapping and bagging produce while reciting recipes. When he's assisted by his fireman son, Valerio, culinary discussions are frequent and often involve clients who exchange recipes. Valerio is a good cook and has his own ideas. He uses a wider range of ingredients than Torquato but his recipes are always simple, just like his father's. "Mix chunks of squash with potatoes and a little rosemary and roast in the oven," was Valerio's advice one day. Baking vegetables in one layer on a nonstick surface prevents the caramelized crusts (the best part) from sticking to the pan. Potatoes pick up some of the squash flavors, and the squash gets overcooked and crispy. I never have leftovers.

> 1 pound yellow-fleshed potatoes, peeled and cut into ¾-inch cubes, about 2 cups
>
> 1½ pounds winter squash, peeled and cut into 1-inch cubes (Hubbard, banana, or butternut), about 4 cups
>
> ¼ cup extra virgin olive oil
>
> 2 tablespoons fresh rosemary
>
> Fine sea salt
>
> Freshly ground black pepper

1 Preheat the oven to 400 degrees.

2 Put the potatoes in a bowl of cold water for 5 minutes to remove excess starch.

3 Drain the potatoes and pat dry with paper towels. Place the potatoes and squash in one layer in a nonstick roasting pan. Drizzle with extra virgin olive oil, sprinkle with rosemary, and season with salt and pepper.

4 Roast the potatoes and squash for 1 hour or until well browned, stirring after 30 minutes to cook evenly. Serve immediately.

Agostina's and the Duke's Marinated Squash and Onions

*E*nrico Alliata, the Duke of Salaparuta, probably wrote his undated *Vegetarian Cooking and Raw Naturism*, a "manual of naturistic gastrophy" in the 1920s. The Sicilian duke advocates the suppression of "degenerate necrophagistic appetites," and stands firmly against eating "dead bodies." But in spite of his radical stance and worldly aristocratic style his Sicilian recipes are wonderful. The duke treats squash like tuna and gives it what he calls the *skapici* treatment, sauced with an onion, vinegar, mint sauce, served at room temperature. His recipe resembles the sweet-and-sour onion sauce, *cipollata*, that I've eaten at Marchesa Anna Tasca's table. She, like the duke, grew up eating the elegant cuisine of the aristocracy along with traditional Sicilian soul food. They ate their *cipollata* on meat or fish, while the less affluent used the same sauce on thickly sliced vegetables. Agostina, who works for Anna, gave me her recipe for winter squash sauced with *cipollata*. She adds a hint of sugar to her sauce that the duke leaves out.

> 1½ pounds squash, peeled and sliced ¾-inch thick
>
> 3–4 tablespoons extra virgin olive oil
>
> Fine sea salt
>
> Freshly ground black pepper
>
> 2 large red onions, sliced
>
> 3 tablespoons red wine vinegar
>
> 1 tablespoon sugar (optional)
>
> 3 tablespoons roughly chopped fresh mint

1   Brush the squash slices with 1 tablespoon olive oil and cook them in a large nonstick skillet over moderately high heat for 5–8 minutes or until well browned. Turn the slices over, lower the heat, cover the pan, and cook for another 8–10 minutes, or until the squash is tender when pierced with a toothpick. Remove the squash from the pan with a spatula, season with salt and pepper, and place on a platter.

2   Put the onions in the skillet, drizzle with 2–3 tablespoons extra virgin olive oil, and cook over low heat until soft.

3   Add the vinegar, sugar, and mint to the onions, season with salt and pepper, stir to combine well, raise the heat to moderate, and cook for 1–2 minutes.

4   Pour the contents of the skillet over the squash and cool. Serve at room temperature.

Zucchini
and
Zucchini
Flowers

*T*he British may try to make zucchini sound like a fancy French vegetable (courgette) but everyone else uses the Italian name. Zucchini is a spring and summer vegetable although it's found throughout the year, far beyond its natural season. Tasteless supermarket specimens, creations like zucchini muffins and baseball bat-sized gifts from gardeners give zucchini a bad name. Dwarf (or is it dimensionally challenged?) zucchini may be cute but don't improve the situation. The key to great-tasting zucchini is early harvesting, because it should be utilized unripe, small, before seeds develop, hence the diminutive "*ini*" suffix preceded by *zucca*, Italian for squash.

Zucchini practice the safe sex of the vegetable kingdom, unisexual yellow-orange flowers on the same plant. Male staminate flowers are on stems, big and flashy; female pistillate flowers are smaller, attached to ovaries that turn into zucchini. Males are sold in Italian markets, destined to be stuffed, deep-fried, cooked with rice, pasta, or eggs. Female fruit is often sold with its flower, which turns brown and dries out after a day or two. Perishable squash flowers of either sex rarely turn up in American markets but home gardeners can harvest fruitless males. In Sicily, tender shoots and leaves, called *tenerumi*, are sold in markets but I've never seen them served in a restaurant, too humble to be taken seriously. *Tenerumi* are said to be digestively cleansing and are usually treated simply, either boiled or cooked with pasta in a simple soup.

It's not easy to sort out how the zucchini, a member of the Cucurbitacae squash and melon family, came to Italy. Some sources claim that zucchini and squash are American, yet there are many classical references that precede the discovery of the New World. Others say that gourds, *Lagenaria* genus are Old World, and pumpkin and squash members of the *Cucurbita* genus are American. A dependable botanical source says zucchini come from South Africa but skirts the squash/pumpkin question. The term squash is used generically in many Italian gastronomic texts, while others differentiate between winter and long squash. The term *zucchetta*, little squash, is used. It was probably an easy transition from long, green Old World squash to shorter, tender, tastier, green New World specimens.

Zucchini is more than 90 percent water, low in calories, high in potassium, but without great nutritional benefits. Italians consider it a safe vegetable for those suffering digestive ills, condemned to eating a bland, boiled diet referred to as "in white." All my usual sources of folklore and home cures are silent on the effects of zucchini, though they've got plenty to say about winter squash.

Although zucchini is available all year long, it's at its best in the spring and summer, its natural season. Fresher is better. Zucchini should be firm with taut, unwrinkled, blemish-free skin. Male zucchini flowers on stems are usually picked in the evening when the flowers are closed. Many cookbooks suggest removing the stamens but all the Italians I asked don't bother so I don't either. Flowers should be soaked in cold water for 30 minutes to refresh and crisp them.

Zucchini are treated with respect in Italian home kitchens although restaurant diners will have a hard time getting beyond boiled or deep-fried zucchini or deep-fried zucchini flowers. Ligurians make a rice and zucchini custard pie. In Campania, they make a simple soup of zucchini and its flowers, cooked with lard, onions, broth or water, served over toasted bread. Zucchini are baked with Parmigiano, stuffed with bread crumbs, meat, or tuna, cooked mushroom-style with garlic and *nepitella*, a kind of wild mint. Sicilians fry zucchini slices and garnish tomato-sauced pasta with them. Neapolitans deep-fry zucchini and marinate with garlic, oregano, and vinegar. Florentines make a "mess," *buglione*, zucchini cooked with tomato until soft and creamy, not a dish for *al dente* vegetable lovers.

Italian regional cultivars include the green of Milan, Italian or Apulian striped, Albenga or little trumpet, Faenza and pale round from Nice. Some of these varieties can be purchased through Pinetree Garden Seeds, Box 300, New Gloucester, Maine 04260, Telephone: 207–926–3400; The Cook's Garden, P.O. Box 535, Londonderry, Vermont 05148, Telephone: 802–824–3400; and Shepherd's Garden Seeds, 6116 Highway 9, Felton, California 95018, Telephone: 408–335–6910; or from Ingegnoli, Corso Buenos Aires 54, Milan 20124.

History

Giacomo Castelvetro, in his summer chapter, refers to ". . . long white squash as big as a large arm, although this size isn't attained by all . . . " He is surely the first recipe writer on record to work with baseball-bat zucchini. Castelvetro advises the English to boil big zucchini, then stew them with onions, oil, and *agresto*, a lightly acidic vinegar.

Florentine Francesco Gaudenzio (1648–1733) cooked in Jesuit monasteries in Spoleto, Rome, and Arezzo. His 1705 *Tuscan Oiled Bread* presents everyday food with vague recipes that often include modifications for fast days. He never mentions quantities but measures the initial boil in a long squash soup recipe with two Miserere, the Fifty-first Psalm, said to take about 3 or 4 minutes, followed by a second boil in broth, finished with oil, salt, pepper, parsley, basil, and *agresta*.

Ex-monk and best-selling author Vincenzo Corrado's *The Gallant Cook* (1773) and *Of Pythagorean Food* (1781) both contain long squash, winter squash, and tender squash shoot recipes. He writes about many varieties of squash, traces their use to the Romans, and recommends peeling medium-sized *zucchette*, slicing, salting, and squeezing to expel bad humors. Some recipes in both books have the same name but are actually quite different. My favorite is Corrado's "Italian-style squash," baked under hot coals or in the oven, dressed with oil, lemon, garlic, mint, and pepper.

Zucchini Recipes

LISA'S GRILLED ZUCCHINI

Grilled, then marinated with parsley, garlic, and extra virgin olive oil

—

FRANCESCA'S ZUCCHINI *CARPACCIO*

Wafer-thin raw zucchini slices dressed with arugula and Parmigiano

—

FRANCO'S PASTA WITH ZUCCHINI AND POTATOES

Pasta is cooked together with zucchini and potato cubes, dressed with chopped arugula, extra virgin olive oil, and Parmigiano

—

ZUCCHINI RISOTTO

TORQUATO'S ZUCCHINI CIGARS

Pan-browned baby zucchini

—

TORQUATO'S ZUCCHINI WITH SPICY TOMATO SAUCE

Buglione Piccante

—

DANIA'S STUFFED ZUCCHINI FLOWERS

—

THE DUKE'S PASTA WITH PSEUDO-CLAM SAUCE

—

TORQUATO'S ZUCCHINI FLOWER *FRITTATA*

Lisa's Grilled Zucchini

*C*ountess Lisa Contini is one of the greatest home-cooks in Tuscany. Her husband, Count Ugo, and many of her seven children work at the family winery and her table is always set for 12 to accommodate visiting family and friends, there to taste Tenuta di Capezzana's fine wine. Count Ugo complains in jest that Lisa's cooking is so good that wine tasters forget to focus on the wine. The estate's extra virgin olive oil, a personal favorite, is an important element of Lisa's *cucina*. She cooks in an easygoing style, changing recipes according to what's in the garden and larder, and is hard to pin down about quantities. But this recipe is too easy and all the ingredients are visible. Lisa slices her zucchini with an electric meat slicer, I use the 3-mm blade of my Cuisinart like a mandoline. She grills the slices on a ridged grill pan, marinates with Capezzana's fine extra virgin olive oil, garlic, and parsley, and serves the zucchini at room temperature. "Leftover zucchini submerged in extra virgin olive oil will keep for a week in the refrigerator," says Lisa.

> 4 medium-sized zucchini
> 1–2 garlic cloves, minced
> 2 tablespoons chopped Italian parsley
> Sea salt
> Freshly ground black pepper
> 3–4 tablespoons extra virgin olive oil

1 Cut the ends off the zucchini and slice lengthwise into thin slices, ⅛ inch thick.

2 Lightly oil a ridged cast-iron grill and place over high heat. Grill the zucchini slices for 2–3 minutes on each side, turning with tongs.

3 Put the zucchini slices on a serving platter, sprinkle with the garlic and parsley, season with salt and pepper, and drizzle with extra virgin olive oil. Serve at room temperature.

Francesca's Zucchini *Carpaccio*

For 4–6 Servings   Appetizer

*H*ow did new-wave raw zucchini *carpaccio*, a vegetarian variation of a Venetian raw meat appetizer, wind up on the menu of Borgo Antico, a popular neighborhood pizzeria around the corner from my apartment? Florentine Francesca Cianci moved to New York and cooked at the restaurant Mezzaluna for 5 years, came home in 1990, and got a job managing Borgo Antico. She added stylish but simple dishes to the menu, using the produce from the farmers at the Santo Spirito market in front of the restaurant. Francesca now cooks at Il Borghetto, an elegant country inn in Montefiridolfi outside Florence, and Borgo Antico no longer serves her zucchini *carpaccio*. But I make it all the time when the farmers at the market sell fresh, just-picked zucchini since it's one of fastest recipes I know, an almost effortless appetizer with no cooking and only five ingredients plus salt and pepper. Each one should be of the highest quality. Fresh seasonal zucchini are imperative and flaccid supermarket zucchini should be avoided. I hand-slice tender zucchini, using a 1-mm food processor blade like a mandoline for thin, uniform results and use a potato peeler to produce curls of Parmigiano cheese. Two medium-sized zucchini, sliced paper thin, can cover an entire platter.

> 2 small fresh zucchini
> ⅓ cup tightly packed arugula, roughly chopped
> 3 tablespoons extra virgin olive oil
> 1 teaspoon balsamic vinegar (optional)
> Fine sea salt
> Freshly ground black pepper
> 1 piece of Parmigiano-Reggiano, about 4–6 ounces

1 Trim the ends off the zucchini and slice into paper-thin rounds on a mandoline, meat slicer, or with a 1-mm food processor blade. *Be careful.* Put the zucchini on a large serving platter.

2 Chop the arugula and sprinkle it over the zucchini.

3 Drizzle with extra virgin olive oil and the balsamic vinegar and season with salt and pepper.

4 Shave curls of Parmigiano-Reggiano directly over the platter to cover the zucchini and arugula. Serve immediately.

Franco's Pasta with Zucchini and Potatoes

For 4–6 Servings · **First Course**

"No one wants to eat this kind of food in a restaurant" Franco Ricatti, owner of the now closed Ristorante Bacco in Barletta, Apulia, told me, "but we make it all the time at home." He described this one-pot preparation of pasta boiled with diced zucchini and potatoes, dressed with extra virgin olive oil and grated cheese, and I begged him to make it for me. The guidebooks love Franco's creative cuisine, prepared with the finest local seafood, lamb, and wild and cultivated vegetables, but he knows that I'm more impressed by simple regional home-style cooking. Franco breaks the spaghetti into 2-inch pieces but I don't bother. And he doesn't use any herbs, unusual behavior in Italy, but I like to add a little parsley or basil.

> 5–6 quarts water
>
> 1 large potato, peeled and cut into ½-inch cubes
>
> 2–3 tablespoons salt
>
> 2 medium zucchini, cut into ½-inch cubes
>
> 14–16 ounces spaghettini
>
> 2–3 tablespoons extra virgin olive oil
>
> Freshly ground black pepper
>
> 2 tablespoons chopped Italian parsley or basil (optional)
>
> ½ cup grated Parmigiano

1 Bring 5–6 quarts of water to a rolling boil. Add the potato and 2–3 tablespoons salt. Cook the potato for 2 minutes, add the zucchini and the pasta, and cook until *al dente* and offering some resistance to the tooth. Bear in mind that the pasta doesn't cook with the sauce in this recipe.

2 Drain the pasta and the vegetables, reserving ½ cup of the cooking water. Put the pasta in a serving bowl, drizzle with extra virgin olive oil, season with pepper, add the optional herbs, 2–3 tablespoons cooking water, and the Parmigiano. Add another spoonful or two of the cooking water if the pasta is too dry. Stir well to combine and serve immediately.

Zucchini Risotto

For 3–4 Servings   **First Course**

*P*rimizia is the word for the earliest examples of seasonal produce, the first to
appear in the markets, precious and much more expensive than those of the
full-fledged season. The spring's first zucchini are a reason to rejoice after a winter
of cabbage, beans, potatoes, and leeks. I have to shop early in the morning if I want
a chance at Torquato's earliest zucchini and thinned-out basil plants from his garden outside town since customers at the Santo Spirito market are as hungry as I
am for a change.

Harry's Bar in Venice makes risotto *alla primavera*, spring-style, with a mixture
of zucchini, mushrooms, artichokes, asparagus, bell peppers, and tomatoes, a lovely
combination of vegetables, but they don't appear at Torquato's stand in the same
season. I make my own version of spring-style risotto with the earliest zucchini and
basil, so delicately flavored that I don't want to combine them with anything else.

1 small onion, chopped

2 garlic cloves, chopped

¼ cup extra virgin olive oil or 2 tablespoons extra virgin
    olive oil and 2 tablespoons butter

1 cup rice for risotto, Carnaroli or Vialone Nano
    (see page 8 for information about rice)

¾ pound zucchini, trimmed and chopped or diced,
    about 2¼ cups

¼ cup white wine (optional)

8–10 cups simmering lightly salted vegetable broth
    (made with 1 onion, 1 garlic clove, 1 carrot, 1 celery
    stalk, and a few parsley stems, cooked for 15 minutes)
    or simmering water

Salt

2 tablespoons chopped fresh basil

Freshly ground black pepper

½ cup grated Parmigiano-Reggiano (and additional
    cheese if desired)

1 Put the onion and garlic in a heavy-bottomed 4-quart pot, drizzle with 2 tablespoons
extra virgin olive oil, and stir to coat the vegetables with the oil. Cook over low heat
until the onion is soft.

2　Add the rice, stir to coat with the oil, and cook for a few minutes to lightly toast.

3　Add the zucchini and stir to combine with the rice. Add the wine if you are using it and raise the heat to evaporate the wine.

4　Add the simmering vegetable broth (or simmering water and a little salt) 1 cup at a time, stirring frequently with a *long* wooden spoon or fork, over highest heat. Boiling risotto attains the temperature of molten lava and it's wise to keep your distance while stirring. Add more vegetable broth when the risotto is still surrounded by liquid, stirring often. After 10 minutes of cooking, begin to add broth ½ cup at a time. Taste the rice after about 15 minutes of cooking. It should be firm under tooth, *al dente*, since it will still cook for a few minutes. The risotto should be a little soupy because the grated cheese, oil (or butter), and final whipping will tighten up the sauce, which should be opaque, bathing the individual kernels.

5　Add the grated cheese and the remaining extra virgin olive oil (or 2 tablespoons butter) and stir energetically with a long-handled wooden spoon or fork over high heat to whip the ingredients together.

6　Remove from the heat, stir in the basil, and season with pepper. Ladle the risotto into individual bowls and let them cool for a minute before serving. Top the risotto with Parmigiano if desired.

Torquato's Zucchini Cigars

For 4–6 Servings   **Side Dish**

*T*orquato Innocenti, my favorite farmer at the Santo Spirito market in Florence, sells his just-harvested, still prickly zucchini with their flowers attached, a sure sign of freshness. He dispenses culinary tips and talks about the benefits of eating his "unmedicated" vegetables, a double-edged sales pitch that always works with me. I find both recipes and vegetables irresistible. Torquato's simple advice for cooking his zucchini was to roast them whole in a "puddle" of oil in a pan and serve with basil. I bought a bag of his smallest cigar-sized zucchini and pan-roasted them until brown, sprinkled them with chopped basil, and loved the results. Fresh, lively zucchini are a must or else zucchini will turn into mush held together by tough skin. Gardeners should pick zucchini before the blossoms open and cook the zucchini with their female flowers attached.

> 8–10 small cigar-sized fresh zucchini
> 2–3 tablespoons extra virgin olive oil
> 2 tablespoons chopped fresh basil
> Fine sea salt
> Freshly ground black pepper

1 Trim the stem end off the zucchini. Those lucky enough to have fresh flower-tipped zucchini should carefully rinse the zucchini without detaching the flowers.

2 Put the zucchini in one layer in a large nonstick skillet. Drizzle with 1 tablespoon extra virgin olive oil and shake the pan to coat the zucchini with the oil.

3 Place the pan over moderate heat and cook the zucchini, shaking the pan to turn them, until browned all over, about 20–25 minutes.

4 Remove the zucchini to a serving platter, sprinkle with basil, season with salt and pepper, and drizzle with 1–2 tablespoons extra virgin olive oil. Serve hot or at room temperature.

Torquato's Zucchini
with Spicy Tomato Sauce
Buglione Piccante

For 4–6 Servings   **Side Dish**

---

*C*rates of round and long zucchini, partially and super-ripe tomatoes of three different varieties, and bunches of basil with dirt-covered roots wrapped in ripped-up magazines grace Torquato's trestle table at the Santo Spirito market at the height of summer. Traditional Tuscans make *buglione*, a "mess" of zucchini stewed with tomato and basil but Torquato's recipe is spiced with *peperoncino* hot red pepper, a big improvement over the blander classic.

> 1 pound zucchini, thinly sliced (2-mm processor blade)
>
> 3 tablespoons extra virgin olive oil
>
> 2 garlic cloves, chopped
>
> 1 fresh hot red pepper, chopped, or dry chili pepper flakes to taste
>
> 1 cup tomato pulp, fresh or canned
>
> 2 tablespoons chopped fresh basil or Italian parsley
>
> Fine sea salt

1   Put the zucchini in a large nonstick skillet, drizzle with 2 tablespoons extra virgin olive oil, stir to coat the zucchini with the oil, and place over high heat. When the zucchini start to sizzle, lower the heat to moderate, and cook, stirring frequently, until lightly browned.

2   Push the zucchini to the sides of the skillet. Pour the remaining extra virgin olive oil in the center of the skillet, add the garlic and hot pepper, and cook for a minute or two.

3   Add the tomato pulp to the pan, stir to combine well, and simmer for 5 minutes. Add the basil or parsley, season with salt, and serve hot or at room temperature.

Dania's Stuffed Zucchini Flowers

*D*ania Luccherini's restaurant/country inn, La Chiusa in Montefollonico, is set in the sweet Tuscan countryside of olives and vines with the hilltop city of Montepulciano in the distance. Dania's cooking is flavorful and elegant without being fussy. I'm wild about her zucchini flowers, stuffed with cheese and briefly braised in tomato sauce. I bake mine in the oven and serve the sauce separately. Piping the ricotta stuffing into the flowers is no more difficult than piping toothpaste on a toothbrush.

> 12 large zucchini blossoms
> 10 ounces whole milk ricotta, drained for 30 minutes in a
>   sieve, if watery
> 1 egg
> ¼ cup grated Parmigiano-Reggiano
> 2 tablespoons chopped Italian parsley
> Fine sea salt
> Freshly ground black pepper
> 1 garlic clove, minced
> 2 tablespoons extra virgin olive oil
> 2 cups tomato pulp, fresh or canned

1 Carefully wash and drain the zucchini flowers. Stamens don't need to be removed.

2 Combine the ricotta, egg, grated Parmigiano-Reggiano, parsley, and season with salt and pepper.

3 Transfer the cheese mixture to a pastry bag or a plastic bag with a ½-inch corner cut off, and pipe the mixture into the zucchini flowers.

4 Put the garlic in a large nonstick skillet and drizzle with extra virgin olive oil. Place over moderate heat and when the garlic is sizzling add the tomato pulp. Cook for 5 minutes and season with salt and pepper.

5 Add the zucchini flowers to the tomato sauce and cook for another 5 minutes. Serve hot.

Note: Alternately, bake the stuffed flowers in a preheated 400 degree oven for 15 minutes or until lightly browned and serve with the tomato sauce.

The Duke's Pasta with Pseudo-Clam Sauce

For 4–6 Servings   **First Course**

*I*n his book *Vegetarian Cooking and Raw Naturism,* the Sicilian Duke of
Salaparuta advocates the suppression of "degenerate necrophagistic appetites,"
and includes international vegetarian recipes. But his best recipes are traditional
Sicilian or vegetarianized versions of classic dishes. The duke's vermicelli with
pseudo-clams is a perfect example of the latter. He feels that the taste of zucchini
flowers resembles the taste of clams. I don't think the duke's recipe really tastes like
clam sauce but I love his pasta anyway.

2 garlic cloves, chopped

1 small onion, chopped

2 tablespoons chopped Italian parsley

2–3 tablespoons extra virgin olive oil

12 zucchini flowers, chopped

1 pinch saffron threads or ⅛ teaspoon powdered saffron,
softened or dissolved in ½ cup hot water

1 cup tomato pulp

Sea salt plus 2–3 tablespoons salt

Freshly ground black pepper

5–6 quarts water

14–16 ounces spaghetti or vermicelli

1   Put the garlic, onion, and parsley in a large nonstick skillet. Drizzle with the olive oil,
stir to coat the vegetables with the oil, and cook over moderate heat until sizzling.

2   Add the zucchini flowers. Stir to combine with the onion and garlic, and cook until
wilted.

3   Add the saffron and water, and the tomato pulp, and season with salt and pepper;
simmer for 5 minutes.

4   Bring 5–6 quarts of water to a rolling boil. Add 2–3 tablespoons salt and the pasta
and cook until it still offers considerable resistance to the tooth, about three quarters
of the recommended cooking time.

5   Drain the pasta, reserving 2 cups of the cooking water. Add the pasta and 1 cup
cooking water to the sauce. Cook over high heat, stirring to combine, until the pasta
is cooked al dente and lightly coated with sauce. Add more pasta water if needed.
Serve immediately.

Torquato's Zucchini Flower *Frittata*

*T*orquato suggested this pan-fried flower *frittata* flavored with basil, which begins with a "puddle" of oil from his own trees. Early birds can purchase small super-fresh eggs from Torquato's own chickens along with zucchini, basil, and garlic.

There are different ways to cook a *frittata*. Liliana, the cook at Castello di Ama in the heart of Chianti, cooks one side, flips it over onto a plate, and slips it back into the pan to cook the other side. Some cooks cover the *frittata* to set the top, flipping it onto a serving dish to expose the browned side. Marcella Hazan recommends cooking the eggs until set, then broiling the upper surface. And flamboyant cooks flip, flapjack-style. A nonstick omelet pan makes the entire process easier.

> About 24 zucchini flowers
>
> 2–3 tablespoons extra virgin olive oil
>
> 1–2 garlic cloves, minced
>
> 2 tablespoons chopped fresh basil
>
> 4 eggs
>
> Fine sea salt
>
> Freshly ground black pepper

1　Soak the zucchini flowers in a sinkful of cold water to refresh and clean. Drain the flowers and pat dry with paper towels or spin in a salad spinner.

2　Put the flowers in a large nonstick skillet, drizzle with extra virgin olive oil, and stir to coat. Cook over moderate heat, stirring occasionally, for 10–15 minutes or until lightly browned. Add the garlic and basil and cook for another minute.

3　Transfer the cooked zucchini flowers, which will have reduced considerably in volume, to a medium nonstick skillet.

4　Mix the eggs, salt, and pepper with a fork and pour over the zucchini flowers.

5　Cook over low heat until the eggs are well set on the bottom but still slightly runny on the surface. Shake the pan to loosen the *frittata*, running a spatula under the *frittata* if it sticks.

6　Put a plate over the *frittata* and invert the skillet to reverse the *frittata* onto the plate. Slide the frittata back into pan to cook the other side.

7　Slide onto a platter and serve hot or at room temperature.

Index